CODY

The Autobiography

Brian Cody
with Martin Breheny

Irish Sports Publishing

Published by Irish Sports Publishing (ISP)
Ballybeg, Kells, Co Meath

www.briancody.net

First published 2009

A CIP record for this book is available from the British Library

ISBN 978-0-9563598-0-3

Printed in Ireland with Print Procedure Ltd
Layout and typesetting: Paul McElheron & Associates
Cover Design: Jessica Maile
Photographs: Inpho Sports Agency Ltd, and Brian Cody's personal collection

FOREWORD

It is a great honour for me to be asked to write this introduction to Brian Cody's autobiography.

This book spells out Brian's philosophies, and his core beliefs. He has put down on paper his life story – as Kilkenny hurling manager – with complete honesty, and I am sure you will enjoy this book as much as I enjoy knowing the author himself.

Sport is a fantastic medium for meeting a whole range of people, and I consider it a privilege to have been in Brian's company on several occasions over the last number of years.

What I have always found inspiring is how uncomplicated he makes life out to be. Though, sometimes, when you meet a man with principles and core values as strong as Brian's, you may not agree with them all, it's always refreshing and inspirational to meet a person like Brian Cody who presents himself to you as he is, with no pretensions to be anyone other than himself.

Brian does exactly as he preaches. On returning to school as a teacher after so many first Sundays in September, he instills in his pupils a love of the game he so passionately cares about.

At the same time, he is always the first to recognise the contributions of all those involved in Kilkenny hurling.

This book is an honest man's own honest account of how he goes about his role as Kilkenny hurling manager. In sport, as in life, that is all you can ever ask for! Honesty.

Declan Kidney

CONTENTS

Chapter 1:	A Part of What We Are	1
Chapter 2:	Foundation Stones	9
Chapter 3:	New Year, Old Values, Cold Comforts	17
Chapter 4:	A Land of Uncertainty	21
Chapter 5:	Go Easy on the Praise, Lads	29
Chapter 6:	Spirit, Respect, Honesty	33
Chapter 7:	Reflection Time	47
Chapter 8:	Judgement Reserved	51
Chapter 9:	Relief and Redemption	56
Chapter 10:	Right Results, Wrong Conclusions	65
Chapter 11:	A Cloud on the Horizon	70
Chapter 12:	A Belt of Reality	75
Chapter 13:	Nothing Personal, Just Business	85
Chapter 14:	God in Kilkenny Heaven	89
Chapter 15:	Doubles and Troubles	93
Chapter 16:	Red Card for Yellow	106
Chapter 17:	Hangover Hill	112
Chapter 18:	In Search of the Treble	118

Chapter 19:	The Scent of Summer	139
Chapter 20:	Sticks, Stones but No Broken Bones	144
Chapter 21:	Panel Power	150
Chapter 22:	Cradle of Dreams	156
Chapter 23:	For the Honour of The Village	160
Chapter 24:	Let the Games Begin	166
Chapter 25:	Swinging Out of the Sixties	171
Chapter 26:	Broadening Horizons	176
Chapter 27:	We Have Lift-off	187
Chapter 28:	Lows, Highs. Myths and Magic	191
Chapter 29:	Living on the Edge?	197
Chapter 30:	Terms of Engagement	203
Chapter 31:	One Goal, Shared Responsibility	211
Chapter 32:	Towards the Final Hurdle	218
Chapter 33:	Mind and What Really Matters	225
Chapter 34:	Nearly There	232
Chapter 35:	View from the Summit	236
Statistics		243

CHAPTER 1

A PART OF WHAT WE ARE

I would abolish the provincial Championships and replace them with a carefully-calibrated mechanism designed to get the most from having the top counties pursuing the All-Ireland title. I have no specific structure in mind but, obviously, it would incorporate a group set-up involving Leinster and Munster counties, plus Galway, Antrim and possibly one other Ulster team. The Hurling Development Committee has done some excellent work in proposing new ideas, but I always felt they came up with recommendations which they felt had a chance of being accepted rather than what they felt was right for the game.

I wouldn't ever be classed as a GAA politician and have no ambitions, whatsoever, to wander in that direction.

The games, the players and the training ground are my domain and I'm quite happy to remain there. However, just because I have no interest in becoming involved in the administrative side – other than how it pertains to the squad I'm managing – doesn't mean that I'm disinterested in what's going on in the wider GAA world.

All GAA members are shareholders in the organisation. It's a sporting co-op where, in theory at least, everybody can have their say. Now, for reasons that escape me – and which are certainly not based on any logic –

it's fashionable, in some quarters, to criticise the GAA.

That annoys me. Like so many Irish people, I enjoy all sports and believe they can live in harmony with each other while fulfilling what should be the basic aim of providing playing opportunities for as many as possible and an entertainment outlet for the rest. The GAA continues to do that and, while it undoubtedly faces tests of resolve into the future, I have no doubt that they will be met with the same sense of steely determination which has underpinned the Association since its foundation.

It's easy to be critical of GAA officials, whether at club, county, provincial or national level, but where would the organisation be without them? I happen to think that, in general, we're well served by the GAA leadership and I hope it continues that way because there are challenges on the horizon which, unless carefully managed, could cause serious problems.

One such issue is pay-for-play. It's impossible to predict accurately how much of a concern it will become, but I would hope that it would be sorted out as quickly and as sensibly as possible so that precious time and energy won't be wasted on it over future years.

Is pay-for-play a possibility? I sincerely hope not, because I believe it would have a catastrophic effect on the GAA. The GAA has a massive presence in every city, town, village and parish in Ireland, but it's a small organisation when compared to the major international sports so to suggest that it could pay players displays a scant knowledge of reality and no understanding of the ethos which has made the Association what it is.

Even if the GAA could afford pay-for-play, there's a fundamental reason why it would be probably the single, greatest disaster the GAA has ever encountered. The organisation is based on the volunteer principle and the unmistakable sense that you're doing something for your club, your school or your county. You're doing it because you want to, not because you have to. It's a matter of local pride and identity.

Now, if an elite minority emerges which is paid for its services then the basic structure is, in my view, under threat. Imagine the impact it would have on clubs if county players were paid: the club facilities were put in place by generations of volunteers who worked hard, the county players who came through them were helped to reach the highest standards by the volunteer coaches and others, but the only ones to be paid would be the elite players.

One of the arguments put forward in favour of pay-for-play centres on Croke Park on big match days, where comparisons are made between people who are paid to work there and the players. It's as simple as this: those who are hired to help run the day have to be paid, they are providing a professional service whereas the players are there of their own volition as part of their sporting pursuit.

Players are there because of the standard they have reached in Gaelic Games, controlled by an amateur organisation of which they are members. They signed up to that when they joined the GAA. Yes, they're generating money, but the facilities which they enjoy were built by the endeavours of those who went before them. Besides, much of the money is derived from other GAA members.

When it comes to players, they should always be looked after properly. No standards can be too high in that regard, but that's altogether different from actually paying them for playing. In my opinion, that has to remain non-negotiable if the GAA is to survive as the successful organisation that it is.

The strange thing is that, while pay-for-play is supposed to be simmering away in the background, I have never actually met a player who was actively campaigning for it. Still, we live in a fast-changing world so it would be naïve to assume that it won't be on the table in some form in the future.

The GPA has claimed it's not pursuing a pay-for-play agenda but, I have to say, they were somewhat unconvincing on it for a while. There has to be some concern that it could be part of a down-the-line vision. Just because something isn't being pushed now doesn't mean it won't happen in five or ten years' time.

I'm no old-fashioned traditionalist but, where pay-for-play is concerned, there's a fundamental principle at stake which, in my view, cannot be compromised. Just in case anybody gets the wrong impression, I'm not remotely anti-GPA. On the contrary, they have done a lot of good work.

The GPA came about, essentially, because it appears that, in some counties at least, players had genuine cause for grievance over various issues. Perhaps it was a case of administrators getting into a comfort zone and not realising that what might have been good enough years ago was no longer acceptable. It may also have been down to a lack of respect for players, another recipe for trouble.

The GPA certainly concentrated minds and will, I have no doubt, continue to play a key role on various projects. All the better if that's happening in co-operation with the GAA, because the greater the harmony the more that gets done and the more everybody benefits.

I can see no reason why a deal can't be struck between the GPA and Croke Park regarding official recognition. If that were sorted out, on a mutually satisfactory basis, then there's great scope for moving forward together rather than in an adversarial manner where each side is suspicious of the other's motives. That merely drains energy.

The last thing the GAA needs is a division between Croke Park and the inter-county players. All sides have enough to do without wasting energy on rows and controversies. That's why I sincerely hope that pay-for-play is nailed once and for all because, if it ever becomes a real issue, the potential for chaos is enormous. And, if that were to happen, the only loser would be the GAA.

There's no doubt that the success of Croke Park stadium encourages those who believe players should be paid. At central level, the GAA is generating the sort of money nobody could have dreamt of some years ago but, oddly enough, that brings its own problems.

History has shown that when a club is struggling financially, its members work much harder than when times are good. It becomes a communal effort and presents a clear challenge to everybody which, in turn, sharpens the focus.

Croke Park's success – not just as a GAA stadium but also as a venue for rugby, soccer and major concerts – has dramatically increased the income levels so, in some ways, I suppose it's inevitable that the pay-for-play question continues to arise from time to time. The sooner it's addressed and destroyed the better for everybody.

I would much prefer to see more energy being devoted to aspects of the GAA which, if sorted out, would have a hugely positive impact. In my view, the biggest test of all relates to the club activity, in particular how to give players more games in summer. The inter-county scene carries most of the glamour but it should never be at the expense of club players. We have nothing without a vibrant club game and the only way to keep that healthy is to provide a consistent flow of action for players.

That has to include a regular flow throughout the summer months. I can never understand counties who close down their club Championships until the county teams are finished because, once that's allowed to happen, club players suffer badly. We try to manage the club scene as best we can in Kilkenny, but it's far from perfect here either.

For all the challenges that arise in an organisation that caters for two major sports using a club and county model, it's fair to say that we get an awful lot right in the GAA. Obviously, I know more about hurling than football and I'd have to say the standard of hurling is extremely high at the top level.

Of course, we would love to have even more counties at the higher end of the market, but we certainly have as many as we ever had, despite grim warnings of a decline from time to time. The key to improving hurling is getting it right at underage level, starting with kids from the time they're old enough to pick up a hurley.

I'm not talking about specialised coaching at that age. Far from it. No, it's all about giving youngsters the opportunity to play the game. Hurling only becomes enjoyable when you start to get good at it, when you're able to knock the ball off the wall and control it. From there on, the enjoyment levels rise in direct proportion to the rate of improvement.

There's sometimes a tendency to get bogged down in training youngsters and to believe that only those with coaching badges can do it properly. Badges don't automatically make a good coach. An instinct for the job and an ability to work with kids is far more important. Giving youngsters the freedom to enjoy the game should always be the starting base in those early, formative years.

In fairness, there's a lot of good work going on around the country as proven by the standard of players that emerge at minor level. It's exceptionally good in many counties.

I believe too that the introduction of the Christy Ring, Nickey Rackard and Lory Meagher Cup competitions have been very positive for hurling as they give counties a target at their own level with promotion as the prize for the winners. That system doesn't lie. It's tiered according to standards, with counties empowered to find their own level, based on how they fare. There's a natural order to it, which works well.

The Liam McCarthy Cup competition is, of course, the main event which makes it all the more important to run it off in a manner which serves hurling best. I'm sorry to have to say that I don't regard the current system as fulfilling that crucial role.

I would abolish the provincial Championships and replace them with a carefully-calibrated mechanism designed to get the most from having the top counties pursuing the All-Ireland title. I have no specific structure in mind but, obviously, it would incorporate a group set-up involving Leinster and Munster counties, plus Galway, Antrim and possibly one other Ulster team. The Hurling Development Committee has done some excellent work in proposing new ideas, but I always felt they came up with recommendations which they felt had a chance of being accepted rather than what they felt was right for the game.

That's understandable, because why should they offer proposals knowing that the vested interests from the provincial Councils would shoot them down? However, if we got away from the provincial-based system, I'm sure that the HDC would devise a very interesting structure.

I'm just as proud of the Leinster Championship as Munster people are of theirs but I still believe it would be in hurling's best interest if both were scrapped. The wrong time to change something is when it's played out. It's far better to freshen things up when they're going well.

Under the current system, winning provincial titles doesn't mean anything like as much as it used to. Tipperary won the 2008 Munster title but lost the All-Ireland semi-final to Waterford. So, which was the best team in Munster that year? I have no doubt Tipperary would have preferred to lose in Munster and win the All-Ireland semi-final.

In 2007, Waterford beat Limerick in the Munster final but lost to them in the All-Ireland semi-final some weeks later so, guess who felt they achieved more that year? We know what it's like in Kilkenny too, having beaten Offaly in the 1998 Leinster final only to lose to them in the All-Ireland final – somehow, I don't think many Kilkenny people saw that year as a glowing success.

The arrival of Galway and Antrim in Leinster is a forward step and shows that there's a mood for change. But, surely, if Galway or Antrim can win their adopted Championship even though they are geographically outside the province it's not really the Leinster Championship anymore.

I would much prefer to see all the McCarthy Cup counties competing against each other, across provincial boundaries. It should be possible to have 'home' and 'away' fixtures so that players get a chance to perform in front of their own people on a consistent basis. As things stand, that's denied to a great many players while the supporters don't get to see games at their local venues.

If the HDC were given a blank canvas for the Championship with no restrictions as to what they could paint on it, I have no doubt they would produce a very interesting picture which didn't have the provincial Championships as a non-negotiable background.

We have had several changes to the Championship structure over the past twelve years, but they have always centred on retaining the Munster and Leinster campaigns as independent entities. I believe the next alteration should involve dissolving that arrangement.

So many aspects of GAA life have changed over the last twenty years that it shows that a willingness to adapt to evolving circumstances is a strongly-held belief among the membership. That's why we should not be afraid to make one more leap for the sake of hurling. I have no doubt that it would be of great benefit.

The courage to change for the right reasons is an essential quality, which has stood to the GAA down the years. As long as it retains that courage – and there's no reason to suspect otherwise – the future is bright. There are some outstanding people leading the GAA and, once they keep a step ahead of the game, the Association can cope with any challenge – except perhaps professionalism if, God forbid, that ever becomes a serious issue.

Nothing represents Irish life quite like the Gaelic Athletic Association. It touches so many people in such a wide variety of ways that its importance can never be over-estimated. It's part of what we are, and a proud part at that.

CHAPTER 2

FOUNDATION STONES

A dressing room without ego is a beautiful place because everybody knows that they're part of something special. However, the minute ego begins to creep into individual thinking then the unity of the place can be shattered very quickly.

I'm in the county management game for over a decade now, and have been lucky enough to be involved with some very successful teams and many outstanding individuals, but I'm still learning. Every day, every game and every training session is different because that's the nature of sport. It's also a major part of sport's enduring appeal for players, managers, spectators and just about everybody who has an interest or any involvement, however large or small.

It's always throwing up something new and challenging while offering solutions to puzzles that might have looked impossible hours, days or weeks before. The trick is to rise with, and to, the challenges, see them for what they are and don't allow yourself to become intimidated by them. It's also vitally important to be able to spot the solutions because they're out there, waiting to be picked up.

There's no one true gospel on team management. There are several right ways of doing things, just as there are several wrong ways, but there are some principles which – certainly in my view – are non-negotiable. What's more, they apply to all levels, all grades and all ages.

All any group can ever hope to achieve is to get the very best out of themselves. That doesn't mean that extracting the best will result in titles or honours but it does bring inner satisfaction to those involved. It's a fact of sporting life in all disciplines that some players are better than others. That's down to natural talent, the initial building block for everything.

However, there's plenty that can be done about harnessing a talent and getting more out of someone. In a squad situation you multiply that by thirty or thirty-five and now you're into a much wider range of possibilities.

To my mind, the first essential is putting in proper foundations and structures: without them, you're at nothing because sooner or later everything comes crashing down if the fundamentals aren't tightly secured. It's vital for a team manager to have all the strands pulling together so that a sustainable momentum can be created and maintained.

It always amazes me when I hear of friction between County Boards and team managements or between County Boards and players or whatever. Friction equals problems and problems equal less efficiency. There's no need to go beyond that because, once you shed efficiency, you're in trouble.

I have always felt that one of the key ingredients in Kilkenny's success throughout this decade has been the sense of unity we have generated and maintained. Of course it hasn't always been peace and harmony – we are, after all, a collection of individuals coming together in a common cause – but we have been able to work our way through difficulties and retain sight of the main targets, realising that unless we all pursued them together they wouldn't be reached. Working through things demands respect and trust from all sides. And, once these elements are present, nothing is insurmountable.

I have enjoyed a good working relationship with the County Board, mainly through its officers whom I have found to be first class people to deal with. Of course, it's a two-way street. I'm the Kilkenny senior hurling manager with responsibility for assembling the best panel, preparing them properly and ensuring that when they take the field they are in with a real chance of winning. Mine is a results-based job but there's more to it than that as I also have a responsibility to the wider game in the county.

A county manager can only deal with the players provided for him by the clubs. He can't buy in players so he's reliant on the local conveyor belt. Clubs everywhere have always taken great pride in producing players who are good enough to get on the Kilkenny team, but they also have to cater for the large majority who will never make it that far.

That's why it's so important for a county manager to acknowledge the role of the clubs and respect their needs. They're not there just to provide him with star players to slot into a county team, nor are they there for the honour and glorification of their star players or the county manager. Clubs love feeding talent into the county system as part of the natural process but, ultimately, their main responsibility is to cater for all their members, which they do extremely well. Coming from a club like James Stephens, I have always been deeply conscious of the role clubs play in the local community. It's important that they be respected because, in the end, the whole structure depends on them. Weaken the club game and you undermine the county scene. Worse than that, you undermine the foundation on which the pyramid is erected.

Just as the county scene benefits from a vibrant club structure, clubs gain when the county team is going well. It increases interest and awareness, which is good for everybody. You'll find it's reflected throughout the country when counties win an All-Ireland title. The attendances at club Championship games over the following weeks usually increase because of the feel-good factor. The battle to become the champion club in the champion county has that extra special edge.

Apart from the need to have a good relationship between club and county so that both continue to prosper and complement each other, it's important that there's harmony purely from a practical viewpoint. Managing a county team is demanding enough without running into problems with the County Board or with clubs. Thankfully, I'm happy to say it's an area we have managed quite successfully in Kilkenny but only because all sides work at it and understand one another's needs. It won't happen automatically and can never be taken for granted.

While good organisation is a key ingredient in a solid county scene, there are others too which I have always held dear. Spirit and respect have to be at the core of what a squad is about. If they're there, they can be harnessed in a very positive way. Respect for ourselves, each other and what we are trying to do as a group has stood to us on many occasions when our backs were to the wall over the years. That's when the group ethic really comes into its own.

As manager, I have got a lot of credit for the successes but I've repeatedly said that it has been – and remains – a massive team effort by players, backroom team and County Board. I play my part but it's no more than that. Players are publicly acknowledged because their feats are there for all to see while the manager also receives recognition, but others often don't, certainly not to the same degree. I could never over-emphasise the importance of the people who have worked with me on the backroom teams. Even if they don't always get the kudos they deserve they know how much they put into it and how loyal they have been to the cause. I certainly do and I appreciate it immensely.

If getting the right people with and behind you is vital in setting up a good management structure, it's also crucial to trust yourself implicitly and run with what you believe is right.

Bring your own strengths and weaknesses to the job and don't get caught up trying to imitate anybody else. If you park your own individuality outside the door, what's the point in going inside at all? You'll come across as weak and indecisive, simply because you are weak and indecisive if you don't trust your own instincts.

Of course, there's a big difference between believing in yourself and allowing ego to take over.

A dressingroom without ego is a beautiful place because everybody knows that they're part of something special. However, the minute ego begins to creep into individual thinking then the unity of the place can be shattered very quickly. From a management viewpoint, it's easy enough to guard against it among players as you'll spot it very quickly and can react accordingly, but what happens if it's the manager's ego which takes over?

Who tells him that he has lost the squad ethic or the sense that he is there to facilitate the players and the county, not the other way around? A manager doesn't need to be constantly showing how much in control he really is. That's not what management is about. Where you have proper squad cohesion, everybody knows what they're at so they should be allowed to get on with it to the best of their ability. Interfering for the sake of showing who has the real power is a sign of weakness. Besides, it can irritate good people who are going about their business in a diligent manner. Upsetting them is scarcely the art of good management.

I have always had an obsession with establishing and maintaining a settled spirit, honesty, drive and determination. Provided they're all in place within the squad, you don't need to have the same team on the pitch all the time. Others can adjust to the core principles and apply them because, as a group, that's what they've learned to do. So when their chance arrives, they're ready to take it both as individuals and as part of the overall unit. They know what's expected and they know how to deliver it.

People talk about the need for centres of excellence to push things on but, to me, it's much more basic than that. The training pitch should be the centre of excellence for players. That's where they encounter every experience that they will ever come across in a match situation. Or at least they should. We try to drive that home all the time in Kilkenny and the players have responded in a very positive way over the years.

Players will buy into that concept very quickly because they're encouraged to take ownership of what they're doing. After all, the training is for them so they need to believe in it and the reasons why they're asked to do certain things. They own the training sessions – the rest of us are facilitators.

I keep hearing of these ferocious training games we're suppose to have where two teams line up against each other in Nowlan Park and I stand in the middle of the pitch with a whistle which I only use for the most heinous of offences. If you believe the stories, these games are supposed to be utterly lawless affairs where every player has to look after himself without any help from the man with the whistle. As is so often the case, the reality is totally different.

Yes, we play 15-a-side games which are intensely fought. What's the point of them otherwise? The whole purpose of training games is to create an environment which will be as close as possible to what the players will experience on match day and you can only achieve that with flat-out engagement.

Inter-county players are very competitive people so it's not difficult to get them powering up through the gears in training. Actually, it's what they want to do. I'm not a big fan of challenge matches against other county teams, which is why our own training games are so important. I don't mind playing other counties to mark the opening of a pitch or for a charity because I think we should be doing that to boost the game when possible, but I don't see a whole lot of value in challenge games simply for their own sake. I much prefer playing among ourselves in Nowlan Park because I believe this works better for us. Others may see it differently but I'm only interested in what works for us.

Competition for places is always pretty intense so there's a real cut to the action. I'm sure that applies in other counties too but, for whatever reason, a degree of mystique has built up around our training games. Mind you, I have always found it amusing that some people who have never seen us training tell wondrous tales of our unruly games. Have they actually thought of how crazy it would be if players were to overstep the mark on a regular basis? Apart altogether from the risk of injury, we would be creating a situation which would leave us badly exposed on match day where official referees were in control.

If our fellas were getting away with all sorts of skulduggery in training, it would be difficult for them to curtail it in matches with the result that the free count against us would be much higher than it is. The truth about our training games is simple. They are designed to replicate match situations as closely as possible so that players can make the transition quite comfortably when they leave Nowlan Park and head for Thurles, Limerick, Croke Park or wherever. The more often you've dealt with a situation in training the more likely you are to cope successfully with it in a match.

Our training sessions are open to the public because I believe they should be. Club and inter-county games are played in front of the public so it makes sense to train in the same environment, albeit in front of much smaller numbers. The only time we had a few closed sessions was before the 2005 All-Ireland semi-final against Galway. So many people were turning up that it grew a bit crazy for a while and we needed to get some specific work done. We haven't had any closed sessions since, and that's the way it will stay. Supporters like to feel part of the scene by dropping in to Nowlan Park to have a look at what we're doing and since they're important stakeholders in Kilkenny hurling they are entitled to do that.

Some people from outside Kilkenny who have come along to see us training commented afterwards on how ordinary the sessions looked. And they are ordinary in many ways, but there's real quality to them too. Or at least we try to ensure that there is.

It's the players' application that defines the quality. They're encouraged to take ownership and drive on as hard and as fast as they can. It's demanding but they find it very enjoyable because they're testing each other all the time. A defender who's marking Henry Shefflin, Eddie Brennan or one of the other attackers in training has to be on his toes to survive just as Shefflin, Brennan and Co. have to be going well to get anything off Tommy Walsh, Michael Kavanagh and the rest of the defenders.

That sort of game tells me an awful lot more about how things are going than challenge matches against other counties. We're lucky that we have so many top class players constantly challenging each other but, ultimately, it's the manner in which they go about their business that's important.

The standards set on the training field are the standards that will be put to the test in games. If the training tempo drops, it will show up on match days. It's all about quality rather than quantity on the training ground. One good session, conducted in the right way with the players fully switched on is worth any number of loose, casual get-togethers.

That's why I'm not especially concerned about how many training sessions we've had but, rather, how good they were. I've often read of teams having a huge number of sessions, as though this exemplified just how well-prepared they were, but it means nothing to me. I'm not into counting sessions but I am into totting up just how valuable each one was. I'm not saying that's the right way but it's my way. And, as I've said, there's no one, true gospel when it comes to team management.

CHAPTER 3

NEW YEAR, OLD VALUES, COLD COMFORTS

The day you pull on a Kilkenny jersey – or *any other jersey – for the first time, is the day you get your opportunity. If you take it, then you decide your own future, not the manager or selectors, since a player who keeps performing well won't be dropped. And even if it doesn't work out, it's still the day you were given an opportunity to represent your county. It's an honour that eludes many, so those who get it should always treasure the experience.*

Sunday, January 18, 2009: *It's good to be back. Well, maybe not on a bitterly cold day like this but we have to start somewhere. It's only a week since we returned from a squad holiday and the delights of San Francisco, Hawaii and San Diego – now, we're in Parnell Park for the first game of the New Year, a Walsh Cup tie with Dublin. Welcome to the real world. A top-of-the-range holiday usually follows an All-Ireland win and, since we've done so well this decade, we've seen the world. This year's trip was outstanding but then they always are. We've been to South Africa, Australia, New Zealand, Thailand and several parts of America over the years and I, for one, deeply appreciate it. I'm sure everybody else in the travelling party does too.*

How many of us would ever have got the opportunity to visit so many places around the globe if it weren't for hurling? We all know it will dry up eventually because it always does. All careers – however successful they might be – come to an end. That applies to players, managers and everybody else associated with teams so it's important to make the most of them while they last.

It's also important to see them for what they are while you're still living through them. Yes, there will be bad days, disappointments, irritations, and frustrations, but it's crucial not to lose sight of one basic fact: those of us involved in sport, certainly in the amateur scene, are there because we love what we're doing. And in the case of Kilkenny hurling, it's our passion, our heritage, our way of life. It's what we do outside work and family.

The team holiday has been a very pleasant part of the scene in the years when we won All-Irelands. In a way, they're performance related. After losing the All-Ireland semi-final in 2005, we took a few days' break in Barcelona. We had won the League and Leinster titles but the season hadn't been a success in All-Ireland terms and we weren't going to behave otherwise and jet off to some exotic spot. We didn't deliver, so we didn't deserve any big rewards. Simple as that.

We work closely with the County Board on destinations and travel arrangements and there's never been any friction. It's a good sign of the set-up. The lads appreciate the opportunity and don't take it for granted. It's a reward for their accomplishments but, once it's over, the search for new goals and new achievements begins. This year, we start on a Sunday afternoon in January borrowed from the Arctic and re-located in Parnell Park.

A decent crowd turned out but then it's a new era for Dublin who have Anthony Daly in charge for the first time. He'll do a good job with them. They'll look up to him as a man who helped Clare to make the breakthrough after so much disappointment, and he can identify with them. He'll know how they're thinking from his own days with Clare before they turned things around in 1995. He also has management experience so he knows what it's all about.

Anyway, here we are in Parnell Park exactly nineteen weeks after last year's All-Ireland final. Nineteen weeks from today, we'll discover who will be our opponents in the Leinster semi-final . The months move on very quickly – it's time to make a start.

People might think that, in the circumstances, Dublin would have a much bigger appetite for this game than Kilkenny, with their players wanting to put down a marker in front of their new manager. That's not the case. Dublin might well be all fired up, but it's the start of a new season for us too and, even if we've only been back from our holiday for a week, there's work to be done. We have lads on this panel who want to prove themselves just as much as Dublin and this is their chance. I always tell players that every career starts somewhere. It could be a Walsh Cup game in Freshford, Portlaoise, Birr or, in this case, Parnell Park. If a player does well, he gets another chance. Make the most of that and he gets another chance and so on.

So, the day you pull on a Kilkenny jersey – or any other jersey – for the first time, is the day you get your opportunity. If you take it, then you decide your own future, not the manager or selectors, since a player who keeps performing well won't be dropped. And even if it doesn't work out, it's still the day you were given an opportunity to represent your county. It's an honour that eludes many, so those who get it should always treasure the experience.

We beat Dublin quite comfortably in the end, probably more comfortably than we deserved but it was one of those days when the goals flew in. It was a good performance, as a mixture of some new faces and All-Ireland winners went about their business in a determined way. Good. They're switched on early.

Anthony Daly remarked to the media later that he couldn't get over how determined the likes of JJ Delaney and Tommy Walsh were and how they had hurled like lads who had never won anything. "Fresh and mad for road," were the words he used.

Glad to see it! I wasn't driving them but they wanted to do it anyway. With lads like that it doesn't matter if it's an All-Ireland final, a first round Walsh Cup game or a puckaround, they're fiercely competitive. It's the only way they know – indeed the only way they have always known – and it's the only way any player should think.

They played like that on a miserable January day because performing to their very best is all that satisfies them. I can't understand players who switch off or go through the motions depending on the game. If it's worth playing, it's worth playing well. That's central to the whole way we do things in Kilkenny so, while others might have been surprised by the driven approach by Walsh, Delaney and others to a first round Walsh Cup game, it came naturally to them because it's the only philosophy they understand.

That's one of the fundamentals of the way we approach things. There's also the enjoyment side which is absolutely vital and which is never over-looked in Kilkenny despite what you might have heard. Playing hurling is highly enjoyable; playing for your county brings it to another level. A player who doesn't grasp that is missing something. Walsh and Delaney hurled as they did against Dublin because, for them, the biggest satisfaction they could get from the day was to play well, win and look forward to the next game. Where would the enjoyment be if they travelled all the way up from Kilkenny to tap around as if it didn't count for anything? More importantly, what would be the point?

There is nothing deep or wonderfully mysterious about it. In fact, it couldn't be simpler – we play every game to win. Besides, if you don't play well, there's somebody behind you who wants your place. And just as every career starts somewhere, every career ends somewhere too. It might even be in a Walsh Cup game.

Back in the dressing room afterwards, the lads couldn't have showers because there was no water. It would be awfully easy to make a fuss, to complain about how this is no way to treat county players. It would, no doubt, have made big headlines the following day but we're not in the business of making headlines, except for our hurling. Besides, what would it have achieved? It seems there was a general problem with water supplies in the area that day so it was nobody's fault that the showers weren't working. Just one of those things. Not one single player moaned or complained about the showers. Good – they have got things in perspective.

CHAPTER 4

A LAND OF UNCERTAINTY

Becoming the first county to lose an All-Ireland final to a team they had beaten earlier hurt Kilkenny deeply. Nor had it been the only unusual aspect of Kilkenny's season. DJ Carey had announced his retirement in January, only to change his mind six weeks later.

Martin Breheny writes: In late September 1998, the Bob O'Keeffe Cup was feeling unloved, uncomfortable and uncertain of its identity as a prize worth cherishing. It was preparing to settle in for a first winter stay in Kilkenny since 1993, yet it couldn't escape the unmistakable sense that the county's hurling supporters weren't exactly ecstatic over its presence among them.

It certainly wasn't the only time that a provincial title had represented the peak of Kilkenny's achievements in a season, but it definitely was the first occasion when they had won Leinster only to see it trumped so decisively by rivals whom they had beaten quite comfortably earlier on.

Kilkenny had won the summer battle with Offaly in Leinster but lost the All-Ireland final re-match in September, resulting in Liam McCarthy resting contentedly with Hubert Rigney and his history-making colleagues.

Not that there was much time for relaxation in a county that had been hoisted high on an emotional gusher after a remarkable season, during which they had lived so many different lives that there were times when they must have had difficulty even recognising who they were. For reasons which will always remain deeply embedded in the Offaly psyche, 1998 was truly special, not just for what it eventually yielded, but also in terms of the adventure on which they embarked to procure it.

Offaly's first All-Ireland success in 1981 could never be matched for its historic dimension and the relief it engendered now that the desert had finally been crossed. The 1985 triumph reinforced their reputation as high achievers who could cope with success and go on to repeat it, while the 1994 win was memorable for the late explosion which shattered Limerick in the final. Those All-Irelands had created a whole new perception of Offaly hurling as a powerful force but, even then, nobody could have envisaged how, in 1998, they would transform what seemed like a seriously lost cause into a glorious conquest.

Clare, the 1995 and 1997 All-Ireland champions, had felt the full fury of Offaly's collective desire to rescue a season that had appeared in disarray after the Leinster final. Offaly's recovery was spirited and effective, and eventually resulted in an All-Ireland semi-final win over Clare at the third attempt.

It was a horrible experience for Clare who took to consoling themselves that they had been the victims of numerous conspiracies in the course of a turbulent season. It wouldn't alter the reality that Liam McCarthy had fled The Banner, but it made the disappointment a little easier to accept, initially at least. In reality though, it was the end of Clare's greatest ever era.

There were no such comforts in Kilkenny as they sifted through the debris of a season that had promised a whole lot more than it delivered. They had beaten Offaly by five points in the Leinster final before slipping quietly away to wait for All-Ireland semi-final opponents. They had watched in amused silence as a rebellion by the Offaly players led to a change of management with Michael Bond replacing 'Babs' Keating, who stood down amid player unrest over comments he made after the defeat by Kilkenny. 'Babs' was replaced by Galwayman Michael Bond.

He was a surprise option but, in less than two months, would prove to have been an inspired choice.

As the drama in Offaly was being played out, a volcano erupted in Munster after the Clare-Waterford final replay. It dominated the agenda for weeks as disciplinary processes which were fiercely resisted by Clare generated an intrigue which reverberated right across the sporting world. Then, there was Waterford's trimming of Galway in the All-Ireland quarter-final, followed by Kilkenny's very close call against Waterford in the semi-final. It certainly wasn't an impressive Kilkenny performance but they had been idle for six weeks after beating Offaly which, at the time, appeared like a plausible explanation for their unconvincing display. In reality, there was more to it than that.

Despite the reservations about Kilkenny arising from the performance against Waterford, they were still warm favourites to repeat the Leinster final win over Offaly in the All-Ireland final. The 'back door' system was only in its second year but, once again, it had facilitated the arrival of a team that had lost a provincial final. However, unlike 1997 when Clare repeated their Munster final success over Tipperary, 1998 had planned a mischievous sub-plot with Offaly emerging as the main characters.

If the GAA deemed it appropriate to allow beaten provincial finalists back into the All-Ireland race, the gods considered it in order to reward them with the ultimate prize. Offaly's 2-16 to 1-13 win over Kilkenny produced two large chunks of history: Offaly became the first team to win the All-Ireland via the 'back door', while Kilkenny became the first county to lose the final to 'back door' entrants.

Inevitably, the defeat led to deep introspection in Kilkenny. Losing an All-Ireland final to Offaly was considered utterly unacceptable, especially since they had beaten them in the Leinster final. Inevitably, the focus switched to manager, Kevin Fennelly and his selectors, Mick McCarthy and Dick O'Neill.

Fennelly was in his first season as manager and, in normal circumstances, would not have come under such fierce scrutiny after an All-Ireland final defeat, especially since the Leinster title had finally been regained after a five-year wait. The trouble was that these weren't ordinary times for Kilkenny.

Becoming the first county to lose an All-Ireland final to a team they had beaten earlier hurt Kilkenny deeply. Nor had it been the only unusual aspect of Kilkenny's season. DJ Carey had announced his retirement in January, only to change his mind six weeks later.

The reasons given for his original decision never quite stacked up in the public mind. Inevitably, there were rumours of a rift between Fennelly and Carey which were robustly denied by both parties. Nonetheless, the whole saga, allied to the All-Ireland final defeat, left Kilkenny people bewildered and disappointed when they set about reviewing the 1998 season. Worst of all, optimism was scarce, even if Kilkenny were Leinster champions.

The county was confused as to how it had lost so much status since winning the All-Ireland double under Ollie Walsh in 1992 and 1993. Back then, they had appeared perfectly primed to continue harvesting high yields but had veered badly off course. More accurately, they were pushed off course by Offaly in 1994 and 1995 and by Wexford in 1996 and 1997.

The 1995 Leinster final defeat was as dismal a day as Kilkenny had experienced for a very long time. Classed as the ultimate shoot-out between the reigning All-Ireland champions and their immediate predecessors, it turned into a disastrous outing for Kilkenny who, after allowing themselves to become wet and miserable while Offaly remained snug in the dressing rooms safe from the pre-match torrents, trailed by 2-14 to 0-5 just after the hour mark. DJ Carey's two late goals weren't even a consolation on a day which marked the end of Ollie Walsh's five seasons in charge.

Offaly had undermined the second half of Walsh's reign but his term in charge was still an outstanding success, having brought two All-Ireland and three Leinster titles, and one National League title back to Kilkenny. He was replaced by Nickey Brennan who ran straight into a Wexford storm in 1996. Kilkenny were eliminated in the first round of the Leinster Championship in a game which launched Wexford on their first successful All-Ireland title trail since 1968.

In 1997, Wexford extended their dominance over Kilkenny, winning the Leinster final by six points after trailing by five points at half-time. The 'back door' offered Kilkenny a reprieve which they availed of in spectacular circumstances when beating Galway by two points in an epic All-Ireland quarter-final in Semple Stadium.

This was one of DJ Carey's finest ever performances as he led a stunning second-half revival which turned a nine-point interval deficit into a two-point victory. Carey scored 2-8 and drew an appropriate response from his colleagues to leave Kilkenny brimming with optimism. However, the upbeat mood only lasted a few weeks as Clare beat them by four points in the semi-final.

Brennan has always contended that the absence of Michael Phelan and Liam Simpson through injury was a huge contributory factor to Kilkenny's defeat. Both had hurled very well against Galway, and possessed the physique and experience required to engage with Clare on the most forceful terms. Whether they would have made the crucial difference remains one of hurling's great imponderables but, suffice to say, their absence was probably a factor in Kilkenny's defeat.

It was to be Brennan's final Championship game as manager although, he did have one more outing in the National League. As part of an experiment aimed at boosting the knock-out stages of the League, the GAA opted to split the competition into a spring-autumn affair. The group stages were played in spring, after which the competition went into storage until August when the semi-finals were played. The final was fixed for October. A solid group campaign earned Kilkenny a place in the semi-final against Limerick which was scheduled for August 24, just two weeks after the defeat by Clare.

Clearly switched off after their Championship exertions and the belief that a League title wouldn't rescue the season, Kilkenny produced a dismal performance, losing by ten points. With a small group of supporters in mutinous mood it was a disastrous evening for Kilkenny. What followed the final whistle was most untypical of Kilkenny, whose innate understanding and appreciation of the game of hurling had always been one of the county's treasured characteristics.

Parking the more honourable traditions on an autumn evening in Nowlan Park, a small section of the crowd vented their anger on Brennan in a manner which discredited the honesty and principle for which the county was highly regarded right throughout its history. They booed the manager and the team, underlining that however much you have done for your county – as Brennan had as a player and administrator – you're not immune from illogical attacks once the blame game begins. Brennan was castigated for, among other things, playing his brother on the team. Canice Brennan was there on his own merits – as he proved afterwards under Kevin Fennelly and Brian Cody – but a section of the Kilkenny following wouldn't accept that, effectively accusing his older brother of blatant nepotism. It was a disgraceful slur on the manager who decided to step down.

Fennelly replaced him and, while there were some criticisms when his first year ended in All-Ireland defeat, he was under no pressure – certainly not at County Board level – to resign. He gave no indication of his plans in the immediate aftermath of the defeat by Offaly, stating that he would take his time before making a decision. Indeed, it was widely expected that he would continue.

A month later, the Kilkenny County Board were all set to re-appoint him for 1999 when he told them that he wouldn't be available due to work commitments. It came as a complete shock to the Board who were now faced with finding a third manager in the space of three years, a most unusual situation in Kilkenny.

It was a strange time in Kilkenny's history because, apart from the managerial upheavals there was also a feeling that a new order had been created, one in which they were playing no meaningful part. But then neither were Cork, who went from 1992 to 1999 without winning a Munster title, nor Tipperary who failed to win a Munster title between 1993 and 2001.

What was happening to the 'Big Three', who had dominated the hurling scene through so much of GAA history? Kilkenny could point to having won four senior All-Irelands and eight Leinster titles since

1980, but Offaly had also won four All-Irelands and nine Leinster crowns in the same period.

Being not only challenged but actually led by Offaly was something Kilkenny had never previously experienced. And if that wasn't worrying enough, the Clare bandwagon, led with swashbuckling certainty by Ger Loughnane had swept through the land at a time when Kilkenny were struggling.

Clare weren't shy about claiming they had brought a new approach to hurling. They did everything with an overwhelming sense of certainty, and even gimmicks – such as announcing a team only to make changes on match day – were highlighted as an example of a new thinking when, in reality, it was no more than gamesmanship.

Clare's two All-Ireland successes had been divided by Wexford's return to power which was presided over by Liam Griffin. Loughnane and Griffin brought such an evangelical zeal to the scene that it was as if they were preaching a gospel which they had personally adapted to their own particular needs.

Stories of Griffin's motivational speeches made him sound like a mixture of Daniel O'Connell, John F. Kennedy and Muhammad Ali. Still, whatever he brought to a previously under-performing Wexford dressing room, it worked! He resigned after Wexford's 1996 success for personal reasons, but the image lived on of a man who, by force of personality, had driven the team through a remarkable campaign to emerge from what seemed like a position of hopelessness. And, in fairness, you couldn't argue with results – Wexford had beaten Kilkenny, Dublin, Offaly, Galway and Limerick to win the 1996 All-Ireland. There certainly could be no allegations of an easy run.

Tales from the Clare front of Loughnane taking his players through physical and mental frontiers that nobody had previously encountered gathered momentum at such an extraordinary rate that it really didn't matter whether or not they were true. An impression had been created that Clare were doing things so differently to everybody else that pre-1995 systems could be tossed into the nearest dump. Loughnane himself did nothing to dilute that view. On the contrary, he played it up, presumably on the basis that the greater the aura he could build around himself and the team, the easier it would be to exploit opponents' weaknesses and insecurities.

It was against that background that Nickey Brennan and Kevin Fennelly had worked during their three years as Kilkenny managers. The Kilkenny underage scene wasn't raising spirits either. The minors went from 1993 to 2002 without an All-Ireland title – a very long time by Kilkenny's standards. The 1993 team won the Leinster and All-Ireland titles impressively but, in terms of feeding into the senior team later on, they enjoyed very little success. The Under-21 grade wasn't especially productive either. Kilkenny won the 1994 All-Ireland title but were beaten by Tipperary in the 1995 final and didn't even reach the Leinster final in 1996 or 1997. Certainly, there was no sign of a conveyor belt ferrying lots of exciting young talent towards the start of a new Millennium.

Indeed, when Fennelly surprised the County Board by declaring that he was not interested in continuing as senior manager in October 1998, Kilkenny hurling was in a strange place. Good enough to win Leinster but not good enough to win the All-Ireland against a team they had beaten earlier.

Against an uncertain background, there was no obvious candidate to replace Fennelly. It was a time for all concerned to reflect and assess exactly who and what they wanted as Kilkenny looked ahead towards the turn of the Millennium. The County Chairman and his fellow power brokers took nearly a month to deliberate before deciding that the man best equipped to take on the enormous challenge was somebody who had no experience whatsoever of inter-county management.

However, there was very little else that he hadn't experienced. It was time to visit The Village and talk to Brian Cody.

CHAPTER 5

GO EASY ON THE PRAISE, LADS

We have to keep the standards high. I *reminded everyone what we are about, that what we had achieved over the years was done on the basis of honesty and genuineness. You have to be so conscious of retaining that, even in a Walsh Cup final in early February. If you don't, you might not get it back later on.*

Wednesday, February 4, 2009: *If I didn't know differently, I would think the lads were deadly serious. Two Tipperary men, Liam Sheedy and John McIntyre are sitting to my immediate left, vying with each other to see who could heap most praise on Kilkenny. If we started to believe all this stuff, dressing room doors would have to be widened to get our heads in. And we could let our prospects of winning anything out at the same time.*

We're in the Dublin headquarters of Allianz, the National League sponsors, for the launch of the 2009 competition and we're lined up at the top table, facing the media and the microphones. When I'm invited, I have always tried to attend the launch of the Leagues because I think it's important to do anything I can to boost them.

The Leagues mark the start of the serious action, so it's up to everybody in hurling to give them whatever lift they can, especially since they're in competition with so many other sports at that time of year. As sponsors, Allianz have always done their best. They have backed the Leagues for many years, even at times when not everybody in the GAA – including some players and managers – afforded the competitions the respect they deserve.

The League has been good to Kilkenny throughout this decade and I'd like to think that we have been good to the League too because we have always put in maximum effort to win every single game. I would have great respect for Allianz for their loyalty to the League but far less for those who have downgraded the competitions, often as a camouflage for a poor performance.

Anyway, Liam, John and myself are lined up at this year's launch and the two lads are trying to hoist Kilkenny to levels I didn't even know existed. They were talking about how high we had raised the bar and how Tipperary and Galway – and all other counties – were struggling to keep up so that they could even touch our coat tails. This business of how far ahead of everybody else we're supposed to be seems to be the thing to say, just as it was with Cork at the start of 2006 as they set out in pursuit of the three-in-a-row, and we all know what happened there.

I don't believe a word of it. Every year brings a new campaign and new challenges and that applies as much to Kilkenny as anybody else. We have done very well this decade so we're there to be shot at by anybody and everybody. That's what happens to teams who do well in any sport over an extended period. It's natural to want to knock them off their pedestals and I would say there's a savage determination out there to beat us this year.

I know that if things were the other way around and some team were bidding for the four-in-a-row we'd be very driven to make sure we made life as awkward for them as we possibly could. It's a natural instinct among all sportspeople.

I know damn well that Sheedy and McIntyre and everybody else have us in their sights. Tipperary beat us fair and square in last year's League semi-final in Nowlan Park and lost just one game all year. Granted, it was a big one – the All-Ireland semi-final against

Waterford – but I have no doubt that Sheedy felt they would have beaten us, had Tipperary reached the final. And why shouldn't he think that? It's his job to move Tipperary on, so he's got to think big.

McIntyre is a hungry manager too who, after years of waiting, has finally achieved his cherished ambition of managing Galway. Now that he has got the big chance, he will stop at nothing to win an All-Ireland, neither will Sheedy nor any of the other managers out there. So, if the two lads think that I'm buying into their propaganda about how far ahead of the rest Kilkenny are, they're definitely off beam.

I don't think like that, I never have and it's most unlikely that I will start now. The past is a different world in all walks of life, and that is very definitely the case in sport.

We played Galway in the Walsh Cup final in Freshford last Sunday and got an early indication of how they have set out their stall for the year. They tore into us with furious intent right from the start. They got the tackles in, closed us down, hunted in packs and made life as awkward as they possibly could. Good luck to them. They would regard it as playing us at our own game and you could sense just how intent they were to put down a marker.

Now that they are in the Leinster Championship, the scene changes somewhat as we could be meeting each other quite early in the summer. Then again, we might not meet at all – it depends on the draw and how we, and they, fare. They led by seven points at half-time last Sunday and fully deserved it because we had allowed them to dominate in all the important facets and phases. Do that against Galway and they'll make it count.

There are days when I don't have to say very much at half-time but this wasn't one of them. I made it very clear that I wasn't happy with what I had seen up to then. The season is up and running so it's not a question of saying it'll come right later, the time to get it right is now. This is a Walsh Cup final against a Galway team who are down here in Freshford to make a point so there can be no dilution of the principles we always try to apply.

We have to keep the standards high. I reminded everyone what we are about, that what we had achieved over the years was done on the basis of honesty and genuineness. You have to be so conscious of retaining that, even in a Walsh Cup final in early February. If you don't, you might not get it back later on.

The response was encouraging. We fought back to bring the game level in normal time and won by two points in extra-time. McIntyre came into our dressing-room afterwards and told us how great we were; I went into theirs and told them how welcome they were to the Leinster Championship. I genuinely meant it too. Leinster Council chairman, Seamus Howlin had also welcomed them from the presentation podium earlier on, so it was a day of goodwill all round, with everyone saying all the right things.

For all that, it was good to beat them. Nobody is more acutely aware than me of what Galway can do when they're at their best and, while it might not have changed the overall view of the hurling world if Galway had left Freshford with the Walsh Cup sitting up front on the team bus, it was something we didn't want to see happening. It might only be early February but it's nice to have the edge. A tiny edge at this stage but an edge nonetheless. Besides, we're due to play Galway in the first round of the League next Sunday so it's better to send them home thinking. Better, too, to have the Walsh Cup in Kilkenny than let it out west to unfamiliar territory.

CHAPTER 6

SPIRIT, RESPECT, HONESTY

Towards the end of the 1990s, analysts and commentators talked as if Clare, or more especially Loughnane, had invented hurling and everything that went with it. Their training methods were supposed to be so far advanced while the rest of the country were trapped in a time warp, reminiscing wistfully about the good old days. The new mantra was: imitate or fail. It was the Clare way or no way!

Spirit, respect, honesty. Not one, not two but all three, locked so tightly together that they're bomb-proof, bullet-proof, fire-proof, storm-proof, flood-proof! They have underpinned all my years as Kilkenny manager and will continue to do so for as long as I'm involved.

They represent the essence of what we are and how we conduct our business. You won't find me preaching to others how they should handle their affairs because that's their concern, but I do believe most sincerely that irrespective of whether it's club or county, college or street, senior, junior, intermediate, Under-21, minor or any other grade, the essentials remain the same. Spirit, respect and honesty! Indeed, they are qualities which will never let you down in any walk of life.

They certainly topped my list of ingredients to take into the Kilkenny dressing room when I agreed to take over as team manager in November 1998. They were the priorities – everything else could be built and worked on as we went along.

Waking up one morning to realise that I had been appointed Kilkenny senior manager was a strange feeling. It was also hugely exciting as I knew it would involve challenging myself in a way I hadn't experienced since my playing days. Even that was different because, as a player, you think essentially of yourself and how you can fit into the overall scheme and pattern with your colleagues. As manager, the responsibilities extend far beyond that.

Managing Kilkenny was something I never envisaged for myself. Not that I thought I wouldn't be able to do it effectively but because it just hadn't arisen and there didn't appear to be any obvious reason why it would or should.

Besides, my period in charge of The Village hadn't exactly been a spectacular success. I had been a selector and full-back when we won the 1981 county senior title but, after following up with an All-Ireland title the following spring, things dipped for us. We lost county finals to Ballyhale Shamrocks in the following two years and didn't get to another final until 1996. That was a long time in the shadows for us, but then Kilkenny is a mighty competitive county at all levels.

I had managed the The Village for some years – including 1996 when we lost to DJ Carey and his Gowran boys in a replayed final – so I had been very busy. I was contented too, not with the results we were getting but in terms of being involved with a club which has always been such an important part of the Cody family's way of life.

I never thought after the 1998 All-Ireland final that my life was about to take off in a new direction towards the county management scene and all that goes with it. As far as I was concerned Kevin Fennelly, who is a first cousin of mine, had been appointed for two years in 1997 and would be continuing for a second year at least. Of course, there was disappointment around Kilkenny after losing the '98 final but Leinster had been won for the first time in five years, which was something to work on. Granted, Kilkenny hadn't played well in the All-Ireland final or for that matter in the semi-final but, nonetheless, we had finished the season as provincial champions and All-Ireland runners-up. Naturally, we wanted both titles but it's a competitive world out there and we had no divine right to win anything. I suppose what frustrated Kilkenny people in 1998 was that, after beating Offaly quite comfortably in the Leinster final, it was all so different in the All-Ireland final.

The Leinster final defeat had caused turmoil in Offaly, resulting in a change of manager with Michael Bond replacing 'Babs' Keating. It didn't augur well for their chances of resurrecting their All-Ireland ambitions. In the space of six weeks, the whole thing had turned around so dramatically that Liam McCarthy was on his way to the midlands and Kilkenny were left wondering what the hell had happened.

In the circumstances, it was obvious that some adjustments were necessary for the following year and I have no doubt that, had Kevin continued, he would have addressed the situation. But, for whatever reason, he decided it was time to go.

I have no idea why Kevin left but even when I heard about his departure, I never thought of myself in terms of a replacement. In stark, blunt terms you could say that my years as The Village manager had been a failure – certainly when it came to winning trophies – so there was no obvious reason why County Chairman, John Healy or the rest of the Board would look in my direction. I hadn't been involved with Kilkenny minors or Under-21s, nor had I ever been approached by any county – large or small – or, indeed, by any other club.

Not that it would have mattered because I wouldn't have left The Village for anything. I would have been quite happy to continue there too, coaching any team at any level but, obviously, when the county job was offered to me it was a challenge and an opportunity I couldn't ignore. How could I? I was being given a chance to manage the senior team in one of the top hurling counties in the country.

Once I got the go-ahead from the Board, I had a massive drive to build a panel, a structure and a system that would forge ahead. There was no question of coming in with a two- or three-year plan and talking about re-building. Instead, the target was to win the All-Ireland straight away. It's what Kilkenny people expected and demanded. However, to achieve that – and to give ourselves a chance of building a platform that would sustain us well beyond 1999 – I felt there was more to it than just planning for one season.

When you're from one of the strong counties, you can always get lucky and win an All-Ireland in your first year as manager but, if it isn't built on something solid and sustainable, it won't last. That's why I was so focused on getting things organised properly. That involved players, County Board, management, medical back-up and all the other many and varied components that go to make up a modern-day camp. I was also determined to bring the clubs and supporters with us too because, ultimately, a county team represents everybody so there has to be a sense of shared ownership. It's not us and them. It's not the players and management operating in isolation from the County Board and the clubs. It's everybody trying to fit the pieces of the jigsaw together to give the county team the best possible chance of reaching their maximum potential while at the same time maintaining a club scene that caters for every player, regardless of talent. Neglect the club scene and the county panels suffer very quickly. Club players have to be catered for too.

All the various elements have to be united, in so far as it's possible. Naturally, there will be disagreements and tensions but once everybody has the same destination in mind it should be possible to work through any problems that arise in the course of the journey.

I knew I could work with the County Board, first with John Healy as chairman and then with Ned Quinn who replaced John some weeks after my appointment. They, and the rest of the Board, were – and are – solid people whose sole aim is to do the best they can for Kilkenny hurling. I'd have to say that about the current chairman, Paul Kinsella who is, of course, principal at St Patrick's, where I teach! Seriously though, it's crucial for a manager to have a good relationship with the Board. It's a two-way street, of course. Just as the Board must facilitate the manager as best they can, the manager has to be conscious of the Board's responsibility which extends way beyond the county teams.

I keep hearing nowadays of managers having liaison people between themselves and the County Board, and between players and management. I can't understand why that's necessary. As far as I'm concerned, it's a recipe for division and is certainly not something we have ever found necessary in Kilkenny. If we did, I'd be off because it would tell me something wasn't quite right. It's far better for everybody to be open and honest. That way, niggly little things are dealt with early and efficiently as opposed to being allowed to develop into something more serious. If I have an issue with the Board, I talk directly to them and if players have an issue with me they know they can raise it with me any place, any time. It was on that basis that I took over in late 1998 and it's a principle from which I have never since deviated.

I don't think anybody who knows me would ever accuse me of being remotely cocky or arrogant and there were definitely no bold statements or predictions about the future when I started out. However, I did have a strong belief in my own talents (if you don't then stay on the terrace and never take a manager's bib) and an even greater confidence in Kilkenny hurling. Having been so closely involved in the club scene, I knew every player in the county. Indeed, being a teacher, I would have seen most of them playing since they were young lads so I knew their strengths and weaknesses. I was lucky in that regard. I just love watching hurling at any age or standard so I had a good grasp of what was out there at the time.

I saw my initial job as instilling a massive spirit in the squad and linking it with respect and honesty throughout everything we did. I wasn't going to borrow from anybody else's philosophy or vision of how thing should be done. I had put myself in the line of fire and would live or die by my own decisions. If it went wrong, I would be gone very quickly. I wouldn't need to be told by the Board either.

I didn't give a damn what Ger Loughnane had done in Clare, Liam Griffin in Wexford or Eamonn Cregan in Offaly over previous years. Clare, in particular, were being held up as the template of a new age in hurling. They had been hugely successful in bringing unprecedented success to the county and in adding a sense of glamour to the scene. Nobody could deny that, or the fact that it was great for hurling to see them emerge from the shadows after so long without a Munster or All-Ireland title.

It was good for hurling, too, that Wexford had re-emerged in 1996, just as it was a very positive development when Galway and Offaly made their breakthroughs in the 1980s. The wider the success base, the better for the game although, as Kilkenny manager, that has nothing to do with me. My job is to help Kilkenny win as much as they possibly can and let every other county look after itself.

Towards the end of the 1990s, analysts and commentators talked as if Clare, or more especially Loughnane, had invented hurling and everything that went with it. Their training methods were supposed to be so far advanced while the rest of the country were trapped in a time warp, reminiscing wistfully about the good old days. The new mantra was: imitate or fail. It was the Clare way or no way!

In the midst of all the hype it was forgotten that, whatever about their training methods, their game plans or their psychological warfare, Clare had a lot of very fine hurlers too, men who would have prospered in any county in any era. You can run hurlers up and down all the hills you like, fill their heads with mumbo-jumbo and indulge in all sorts of gimmicks but you won't have anything unless they are good players in the first place. Sometimes, I think that tends to be forgotten about the Clare team of the 1990s. Those boys were seriously good hurlers.

Still, the clear message from the commentating classes was that Kilkenny – and other counties too – were being left behind when it came to training methods and the various ingredients that go to make a successful set-up. Personally, I didn't take the slightest notice of what I regarded as pure nonsense. In one ear and out the other! That was why I had absolutely no hesitation whatsoever in asking Mick O'Flynn to remain on as physical trainer when I came in. Mick had been there for years and knew exactly what he was doing so I was delighted to keep him on board because he was a trainer of the highest pedigree and ability.

Then there was the matter of who I would invite in as selectors. When I was interviewed for the position I wasn't asked who I planned to bring in, which was just as well because I hadn't even thought about it. Where was the point until I had actually got the job?

Nowadays, it's common in some counties for management teams to come as a package with the manager declaring well in advance who he will have with him as selectors, trainer, coach etc. It's almost like an American Presidential campaign where the announcement of a running mate for the candidates is regarded as crucial to their prospects. It might work in politics but, in my view, it's far too orchestrated when applied to county team management. A manager should be appointed on his merits and if he's deemed good enough to be handed the responsibility he should be trusted to get the right people with him. Still, if counties want to go down the 'package' route that's their business. All I'm saying is that I don't believe in it. Thankfully, neither did Kilkenny who didn't raise the issue in our discussions before I was appointed.

Of course, it's vital to get the right selectors – as indeed it is to appoint the right people in other positions – so I thought long and very hard about my choices and eventually decided to ask Ger Henderson and Johnny Walsh if they were interested in giving it a go. I wouldn't have been particularly close to either of them but I knew they would bring three qualities to the job – honesty, independence and, of course, a great knowledge of hurling. I didn't want 'yes men' around me who would agree with everything I said just to give the impression of unity. No, I wanted men who would say "You're wrong there, Brian, and here's why". When Ger or Johnny said it I knew it came from the heart and was motivated exclusively by the desire to do the right thing for Kilkenny hurling. Not that I need have worried because I couldn't think of two more unlikely 'yes men': when those boys wanted to make their point, they did it, whether you liked it or not.

I had, of course, hurled with Ger for years but other than meeting him casually at games I wouldn't have had much contact with him after my playing days were over. However, I knew more than enough about him as a man to understand that he would be a huge asset. The energy, drive and determination he brought as a player would prove mighty valuable on the sideline, training ground and at selection meetings.

Johnny hadn't been a county hurler but was a hugely effective performer with Ballyhale Shamrocks for many years. He knew the game inside out and, like Ger, he was never going to be anything less than strong-minded and independent. Together, they made a powerful combination.

Dr Bill Cuddihy, had been team doctor since the mid-1980s so I was more than happy when he agreed to stay on. The Cuddihy name had been synonymous with Kilkenny hurling since the 1950s as Bill's father, Kieran, was team doctor for over twenty-five years. Bill's older brother, Johnny took over from his father before Bill took on the onerous mantle in 1985. If ever a family deserved credit for services to Kilkenny hurling, it's the Cuddihys.

When I walked into the Kilkenny dressing-room for the first time as manager, I knew I was going to be checked out and tested by the players. Lads like DJ Carey, Pat O'Neill, Willie O'Connor and John Power had won All-Ireland medals in 1992-93 while several others had established themselves in subsequent years, so it wasn't as if I was starting with a brand new panel. After all, they were reigning Leinster champions and beaten All-Ireland finalists so they were used to operating at the very highest level. Losing to Offaly didn't make them bad players but now they found themselves dealing with a new manager, which must have been strange for them as it's unusual to have a changing of the guard after winning a provincial title and reaching the All-Ireland final. I knew I had to win them over as quickly as possible so that we could have a real go at the 1999 Championship.

I couldn't have bluffed them even if I'd tried, which I had no intention of doing anyway. I made no promises other than to work as hard as was humanly possible to win an All-Ireland. I wasn't entitled to any respect as a manager unless I earned it and there are no blueprints or quick-fix guides on how to do that, so I decided to remain loyal to my instincts.

Everything was to be built on spirit, respect and honesty. I would be myself with the players and hoped that they would be the same with me. There were a lot of high-profile managers around at the time but I had no interest in being half of this or half of that, or basing my way of doing things on this guy or that guy. I was prepared to learn from everybody but I wouldn't ape anybody. I wasn't going to look at how others had won All-Irelands and say, sure we'll do that down here in Kilkenny too. No, this was about sinking or swimming by doing it my way and the way I felt was right for Kilkenny.

I had to earn the respect of the players but they had to earn mine too. Whatever perceptions players may have had of themselves were of no interest to me. This was a new scene where everybody would have to operate on the basis of the present and the future, not the past. Places would have to be fought for and earned and there was no question of going into the job with pre-conceived notions. It was a clean slate where it was up to everybody to make their mark.

As a matter of respect, I deemed anybody who had played in the 1998 All-Ireland final as being worthy of a place on the initial panel. If they had won the Leinster title and got Kilkenny to the All-Ireland final they were entitled to be given a chance. However, it would be no more than that. What they had achieved up to then opened the first door but they would have to knock the others down themselves.

We had to make changes too, of course. John Power, who had two All-Ireland medals from 1992-93 wasn't on the panel for some reason in 1998 but I reckoned he still had a lot to offer. He was still only thirty-one years of age, had minded himself like a professional and was as driven for the cause as ever.

Eamonn Kennedy had been doing well at club level and was another I felt could bring something to the panel. He was going on twenty-seven years of age at the time and the talk around Kilkenny was that he wouldn't make it as a county player. Apparently he was too slow, one-handed or whatever! Right. Let's bring him in and see if all that's true. Of course, we knew it wasn't and he went on to become a fine centre-back. It's amazing how a player can get a reputation which becomes difficult to shake off. Just because he hasn't established himself on the senior team by his mid-twenties doesn't mean that he won't, although that tends to be the general thinking. Like other perceived wisdom, I ignored it and, in the case of Eamonn Kennedy, it was definitely the right thing to do.

It didn't require much managerial insight to decide that it was time to bring in a young fella from Ballyhale by the name of Henry Shefflin. He turned out to be a fairly handy addition to the Kilkenny scene! It was clear for several years that Henry was something special which, in itself, brought added pressure on him but he handled it brilliantly from the start and has continued to do so right to the present day. It was certainly my good luck that, just as I was taking over as manager, he was ready to step onto the senior scene.

I have always said to players that every career starts somewhere, sometimes in circumstances which could never have been foreseen: clearly that wasn't the case with Henry, he was always destined for greatness. Others have to take a different route and grab the chance when it arrives. There are also times when circumstances take on a life of their own, as if pre-ordained by forces way beyond human control.

Take the case of James McGarry. He was sub to Joe Dermody in 1998 but, when it came to forming a panel for 1999, I decided to replace James with Martin Carey who is, of course, a younger brother of DJ. I wrote to James, telling him that he wasn't included, something he has reminded me of many times over the years.

Shortly afterwards, Joe picked up an injury and James was invited back into the panel. We saw him as No.2 but his chance arrived when Martin got married and went away on honeymoon. Over to you now, James. Right man, right place, right time, right attitude! He played extremely well over the next few weeks, held on to the position and went on to become one of the best goalkeepers in the history of the game.

If ever there was an example of how to take a chance when it presented itself, it was James. He played himself into a position where he couldn't be dropped, irrespective of who we might have considered to be No.1, 2 or 3 at the start. Also, he could have sulked and refused to return when Dermody got injured. It might have looked to McGarry that we had made up our minds on who our goalkeepers would be and that he was being used to fill in but had no chance of staying there long term. It was never that way because that's not how I do business but since James didn't know me at the time it would be easy to understand why he might have thought differently. I make calls as I see them but, ultimately, the only judgement that counts is based on how a player performs. McGarry got his opening because Dermody was injured and Carey was unavailable. It was a mix of circumstances but he grabbed his opportunity and made the most of it.

Imagine if he had sulked when he was left off the panel and refused to come back for what he probably thought was a short-term arrangement designed to help us rather than him. He would have missed out on what developed into a glorious career and Kilkenny would have been without an exceptionally gifted goalkeeper. The record books might have looked different too. And not to Kilkenny's advantage either.

Instead, he came back determined to prove that he was the best around. The moral of the story for any player of any age is to believe in yourself, don't sulk if things aren't going your way and hang on in there because you never know when, or how, your opening will come.

Having put the panel and structures in place for 1999, I knew that there would be no honeymoon period. I was a new manager which usually carries a period of grace but I wasn't going to be given much time to settle in. Losing to Offaly in the '98 All-Ireland final had hurt Kilkenny very badly so the pressure was on straight away.

We won Leinster with a lot more ease than would have been expected. We dominated Laois from the start but it was even enough against Offaly up to the half-hour mark. The game swung on goals we got just before and after half-time. DJ Carey landed one just before the break and Brian McEvoy hit another a few minutes after the re-start and we eventually ran out ten point winners.

The win over Offaly was very significant. They were the reigning All-Ireland champions and, after what happened to Kilkenny the previous September, there was a lot of nervousness around but the lads settled well and never allowed Offaly to assert themselves.

We scored a total of 11-35 against Laois and Offaly which was very pleasing, even if we knew the day would come when we would be involved in a low-scoring battle where other qualities would be required.

We beat Clare in the All-Ireland semi-final in what was a very satisfying win because while they weren't Munster champions, they were still a very formidable side, most of whom had won two All-Irelands over the previous four years. Besides, it was time for Kilkenny to put down a marker and show that our style, values and principles weren't as obsolete as some of the hurling cognoscenti of the time would have you believe.

It set us up for an All-Ireland clash with Cork whose rate of improvement under Jimmy Barry-Murphy that summer had been quite remarkable. They had come off a disappointing run where they hadn't won a Munster title since 1992 to finally beat Clare before wearing down Offaly in the All-Ireland semi-final.

Cork-Kilkenny finals always generate their own magic and this time the media found an extra hook for the build-up in the fact that Jimmy and myself were the managers. We had been captains in the 1982 All-Ireland final which might have made a nice line for the media but which was never going to have even the tiniest bearing on the 1999 final.

Unfortunately so in my case, because whereas Kilkenny beat Cork seventeen years earlier, we lost this time in the most disappointing circumstances possible. There's nothing more disappointing than a one-point defeat in an All-Ireland final because it makes you re-visit every bounce, every deflection, every missed chance, every decision!

You always hope for a dry day for any game, but most especially in an All-Ireland final where the stakes are at their highest. We didn't get it in 1999. Instead, it was wet, dank and unpleasant which no doubt contributed to what was the lowest scoring final since 1987. And yes, Kilkenny lost that one too, going down to Galway!

If I'd been told in advance that we would concede just thirteen points to Cork, I would have been quite happy as you would always expect to score more than that. We had, after all, hit Offaly for 5-14 and Clare for 2-14. That pair had won three of the previous four All-Ireland titles between them so we looked in pretty good shape to rack up a decent score against Cork. Certainly, we would never have envisaged our strike rate dipping to just a dozen points.

The final really was a strange game. It was close on twenty minutes before we even scored – Cork only got one point in the second quarter and actually managed just one point from the twenty-second to the fifty-third minutes. It wasn't that we didn't have chances to score in the first quarter, but we didn't take them and, as events transpired, we paid dearly for it even if we did succeed in putting ourselves in a winning position midway through the second half.

We led 0-10 to 0-6 at the three-quarter stage and were still two points clear coming up to the hour mark, but then conceded five points on the trot which won the game for Cork. Scores were hard to come by so what made our defeat all the more disappointing was that we surrendered a decent lead without conceding a goal.

We had no excuses, mind you. As far as I'm concerned the better team always wins the All-Ireland final. It's about who scores the most and if you're behind your opponents at the end, you don't deserve to win. You can fool yourself into thinking otherwise but that's the truth.

You can make excuses, look for scapegoats or just claim it was down to bad luck but it changes nothing. You lose, you accept it, you move on. As usual, some bizarre claims were doing the rounds after the 1999 final, principally that we had been over-confident.

Quite why that should be the case is beyond me, but then post All-Ireland final analysis doesn't always major in common sense. Of course, we weren't over-confident. Instead, we were beaten by a Cork team that played marginally better on the day. Sorry if that explanation doesn't suit the forensic hurling scientists who attempt to dissect what is a simple game into minute particles, but it happens to be the truth. Painful for us in 1999, but the truth nonetheless.

While it's pointless going through every detail of a game – whether you win or lose – it is important to learn from the overall thrust and to adapt accordingly. When I reflected on the 1999 final I felt that we weren't, if you like, ruthless or savage enough. Obviously, I use those words in a mental rather than physical context. It manifested itself when we were four points up with a little over a quarter of an hour remaining. We didn't produce the sort of phenomenal interaction between everybody to make sure we didn't allow Cork back into the game. It wasn't that they got two quick goals, or even one for that matter.

Goals can change games very quickly but this time Cork picked us off point for point which was the most disappointing aspect from our perspective. I'm not taking away from Cork in any way but the harsh reality for us was that we had to live with the fact that we didn't perform as we should – or could – have in the closing stages.

Naturally, I examined my own role in the defeat. The game was there for the taking and we didn't do it so I had to answer the hard question: was there anything extra I could have done as manager?

The answer to that question always has to be yes, because if you think you have done everything right and you still lose, you'll never move on. Even if you're up against a better team you have to think that there's something you could have come up with to help the players.

There's no doubt that the 1999 final defeat was a big learning experience for me. We needed to be mentally harder, more attuned to what was required to squeeze the very last drop of efficiency when the fire was at its hottest. We had failed that test in the final ten minutes against Cork so it was up to me to find a way of getting it right next time.

For most of the players it was a second successive defeat in the All-Ireland final which was difficult to stomach. Granted, they had come very close but there are no prizes for second place, and very definitely not in a county like Kilkenny where expectations are always high.

Still, the reaction from the Kilkenny public was disappointed but positive. At least that was the sense we got when a huge crowd came out to welcome us home on the Monday night. I told them that, come hell or high water, we would be back with the McCarthy Cup next year.

Every manager says the same in those circumstances but it was definitely something I totally believed in. I had learned a few things that season which would be of use in the future. I also felt there was enough scope in the county to strengthen the panel so if we could bring it all together we had a right good chance of beginning the new Millennium with an All-Ireland. The alternative was unthinkable.

For now, though, I was left facing the unquestionable truth that I had failed my first All-Ireland test as a manager. Already, the pressure was increasing. Fail in 2000 and my days as Kilkenny manager would probably be over.

CHAPTER 7

REFLECTION TIME

The Kilkenny players would later admit that having to stand in the pouring rain as Cork captain, Mark Landers, received the Liam McCarthy Cup was close to torture. They wanted to scurry into the dressing rooms but it would have been noticed and converted into an accusation of ungraciousness in defeat. So, instead, the Kilkenny players and management stood and listened as Landers raised the cup, yelling excitedly to the Cork supporters, "Welcome home, Liam McCarthy!"

Martin Breheny writes: While Brian Cody may have been convinced after the 1999 All-Ireland final that Kilkenny would launch the new Millennium by winning their twenty-sixth title, the rest of the hurling world was not quite as convinced.

Granted, Kilkenny had come up just one point short against Cork, but this was their second successive defeat in an All-Ireland final. The circumstances were different to 1998 but the outcome was the same. The unthinkable had happened – it appeared Kilkenny had grown accustomed to losing All-Ireland finals.

In the history of the Championship, eleven teams had lost successive All-Ireland hurling finals but only three (Kilkenny, 1947; Cork, 1984; and Galway, 1987) had come back to win at the third attempt, proving just how difficult it is to shake off back-to-back defeats and emerge as a winning force third time out.

It was certainly unfamiliar territory for Kilkenny who had to look back to the 1940s for the last time they were facing that situation. They had lost the 1945 and 1946 finals to Tipperary and Cork respectively, but succeeded in avoiding the embarrassing treble in 1947 beating Cork by a point in one of the game's great contests.

Now, fifty-three years later, Kilkenny faced the prospect of beginning the new Millennium by suffering a third successive All-Ireland final defeat, something no county had ever endured. First, of course, they would have to reach the final.

Offaly were still a formidable force, anchored by players who had enjoyed many happy experiences against Kilkenny. And while Offaly had lost the 1999 Leinster final to Kilkenny by ten points, they had proven that their resolve and ambition levels were still high by running Cork to three points in the All-Ireland semi-final.

They actually led Cork by two points with eight minutes remaining before conceding five points from there to the finish. A few weeks later, Kilkenny would be hit by a five-point blitz by Cork late in the final so, by the end of 1999, Kilkenny's Leinster final win over Offaly didn't look as significant as it might have appeared in mid-July. At least that was the spin being put on it by Offaly, whose sense of self-worth was never in doubt.

They had enjoyed a series of successes throughout the 1990s and, while some great players were coming towards the end of their careers, they still felt they could take some of the magic into the new Millennium.

It was different in Wexford's case. As the decade that had brought them a remarkable power surge in 1996-97 drew to a close, they had spun into a steep decline. They had been thrashed by Offaly in the 1999 Leinster semi-final and, frankly, the signs for the immediate future didn't look bright. It all added up to the likelihood that Offaly still represented the most serious threat to Kilkenny in Leinster.

Unlike most of the Kilkenny players who had played in both 1998 and 1999, Cody hadn't been part of the first defeat so he didn't have to share in any of the responsibility for it. And, since the second one was by the narrowest margin, his optimism for the 2000 campaign appeared well-founded, provided of course that successive defeats hadn't irreparably damaged the players' confidence.

The unchallengeable reality was that Kilkenny had failed twice in finals. While they came up just one point short against Cork in 1999, the manner in which they allowed a four-point advantage to be wiped out in a low-scoring game hinted at problems with their collective resolve. Ultimately, that was proven not to be the case, but it wasn't easy to see any silver lining in the dark clouds that hung over Croke Park during the presentation ceremony.

The Kilkenny players would later admit that having to stand in the pouring rain as Cork captain, Mark Landers, received the Liam McCarthy Cup was close to torture. They wanted to scurry into the dressing rooms but it would have been noticed and converted into an accusation of ungraciousness in defeat. So, instead, the Kilkenny players and management stood and listened as Landers raised the cup, yelling excitedly to the Cork supporters, "Welcome home, Liam McCarthy!"

Losing an All-Ireland final is always a huge disappointment, all the more so when the margin is just one point. Unanswered and unanswerable questions swirled around in the heads of the Kilkenny players as they stood in silence through those horrible minutes as Landers went through his victory speech. "Why didn't referee, Pat O'Connor play a little more stoppage time? Would we have scored the equalising point if he had? Where could we have made up the difference in the course of the game? How would we have fared in a replay?" The speech was no longer than usual but it seemed, to Kilkenny, as though it went on forever.

And yet, in its own way, the excruciating experience may have helped provide the hardening agent which would make such a difference in future years.

While Cody wasn't subjected to any major criticisms for his handling of the final, he didn't escape totally. He had replaced John Power and

Charlie Carter with PJ Delaney and Niall Moloney five minutes from the finish, a double substitution designed to freshen up the attack but which inevitably didn't find favour with supporters of the two long-established stars. Others wondered why he waited so long. If he was going to make changes why not do it earlier? Not that the questions or the questioners bothered Cody.

He took the Kilkenny job on the basis that he would do it his way alone. And while an All-Ireland title hadn't been delivered in the first year, substantial progress had been made not just in terms of how the team was shaped but also in the ancillary services that go to make up a modern camp.

Nevertheless, even after one season, time was already beginning to run out for him. An impatient county wanted an end to the barren years. Indeed, failure to win the All-Ireland in his second year would probably have led to another change of managerial direction. No pressure then as Cody began planning for 2000!

CHAPTER 8

JUDGEMENT RESERVED

It must have been strange for him watching *Waterford recover so quickly and make it all the way to the All-Ireland final last year. I have no idea how he felt on All-Ireland final day, but then I've never managed outside my own county. I presume that working with an outside club or county brings a different type of loyalty, but it's a scenario I know nothing about. The Village and Kilkenny are all I know, or want to know for that matter.*

Sunday, March 1, 2009: *I have my doubts about the experimental rules. Six lads sent off in our game with Waterford in Walsh Park today and none of them deserved it. Tommy Walsh, Jackie Tyrrell, Eoin Kelly and Seamus Prendergast were back in the dug-outs after twenty-five minutes and you wonder, for what?*

A bit of a skirmish and four of them were on yellow cards and heading for an early shower. Will that improve hurling? Will it make more of a spectacle? Will it make it a better game? Will it make it safer? What are we at here? Hard to understand but let's be patient and give the rules a chance to settle in. Maybe things will ease out when referees and players get fully used to them. I wouldn't be very confident, mind you, but we'll see.

Eddie Brennan and Declan Prendergast were sent off on straight reds in the second half. No need for that either. Imagine being told for the first time about this great game called hurling. Fastest field game in the world and all that. A game played with honour and integrity. A game where physicality is allowed within a clearly defined set of rules which have applied for years. Then you learn that six of the thirty players are sent off during a game between the two best sides in the country in the previous Championship: you'd think there was something seriously wrong with the rules, which there isn't. But we're back in experimental mode, after yet another rules revision exercise so we have to live with it – for now at least.

The media ask for my reaction to the sending-offs afterwards, but I hold my counsel. They were probably expecting me to cut loose and make headlines for the following day, but I didn't. I said from the start that I'd reserve judgement on the experiments and I'll abide by that. Not that my silence should be interpreted as support for the change.

We played Limerick two weeks ago and saw neither yellow nor red cards for either side. I couldn't spot where the big difference was between that game and today's but, obviously, the referees could. Either that or they implemented the rules differently, which was probably the case – not deliberately, of course, but in terms of how they interpreted situations. Six cards to none! It makes you wonder. I'm not convinced these rules are going to work and the fear is that a fella could get sent off early on for a clumsy challenge where there wasn't even the slightest intent to foul. Is that where we want hurling to go? You were a bit awkward on that challenge, now I know you didn't intend to hurt or even foul your opponent but you caught him a bit high, so off you go!

Claiming that the new sanctions will make players more careful – as those who drew up the new rules are – is all very fine but how careful do you want? Do we want players to be afraid to tackle in case the referee decides a yellow card offence was committed? I thought hurling was a physical game where lads were allowed to go into tackles fairly and squarely without being fearful of being shown a card for merely doing a job they had been taught when they were kids.

I came out strongly against the 'sin bin' experiments a few years ago (remember how the bins were full of players for ten-minute spells) because I thought they were mad. If I recall rightly, JJ Delaney got sent off two or three times in a few weeks so, if you didn't know him better, you'd think he was a vicious hit man with evil in his heart. Now is that the JJ you know? No, me neither. It was ridiculous stuff that gave common sense a bad name, and I said so at the time. The experiments were proved to be a complete sham, and were dumped. Rightly so.

The latest experiments appear to me to be more designed for football than hurling. I watch football but I wouldn't consider myself sufficiently qualified to comment on whether they should apply there or not, but I do know that you can't have 'catch all' rules for two sports with so many clear variations. Other than being governed by the same association, hurling and Gaelic football have little in common and the rules – and their application and interpretation – should reflect that.

Waterford beat us by four points today and fully deserved it. After what happened in last year's All-Ireland final they were that bit more fired up than us, and it showed. We led early on but, once they got going, they were the better side. We only played in fits and starts. To be honest, we weren't competitive enough and the lads know that.

Still, it has provided us with a focus. With only the top two in with a chance of winning the League, you can't afford to drop too many points in this group, so we'll need to bounce right back very quickly. We should have played three games by now but we missed the opening day game against Galway on February 8 because of the bad weather. We knew when we left Kilkenny on the Sunday morning that there was a danger we wouldn't get very far. The roads were icy, snow was falling heavily and showing no signs of stopping. It took a long time to even get as far as Durrow, so there was nothing for it except to 'phone ahead to Galway and tell them we couldn't make it. The weather was okay in Salthill but it would have been too dangerous for us to continue and, anyway, we probably wouldn't have made it on time.

Since it was the first game of the new League season it was disappointing to miss out, although both Galway and Kilkenny could probably have done without meeting each other twice in a week (we had met in the Walsh Cup final the Sunday before). Still, you always hate when a game has to be cancelled because, apart from the inconvenience on the day, it isn't always easily to re-schedule.

The postponement meant that our first League game was at home to Limerick a week later where we won by a point and were lucky to do so. We were 0-6 to 0-1 up early on, but they came right back into it and won a huge amount of possession, especially in the second half. It was one of those days where all a team can do is hang on and hope the breaks will come their way, which they did for us in the end as Michael Grace clipped over the winning point deep in stoppage time.

Limerick will have been disappointed because it was a game they could have so easily won, and which would have set them nicely for the rest of the campaign as they had beaten Clare in the first round. Justin McCarthy was in charge of Waterford the last time he was in Nowlan Park last spring for the National League quarter-final, but he's in the Limerick corner now and has obviously settled in very quickly.

You get to know some rival managers over the years but for no obvious reason Justin isn't someone I would have had much contact with. Other than patrolling the same sideline and meeting him at the launch of the Allianz Leagues or some other function, I wouldn't have encountered him very much.

I would have great respect for him, though, and felt he got rough justice in Waterford last year. I have a policy of keeping my nose out of other counties' affairs but would have sympathy for Justin, on a personal basis, because what happened wasn't nice. He had done a hell of a lot for Waterford – even the players who eventually wanted him out admitted that – so it was sad to see his term come to such an abrupt and controversial end. That's not the way any manager wants to have his regime ended. It goes to show that you never know what the future holds. Justin wasn't the first manager who either resigned or was forced out in mid-season and he won't be the last. Times really have changed in the GAA, but that's the way of the world nowadays.

It must have been strange for him watching Waterford recover so quickly and make it all the way to the All-Ireland final last year. I have no idea how he felt on All-Ireland final day, but then I've never managed outside my own county. I presume that working with an outside club or county brings a different type of loyalty, but it's a scenario I know nothing about. The Village and Kilkenny are all I know, or want to know for that matter.

The postponed clash with Galway has been re-fixed for next Sunday and now that we've lost to Waterford it means there's no more room for error. Early pressure then, because Pearse Stadium is never an easy place to take points. Lose twice in this group and we probably won't make the final. I most definitely don't want that to happen because, apart from maintaining our policy of taking the League as seriously as it deserves to be taken, I want to keep hurling into early May. More than that, I don't want to allow a losing habit through the dressing room door. Uninvited guests tend to hang around and don't take kindly to being asked to leave.

Galway lost to Dublin in their first game but put a big score on Cork, so they'll be ready for this one. Portumna's win over Ballyhale in the club semi-final will be a boost to them, even if they won't have any of the Portumna lads. Those who were in Thurles for the club game last Sunday will know why I regard Galway as such a dangerous side.

Portumna were absolutely brilliant. They have pace, strength, plus a great sense of togetherness – and that's without mentioning they also have some brilliant hurlers. To be honest, I wasn't surprised they won because Shamrocks hadn't played all that well in Leinster. Yet, they were hot favourites to beat the reigning All-Ireland champions. It goes to show that anyone who takes notice of the odds is only fooling themselves. Games are won on the field, not in a bookies' office.

Portumna were far superior and I have to say I'll be very, very surprised if they don't beat De La Salle in the final. On last Sunday's form, they're definitely the best club team around.

When Joe Canning and some others come off that Portumna team and into Galway jerseys, they're going to make one hell of a difference. Still, they won't be playing for Galway next week which is good news for us. We need to win up there to really kickstart the season.

CHAPTER 9

RELIEF AND REDEMPTION

The pained grimace on his face changed suddenly as he shot a startled look up at me. It was as if I had told him that he had been stripped of the captaincy and was being sent home.

"No way, Brian, no way. I'm staying on. I have to." He paused for a few seconds as if thinking of the punch line. "Tell you what, Brian. My man won't touch the ball in the second half. I guarantee you that."

"Alright, Willie. If you say it, that's good enough for me."

"Right so, let me out there."

Driving home from training one night about two weeks before the 2000 All-Ireland final I remember thinking that I had nothing left to do with the squad except look after the organisational side of things. They were so focused, so driven, so consumed by the desire to win that they just weren't going to be stopped.

It didn't matter who they were playing – this was going to be their final. Next night in training I told them that I could disappear for the following two weeks and let them get on with it. I didn't matter anymore. In fact, nothing mattered any more except winning the final. The squad had matured to a degree where they knew and accepted what it took to be successful. They had taken control of their own destiny and weren't going to be denied.

The defeat in the 1998 All-Ireland final and, even more so, in 1999 had helped enormously in that process. The '99 defeat had very definitely made me aware of what was required from my end of the operation. In fact, I still remain convinced that if we had won the '99 final we wouldn't have enjoyed as much success afterwards.

As a manager, I might have felt this is all quite easy. First season in charge and Liam McCarthy is back in Kilkenny. Happy days. Instead, I had to deal with defeat and work out how it could be avoided the following year. Reality had arrived in my first season and I had to admit to myself that I had failed. The final had been there for the taking and we should have been able to close it out but we didn't. As manager, I had to examine why that happened and what we needed to do to avoid a repetition. We needed to be more ruthless, more clinical and more aware of our responsibilities as a group and as individuals when the pressure points arrived. We hadn't done that in the closing stages of the 1999 final against Cork and paid the ultimate price.

One of the more unusual aspects of the aftermath of that defeat was the attitude among the hurling public outside Kilkenny.

I sensed that they felt a bit sorry for us. That was a bit surprising, given Kilkenny's many successes over the years, but I suppose there was a degree of sympathy for the players on an individual level after losing two successive finals. As for the new manager, he had something else to cope with. People took to complimenting me on being a good loser! It was said with the best of intentions but I absolutely despised it, not least because it wasn't remotely true. We were all gracious in defeat, as any squad should be, but that was as far as it went. Deep inside we were feeling low, empty and deeply, deeply frustrated. Bloody hell, this was the second final defeat in a row.

Anyway, what's a good loser? People who aren't upset by defeat? Somehow I doubt if that particular species actually exists and, if it does, it most certainly wasn't to be found in Kilkenny towards the end of 1999. I couldn't come to terms with the fact that anybody might feel sympathy for us. It was something the Kilkenny hurling fraternity wasn't used to and we weren't planning on changing that particular trait.

As luck would have it, the 2000 National League programme pitted us against Cork in the first game. It was exactly the start we wanted to get the season going. If we lost, there would be plenty of time to work our way back into the season, but if we won it would make an early statement of our intent.

Either way, it would be good for us. Predictably, the Kilkenny public turned out in droves to get an early look at how things were going. There were over 10,000 people in Nowlan Park with the majority of them from Kilkenny, all eager to see how we had wintered. That brought its own demands, but then 2000 was always going to be about intense pressure so it was better to get used to it from the start.

There were times in that game when I thought we would be blown away. As befits All-Ireland champions, Cork had a massive confidence and swagger about them and looked so powerful in everything they did that we had to hurl brilliantly to match them. We led all the way and eventually won by four points, but it took an incredible effort to do it. On a few occasions Cork looked as if they were about to get a run on us but we dug in, deep and determined, and saw it through to the finish. You could sense the fierce drive and unity within the group that day – clearly they were hungry for action and had taken their frustrations from the previous September into the new season. If they hadn't, Cork would have ground them into submission. They tried hard, too, and hurled very well, but we were not going to be denied.

I had a warm feeling for the season ahead after the Cork game. There was still an awful lot of work to be done, but the manner in which the players had gone about their job that day was really uplifting. As it happened, we later lost to Waterford and Wexford and didn't make the League semi-finals. I have always placed a considerable emphasis on the League and would have definitely liked that particular spring campaign to last longer, so it was a bit disappointing.

Nonetheless, there was a great spirit in the camp and a realisation that we were men on a mission. We drove forward in unison, management pushing players and players pushing management in their own different ways. A common goal had been set and nothing was going to deflect us from achieving it.

The more demands we made on each other, the better it worked. Everything down to the last detail was geared to give the team the best possible chance of performing to the absolute peak of their talents.

Willie O'Connor was captain that year and he became a strong influence. He was Glenmore's nomination for the honour after they won the 1999 county title and it worked out brilliantly. We have always operated the system in Kilkenny where the county champions nominate the captain and while some people are critical of it, I have no problems whatsoever with maintaining a tradition that has served us well. Maybe that sounds old-fashioned but, so what? It's up to other counties to run their affairs as they wish but we have remained loyal to the link between county champions and the captaincy, and I see no reason why it should be changed. I benefited from it myself in 1982 when our club success the previous year gave me the opportunity and the great honour to captain Kilkenny in what turned out to be an All-Ireland winning year. Maybe that has coloured my view, although I don't think that it has.

It's a massive honour for the county champions to be allowed nominate the Kilkenny captain for the following year and, since clubs are the very bedrock of everything we do, it's right that they should continue to enjoy that perk. I certainly have always been comfortable with the arrangement. As far as I'm concerned it's a case of if it ain't broken, don't fix it. The manager may not always get the man who, in different circumstances, would be his personal choice, but that has nothing to do with it. This is about how we do things in Kilkenny and if it has served us well up to now, why change it?

Of course, too much is sometimes made of the role of captaincy in terms of the leadership he is supposed to provide. Yes, it's important, but you need a lot more than one leader in the dressing room. While whoever actually leads out the team and takes the toss is the recognisable face of on-field leadership, others have just as much responsibility. In Kilkenny, we have been lucky to have lots of leaders in the squad so I never worry about who emerges as captain from the county champions.

There was certainly no need for concern in 2000 because Willie O'Connor was brilliant in the job. He was a big influence on the whole scene but then we had other experienced leaders in every line, men like Peter Barry, Andy Comerford, John Power and DJ. These guys were strong-minded individuals who generated huge respect among their colleagues and who knew exactly what was required.

One example of Willie's attitude as a captain – and, indeed a man, – stands out from the 2000 campaign. He took a terrible wallop just before half-time in the All-Ireland final and he had actually cracked a rib, although we didn't know that at the time. Anyway, we were in the dressing room at half-time and Dr Bill (Cuddihy) was bringing his own brand of magic to bear on Willie, who was lying on the bench hardly able to breathe. To be honest, I was quite worried about him.

I talked to the selectors about how we'd re-organise the full-back line now that Willie was coming off. "We'll get Sean Meally on and take it from there." I walked over to our stricken captain and said, "You can't continue in that state, Willie".

The pained grimace on his face changed suddenly as he shot a startled look up at me. It was as if I had told him that he had been stripped of the captaincy and was being sent home.

"No way, Brian, no way. I'm staying on. I have to." He paused for a few seconds as if thinking of the punch line. "Tell you what, Brian. My man won't touch the ball in the second half. I guarantee you that."

"Alright, Willie. If you say it, that's good enough for me."

"Right so, let me out there."

He was as good as his word and went on to hurl a great second half. There was absolutely no way that he was going to sit out the second half of an All-Ireland final while he could still breathe. It was pure mind over matter and to hell with the pain and discomfort. He had waited all his life for the chance to captain Kilkenny to an All-Ireland final win, and he was damned if he was going to allow an injury to stop him.

If you look at the pictures of Willie raising the cup after being presented by the then GAA President, Sean McCague, you can see that he was grimacing. In fact he was in bloody agony but staying on the pitch and seeing the final through to the end was all that mattered. It summed up the spirit and hunger which was in the camp that year.

We could never have known at the start of the Championship that we would end up playing Offaly twice. But then they had been such a regular feature of Kilkenny's summers for so long that it was scarcely surprising that once the All-Ireland qualifier system was introduced there would be regular double-ups between us.

We beat them by eleven points in the 2000 Leinster final, a margin that didn't do justice to their efforts for forty-five minutes. We led by three points at that stage but pulled away from there on. Naturally, there was a tendency to write Offaly out of the All-Ireland equation after that but I had a strange feeling that we hadn't seen the last of them. They had a very experienced team with an awful lot of pride and, as they showed in 1998, they knew how to re-build a season after losing in Leinster.

They did just that in the most dramatic circumstances by beating Cork in the All-Ireland semi-final. The general view before that game was Cork would win and set up a repeat of the 1999 final, but Offaly blew that theory apart. Their performance against Cork was as good as anything they had produced for a long time.

Their second half, in particular, was excellent as they pared back a three-point lead to win by four. It was Offaly at their determined best while the quality of their point-taking made it abundantly clear to anybody who doubted it that they were still an outstanding team.

Not that we could pay too much attention to Offaly at that stage as we still had to face Galway in the other semi-final. They had beaten Tipperary in the League final and All-Ireland quarter-final, so their form line was convincing. It was my first time to meet them in the Championship as a manager and knowing what Galway teams are capable of, I was apprehensive. Any team that beats Tipperary twice in two big games in the space of a few months has to be good. They hurled well for a long time against us but – as we had done against Offaly in the Leinster final – we finished strongly and won quite convincingly in the end.

One of the strange things about the build-up to the final was that the public seemed to place much more store on our Leinster final win over Offaly than on their elimination of the All-Ireland champions. I certainly didn't. Offaly still had most of the team that had beaten Kilkenny in the 1998 All-Ireland final; indeed many of them were there in 1994 too so they knew how to win finals.

This was a serious hurling force, as they had repeatedly proved through the 1990s. The Whelahans, the Dooleys, Johnny Pilkington, Michael Duignan, Kevin Martin, Kevin Kinahan – real winners who never knew when they were beaten. They were big day men who would be well capable of blocking out what happened in the Leinster final and replacing it with the positive experience of the All-Ireland semi-final.

We approached that final in exactly the same way as we would have if Cork were our opponents. I was quite confident that if we hurled to our peak we would win because the mood and the application were so good, but we still had to perform on the day. It was all about performance and, as we came closer to the final, I was as convinced as you possibly can be in these circumstances that, unless Offaly produced something truly sensational, we would beat them.

Everything was in place – now all we had to do was keep ticking over at the right tempo. We had a slight hiccup on the Sunday before the final when news reached me that Stephen Grehan had turned out in a soccer game for a local club.

Stephen had done very well in our half-forward line all summer and would have been on the team for the final if events didn't take a regrettable turn. He was a very committed fella who never put a foot wrong up to then but, for some reason, he allowed himself to be persuaded to play a soccer game that Sunday. It seems he was out for a jog, came upon the game and took a chance on playing for the second half. It was just one of those things but it had regrettable consequences for him.

I met him and discussed the situation and he accepted straight away that he was wrong. It gave neither me nor the rest of the selectors any pleasure to have to leave him out of the final but we felt we had no option.

He took it like a man even though it was hard on him, but he knew why he was omitted. Still, he continued to be an important part of our set-up afterwards and came on as a sub a few times in the 2002 Championship.

The record books show that we won the 2000 final by thirteen points which, I'm told, was the highest winning margin since Tipperary beat Antrim in 1989. It might have looked easy, but I don't recall it like that. After all, we were playing Offaly and you never knew what shock they had in store for you, irrespective of how far ahead you were. We made a great start with DJ (Carey) darting in for an early goal. We built on it from there and while Offaly staged a revival in the second half they were too far back to really trouble us.

The early blitz knocked them off line and, once we got in front, there would be no looking over our shoulders. We had trained all season to press on and exploit every advantage that arose. That's important against any team at any time but was more so against the Offaly team of that period whose resilience was quite remarkable, and who had no doubts whatsoever about their capacity to beat Kilkenny on a given day.

I never thought, during 2000, of the possible consequences of not winning the All-Ireland title because I felt we were plenty good enough to take it. There wasn't a remote speck of cockiness about what we were doing but it was as if the experiences of the previous year had provided the catalyst to drive the whole camp on to another level.

Besides, how could the players live with the stigma of being the first Kilkenny group to lose three successive All-Ireland finals? And how could the manager explain it away either? Protesting that I wasn't in charge in 1998 and could only share in the responsibility for two defeats wouldn't have made any difference as I was led to the door by the ear.

There's no doubt that the team performed excellently in 2000. I know that there were whispers about how we had won the All-Ireland without beating any Munster opposition, but that wasn't our fault. Munster's top two, Cork and Tipperary had been beaten by Offaly and Galway respectively so we could only play what was put in front of us. We had no control over who reached the All-Ireland semi-final or final, and the fact that it wasn't Munster opposition on either front was down to the fact they weren't good enough to beat Offaly or Galway.

Would Cork or Tipperary have done better against us than Galway or Offaly? I don't know and I don't care. Results don't lie. I said it a year earlier when Cork beat us in the final and the same applied in 2000 when we won.

Let's put it this way – Kilkenny didn't feel in any way self-conscious about being crowned 2000 champions. We had earned it.

CHAPTER 10

RIGHT RESULTS, WRONG CONCLUSIONS

If you're properly tuned you keep going with the *same determination from start to finish. Bring it down to man-on-man. Whether you're twenty points up or twenty points down, the challenge is the same. Say, for instance, you're the full-back and your team is so comfortably ahead that there's no chance of being caught. The ball is dropping between you and the full-forward so, are you going to say, "I don't care if he catches it over my head, turns and sticks it in the net – sure we're going to win anyway"? No bloody way. You want to soar ten feet into the air, grab the ball and drive it down the field.*

Monday, March 30, 2009: *It has been a good month. The early setback against Waterford has had the desired effect. We've played three games since then and won them all, so we're back on track for a place in the League final.*

We've beaten Galway, Tipperary and Clare and already there's talk about how we're putting down markers for the Championship. Now, what that means exactly is a mystery to me, but there you go. Kilkenny are putting down markers, stamping their authority, grinding down the opposition, asserting themselves in a forceful manner. Take your pick as to which suits your particular viewpoint. I will: they're all nonsense. Pure, undiluted, straight-forward nonsense.

We hurl to win games not to make statements about future intentions. Isn't that what everybody does? The Tipperary game cranked up the daft theory that we were so annoyed over losing to them in Nowlan Park in last year's National League semi-final that we had vowed vengeance this time.

And there was I thinking that our only motivation was to pick up the two points we needed to keep pace with a fast-moving League. Of course the lads were conscious of the previous year's experience and were determined to make sure there was no repeat but that's what you'd expect from any player. If we weren't disappointed with what happened in last year's League semi-final, it would be worrying. We play every game to win it; we play every competition to win it and we failed in last year's League. Tipperary went on to win the title so, yes, we were disappointed by our efforts against them.

The lads are playing county hurling, for God's sake. It's the same everywhere else from Antrim to Cork, from Galway to Dublin, from Offaly to Wexford. They set their own targets, agendas and priorities and if they fail they're disappointed.

Here's the truth about the Tipperary game yesterday week. We didn't go out to grind them down (I hate that phrase but it keeps getting mentioned) or to make some sort of statement. We went out to play as well as we possibly could and see where it took us. As it happened, it steered us through a remarkably efficient first half where we scored 5-9. The team got a standing ovation as they left the pitch at half-time but, to be honest, I hardly even noticed because I have no interest in that type of thing and neither have the players.

They know how thin the line is between success and failure so getting standing ovations at half-time in a League game in March has to be seen for what it is – nice, but irrelevant. The lads hurled exceptionally well in the first half and Tipperary didn't come anywhere close to being as good as they can.

Put the two together and you have the reason for the big half-time difference. We were competitive, strong and we fought for every ball. It resulted in an excellent thirty-five minutes which had everything to do with lads playing well and bore absolutely no relation to putting down markers or grinding the opposition into oblivion. Even when you play very well, you don't expect to be so far ahead at half-time and certainly not against a team like Tipperary. It just happened for us that day.

We were very ordinary in the second half and, no, I wasn't happy with it. That might sound strange when we ended up winning so easily but it's not as simple as that. The general view was that we eased off in the second half, comfortable that the points had been secured but the reality was that Tipperary played better than us.

Our lads would admit that. The notion that a team which has built up a big lead decides to sit on it and doesn't really care if the opposition do better than them, provided there's no danger of completing a comeback, is something I find hard to understand.

Go back to last year's All-Ireland final against Waterford. People remarked afterwards that our lads were competing just as hard in the last five minutes as they were in the first five minutes although the match had long since been decided. The reality is that you don't go out to play for forty, fifty or sixty minutes.

If you're properly tuned you keep going with the same determination from start to finish. Bring it down to man-on-man. Whether you're twenty points up or twenty points down, the challenge is the same. Say, for instance, you're the full-back and your team is so comfortably ahead that there's no chance of being caught. The ball is dropping between you and the full-forward so, are you going to say, "I don't care if he catches it over my head, turns and sticks it in the net – sure we're going to win anyway"? No bloody way. You want to soar ten feet into the air, grab the ball and drive it down the field.

Can you imagine Noel Hickey being careless in the closing minutes of last year's All-Ireland final? Of course not – it's not the way winners think.

If you're a full-forward and you've scored three goals and your team is well ahead, would you be happy to let the full-back catch the next ball over your head? You want another goal because it's a great feeling to grab that ball, turn and lash it to the net. It's what you're programmed to do.

If you're really right for a game you get lost in what you're doing. I don't like the phrase 'in the zone' because I'm not sure what it means. I prefer to think of it as getting lost in the game. Nothing else matters except the next time the ball comes your way. The ball ... the ball ... the ball. It's all you want. If you have the ball you'll be dominating your opponent, which is also part of the thrill. And if you're dominating your opponent and your colleagues are doing the same, you're winning, which is what it's all about.

It's a contest – you against your opponent, your team against theirs. Switch off and you never know what will happen, even if you have a big lead. So, even if you're so far ahead that you can't be caught, you've got to press on anyway because to do otherwise is to take the lazy way out and betray your naturally competitive instincts.

You can analyse teams or performances any way you like but, ultimately, it comes down to players going out and doing their very best for the full game. If it's going against you, you've got to have the mental strength to fight back, however high the odds, and if you're winning you must press on. You're on stage, performing, and you'll carry on until the final whistle. It's what you do, it's what you feel, it's why you work so hard to get ready for games.

We did it against Waterford in last year's All-Ireland final but not in the League game against Tipperary yesterday week, where we let our standards drop in the second half. Still, it was a convincing win and I was very pleased with the first half, but it had nothing to do with a pre-planned obsession to run Tipperary into the ground. In truth, it was as simple as one side playing very well for the first half and building up a lead that wasn't going to be overtaken.

We weren't nearly as sharp against Clare yesterday. We won handily enough but Clare made a lot of mistakes which made it easier than it might have been. Much the same applied to our game up in Galway three weeks ago.

The weather was terrible so there was never any chance of an open, free-flowing game. We got on top early on and pulled away in the second half. Galway were well below full strength and didn't play well at any stage, and we weren't especially outstanding either.

As with the Tipperary game, we were supposed to be highly driven to make a bold statement against Galway. Sorry, wrong again. Yes, we wanted to win. Yes, we know from bitter experience that Galway are a team who can do us damage. But we didn't talk about that or the need to put them in their box on home ground. Our lads know what's expected of them and that applies to every game they play. We don't create artificial motivations. As far as I'm concerned, there's enough incentive to perform every time a player pulls on a Kilkenny jersey. The lads know that too.

As the last three results have shown, they are also well aware of the responsibilities they carry. But then competition for places is very intense. That's a huge driving force among the squad because they know that every chance that presents itself has to be taken.

We're lucky to have a lot of very good players and that keeps the tempo high all the time. So, while some might think that it's all about putting down markers and trying to gain a psychological edge over the opposition at this time of year, it's actually a whole lot simpler. Lads are fighting for places and are working hard to get to the top of their particular queue. They're also trying to win League games, which is all any county can do in March.

As I said, it has been a good month.

CHAPTER 11

A CLOUD ON THE HORIZON

That McGarry went through his career without ever being selected as the best goalkeeper in the country in a given year continues to be a source of annoyance in Kilkenny, where it's felt that his role was never fully understood or valued in the wider hurling world. Kilkenny remain especially unimpressed by the argument that, because he played behind such outstanding defenders, he had less to deal with than other goalkeepers and would contend that part of the reason the defence was so solid was because of the stability which McGarry brought in goal.

Martin Breheny writes: Kilkenny won nine Vodafone All Star awards in 2000 – four defenders, one midfielder and four forwards in an even spread that underlined the symmetry of a powerful force that had won their four Championship games by an average of almost twelve points.

It was only the second time in the twenty-nine-year history of the scheme that one county had harvested such a large yield. Kilkenny were also the first to take nine awards in 1983 after they had won the All-Ireland two-in-a-row. Coincidentally, the spread between 2000 and 1983 was identical: two full-backs, two half-backs, one midfielder, two half-forwards, two full-forwards.

Noel Hickey, Willie O'Connor, Eamonn Kennedy, Peter Barry, Andy Comerford, Henry Shefflin, Denis Byrne, Charlie Carter and DJ Carey all won awards in 2000, leaving James McGarry, Michael Kavanagh, Noel Hickey, Philly Larkin, Brian McEvoy, and John Power, as the six of the All-Ireland final starting team who didn't make it.

Power and McEvoy had already won All Stars while Kavanagh, Hickey and Larkin would be honoured in later years, but McGarry was never selected, repeatedly losing out to Brendan Cummins, Davy Fitzgerald, Damien Fitzhenry and Donal Og Cusack.

That McGarry went through his career without ever being selected as the best goalkeeper in the country in a given year continues to be a source of annoyance in Kilkenny, where it's felt that his role was never fully understood or valued in the wider hurling world. Kilkenny remain especially unimpressed by the argument that, because he played behind such outstanding defenders, he had less to deal with than other goalkeepers and would contend that part of the reason the defence was so solid was because of the stability which McGarry brought in goal.

Nevertheless, by the end of 2000, spats over All Star selections didn't in any way dilute the sense of satisfaction and fulfilment which settled over Kilkenny. The Liam McCarthy and Bob O'Keeffe Cups were happily ensconced, nine All Star awards had been collected and DJ Carey was named as Hurler of the Year for a second time. He had been overlooked for a place on the 'Team of the Millennium', but Kilkenny could live with that even if they thought that he should have been selected.

The All-Ireland winning squad headed to Thailand on the first of many exotic holidays they would enjoy in subsequent years and, as they looked back at the dormant hurling landscape they had left behind, they could feel confident about the future. Others would improve, but Kilkenny felt they had plenty of scope for improvement too.

They had won the All-Ireland title without playing 1999 All-Ireland champions Cork – or Tipperary, who had run Cork very close in the 2000 Munster final before losing to Galway in the All-Ireland quarter final. But that was the luck of the draw and, besides, Kilkenny believed they would have beaten any opposition once they established full momentum.

They lost to Cork and drew with Tipperary in the 2001 League, but wins over Wexford, Laois, Derry and Waterford took them safely through to the semi-finals where they drew Clare. They were hammered 2-21 to 3-8. Twenty-three scores to eleven. The margin of defeat could have been considerably higher as at least two of Kilkenny's goals were down to defensive errors by Clare rather than any great creativity by the attackers.

Admittedly, Kilkenny could point to mitigating circumstances – seven, actually, in the form of Willie O'Connor, Philly Larkin, Brian McEvoy, Denis Byrne, Charlie Carter, DJ Carey and Henry Shefflin, none of whom started for various reasons. Not even Kilkenny could cope with such a talent drain.

If losing by ten points to Clare wasn't the way Kilkenny wanted to sign out of the spring campaign, it didn't spark any long-term worries. Once they returned to full strength, it would be a different story.

Besides, there wasn't much happening in Leinster to suggest a serious threat to Kilkenny's bid to win four successive provincial titles for the first time since the early 1970s. Wexford and Offaly had indifferent League campaigns, while Dublin and Laois were basement cases in their respective groups.

The signs for Offaly were ominous. It was as if re-launching the 2000 season by beating Cork in the All-Ireland semi-final was to be the final act of defiance by a great squad that had been so efficient throughout the previous decade. In truth, that turned out to be the case. Offaly hammered Wexford in the 2000 Leinster semi-final, but have beaten neither Wexford nor Kilkenny in any of the subsequent nine Championships.

Kilkenny's retention of the Leinster title in 2001 turned out to be an even more routine operation than expected. They swatted Offaly away in the semi-final, winning just as easily as the twelve-point winning margin suggested. It was a performance which left Offaly manager, Michael Bond, stretching for superlatives to describe their conquerors:

"Awesome. That's the only word to describe them. Kilkenny are a far better side this year than last year. They are as physically strong as any Kilkenny team I have seen going right back to the 1970s but, as well as being strong, they're also very skilful. They punished every single mistake, but then they nearly always do."

The bouquets were piled even higher after the Leinster final where Kilkenny out-gunned Wexford by thirteen points, while looking as if they were hurling contentedly within themselves. In truth, they were playing to a beat which Wexford couldn't hear.

"How do you stop them? If there's a way, it hasn't been discovered either this year or last year. In the past, Kilkenny had small, first touch players. But they have big men now and their touch is still good," said Wexford manager, Tony Dempsey, before suggesting that maybe it was time to take a different approach to the Kilkenny question. "It's going to take a little bit of research. I think it might be a subject for a PhD or something," he said.

Kilkenny had won the Leinster title by scoring a total of 5-40, conceding just 0-30. Add that to the cumulative score from their juggernaut drive through the previous year's Championship and it left them with a staggering return from six games – For: 17-111; Against: 2-84.

The winning margin had ranged from a high of fifteen points to a low of eight, while averaging neatly at twelve. It was new territory in terms of dominance over Leinster opposition, in particular.

As Kilkenny headed home on the evening of Sunday, July 8, 2001 to the sound of Dempsey's ringing endorsement of them as a wonder team after winning the Leinster final, they felt extremely comfortable about themselves. They had six weeks to wait until the All-Ireland semi-final, but Kilkenny were used to that. They knew how to handle it and it had never been seen as a problem in the past, so it was unlikely to be one now.

In between, they would see Galway rack up a big score against Derry in the All-Ireland quarter-final, but that was to be expected. They would also see Wexford, who had looked way out of their depth in the Leinster final, produce a great performance to beat Limerick in the quarter-final and an even better one to earn a draw with Munster champions, Tipperary, in the semi-final before losing the replay.

The fact that Wexford came so close to beating Tipperary in the drawn game merely served to reinforce the view that Kilkenny were quite some way ahead of all the contenders. After all, they had beaten Wexford by thirteen points in the Leinster final. So, as Kilkenny headed to Croke Park for the semi-final clash with Galway on Sunday, August 19, there was no sense in the hurling world that a major shock was imminent.

Croke Park had cut up badly after a deluge during the Tipperary-Wexford replay on the previous day and, while the weather was much improved twenty-four hours later, the surface was very heavy. That certainly wasn't seen as an advantage to Galway for whom speed and agility in attack would have been regarded as crucial weapons. Kilkenny favoured the quick sod too, but they seemed better equipped to improvise as the need arose.

Pundits and punters alike were convinced that Kilkenny would be quite comfortable against an erratic Galway side, which had come up eight points short against Kilkenny a year earlier. The big question was, how good would Kilkenny look as they went about setting up a first All-Ireland final clash with Tipperary since 1991?

A crowd of 34,301 were in place when Limerick referee, Pat O'Connor, checked his watch and turned to face four jostling midfielders. Kilkenny had their vastly experienced pair, Andy Comerford (27) and Brian McEvoy (28) lining up against Galway's new and youthful pairing of David Tierney (21) and Richie Murray (19).

Most would have expected Comerford and McEvoy to put down an early marker and establish a platform from which Kilkenny would prosper. But even before the ball was thrown in there were signs that this was a different Galway team to the 2000 model. The young Galway pair were making it clear they meant business as they jostled into their opponents.

A game that would have a big influence on Kilkenny's decade was about to begin.

CHAPTER 12

A BELT OF REALITY

I told them that was the real team. They looked at me in disbelief. I knew they didn't believe me, but I was telling the truth. As far as I was concerned, we had started with a clean slate after 2001 and were building a team from the bottom up, not from the top down. Nobody had secured a guaranteed place – they all had to earn it. It was said afterwards that I had made up my mind about certain players following the 2001 defeat by Galway, and that they weren't going to be used under any circumstances from there on.

I never saw it coming, but once it arrived I knew immediately that we weren't ready for the ferocious storm that had hit our shores. The 2001 All-Ireland semi-final was only a few minutes old but it was already heading for an inevitable conclusion. The next sixty-five minutes would be bloody torture, but there was no way of dodging it, or even easing it.

I was standing on the sideline watching a Galway side – most of whom had been on the team we beat by eight points a year earlier – bully the hell out of us. Quite legitimately, it must be said. They had so much fire and energy in them that it was clear from the throw-in that Galway 2001 were a totally different proposition to Galway 2000. These guys were driven and had set an agenda for which we had no coherent response. They had a man sent off in the first half but it made no difference whatsoever. Hell, they even out-scored us in the long period when we had an extra man. Fifteen against fourteen and we still couldn't get close to them.

I got a sense at the throw-in that we were in trouble. And it got worse from there on. They whipped into every tackle, hunted in groups, supported each other all over the field and just couldn't get enough work. They were quick, sharp and aggressive. We conceded an early goal from a Eugene Cloonan free and didn't score from play for nearly half an hour. That's one hell of a long time, all the more so when you're standing on the sideline knowing that it most definitely isn't going to be your day. Even when Galway corner-back, Gregory Kennedy was sent off I never felt that we could turn things around.

An extra man should be an advantage – especially over a lengthy stretch – but this time it wasn't. In fact, it made no difference whatsoever to us. Numerical strength wasn't going to rescue us that day. Our players were doing their best to cope with the blitz but it was always going to be a lost cause.

It was tough going for the lads and sheer torture for me, because I'm watching all this going on and thinking, "this is all my fault".

Croke Park was a mess that day. Torrential rain before and during the Tipperary-Wexford All-Ireland semi-final replay the day before had left the surface like a bog. In fact, I'm told that it was the state of the surface over the weekend that convinced the GAA to replace the old surface with a new modern pitch which doesn't cut up. It certainly cut up that day. There were times when the ball stuck so deep in the ground that players had to dig it out.

Not that the conditions made any difference to us on that particular Sunday. In fact, Galway's superiority would probably have been greater if the pitch was playing fast and true, and the ball was zinging off the surface. The better the conditions the more it suits a team that's going well but, quick or slow, Galway were on top that day.

Galway re-shaped their line-up after Kennedy was sent off and played with five forwards from there on but they still continued to torment our backs. They kept the tempo up right through the game and won by five points which, quite honestly, flattered our efforts. It was an incredibly frustrating day for me because I didn't have to look very far for the reason we performed so badly. It was all down to me.

I promised myself when I took on the Kilkenny job that honesty would be a cornerstone of everything and now was definitely a time to bring the starkest candour imaginable to the review of what happened.

I'm not in any way taking away from Galway's achievement but I had made it easier for them than they could ever have expected. People claimed afterwards that after beating them by eight points the year before we were over-confident.

Absolute rubbish. I have always had huge respect for Galway and would never have taken them for granted. How could I, for God's sake? They have been a serious force for a very long time and have repeatedly proven that when they get their game right, they are virtually impossible to stop. They had won the League and beaten Tipperary in the Championship in 2000, so everybody knew exactly where they stood in the pecking order.

What disappointed me most about the 2001 semi-final was that I didn't know whether or not it was one of those years when Galway had built something special. Their performance in the All-Ireland final where they lost to Tipperary suggests that it wasn't. They hurled well enough but Tipperary didn't have to produce anything especially memorable to beat them. Kilkenny – or rather, I – had handed them a huge opening which they fully exploited in the semi-final.

There were probably people in Kilkenny who thought that Galway would be relatively easy pickings, but that didn't apply in my case. To be fair, the Kilkenny players didn't think that way either. It wasn't as if they had lost the run of themselves after winning the 2000 All-Ireland. They were more relieved than anything else after losing the previous two finals, so there was certainly no question of getting ideas above their station.

We beat Offaly and Wexford by big margins in the 2001 Leinster Championship where harder tests would have stood to us, however we still thought we were ready for Galway. Clearly, we weren't. Even when they had Kennedy sent off they didn't flinch or lose any momentum. We were only a few points behind at half-time so Kilkenny supporters were probably thinking that everything would be sorted out in the dressing room and that we would be a different side in the second half.

It's never that simple. There's no magic formula you can call on to change games or mindsets and certainly not when the opposition have ripped the initiative from your grasp. Galway had grabbed it so tightly that not even a crow-bar could prise it away from them. We were second to the ball, slower to the breaks and made nothing happen for ourselves. The only way we could have won that game was if Galway seized up for some reason. They didn't. The spirit and will in which we had prided ourselves over the previous two years simply wasn't as great as theirs. It was a valuable lesson for all of us, but especially for me. We tried to re-focus at half-time, but I think everybody knew the extent of the problem and realised that however hard we tried it wasn't going to be solved that day.

I made it quite clear in the post-match interviews that I took responsibility for the defeat. This was no time for making excuses. It wasn't a question of shielding the players for any reason other than they were entitled to it: what had happened wasn't their fault.

I am responsible for having the spirit right on any given day and, when it's not, I have to take the blame. A team can lose a game even when everything has gone perfectly in the build-up. When that happens there's nothing anybody can do except to accept it and move on. That's how sport works and everybody accepts that. However, what happened in 2001 left me with a horrible, empty feeling. It was my job to have the team ready – mentally and physically – for whatever was thrown at them and the simple truth is that we just weren't ready for what Galway brought to Croke Park that day.

Afterwards, I wanted to make sure that not even a tiny fraction of the blame was attached to the players and once that was done I set about considering what to do next. We had been out-fought which, to me, is always a cardinal sin. So, I had to ask myself if I was the right man to take the squad on. If I failed them once, could it happen again? Did I want the job? Had I the stomach for it? Was this some sort of watershed?

I had been in charge for three years and we had won one All-Ireland, lost a final and a semi-final. We had also won three Leinster titles. It might appear like a good return but to be blown away – as we were against Galway – went against everything I held as being central to what we were about. Where was the honesty, the genuineness, the spirit that had been there for the previous two years?

I wouldn't be the sort to bare my soul in situations like this so I talked to nobody about how I felt, except my wife, Elsie. In any event, there wasn't much point talking to people within the game in Kilkenny as I wasn't at all sure I wanted to return as manager the following season.

In fairness, nobody in the County Board put me under any pressure. They were hurting too, but I knew they wanted me to continue and I also felt the squad were happy for me to remain on. The only doubts were mine, and it took an awful lot of soul-searching and reflection before I decided to press on.

One of the main puzzles I had to work out in my own mind was why we performed so badly against Galway. The more I analysed it, the more I came to the conclusion that I had allowed standards to drop. Not in an obvious way but in little things, maybe like a fella turning up late for training for no good reason and getting away with it. Despite what people may think, I don't have hard and fast rules for everything and won't savage a player if he's late for training, provided he has a good reason for it. We're all amateurs and have lives outside hurling whether in work, college or whatever, so there will be times when a player is late for training or might not make it at all.

That's understandable but what can never be tolerated is sloppiness. For example, there's a huge difference between being late for training for a genuine reason as opposed to being late because a player didn't plan things properly. I'm not saying there was an epidemic of late arrivals in the 2001 season because there wasn't, but I'm using it as an illustration of how small things were let slip a little. It was only when I saw the results of that that I realised how damaging it had been.

Also, we had all become very friendly as a group. That was inevitable after being together for a few years and winning the 2000 All-Ireland. There was nothing wrong in being friendly but, maybe, I had let it all become a bit too nice. Training appeared to have gone well in 2001 but clearly there was something missing, otherwise we would not have been left so hopelessly exposed when Galway tore into us.

Somewhere along the line the standards that we had carefully set together had dropped. The ruthlessness – and I dislike using that word because of its connotations – wasn't there. That 'savagery' – and again I use the word in sporting terms – to win was down by a tiny fraction. When that happens at the highest level, you're blown away when you come up against a talented, determined team. That's precisely what happened to us against Galway.

Without realising it, we had gone a little soft. We were one grand happy bunch who had won the All-Ireland and, as we discovered in the most painful manner imaginable, the day you get cosy is the day you hit the wall. Very painfully, too. That softness didn't take us over in an obvious way but it infiltrated just enough to do damage. It's like rust just beneath the surface, you mightn't be able to spot it but it's doing damage that will have an effect where you're least expecting it.

Once I decided to remain on I knew it was time to shake up the entire scene. The cosy atmosphere had no place in the re-build. It was clear that there was a massive challenge out there to get back to the top so there could be no short-cuts, no compromises and definitely no looking back. We had learned our lesson in 2001 – now it was time to use it in a meaningful way.

We ran an excellent League campaign in 2002 which was exactly what we needed. The only game we lost in the group stages was against Galway – yes, them again! They beat us by six points in Ballinasloe, but we weren't too concerned about it as the game turned on the sending off of John Hoyne. It wasn't really a six-point game as anybody who was there would realise.

We beat Clare in Ennis in a really good game a fortnight later, and I remember how Martin Comerford, in particular, went especially well. We had quite a few new faces aboard that day and afterwards I was asked by reporters when the 'real' Kilkenny team would be back on duty.

I told them that was the real team. They looked at me in disbelief. I knew they didn't believe me, but I was telling the truth. As far as I was concerned, we had started with a clean slate after 2001 and were building a team from the bottom up, not from the top down. Nobody had secured a guaranteed place – they all had to earn it. It was said afterwards that I had made up my mind about certain players following the 2001 defeat by Galway, and that they weren't going to be used under any circumstances from there on.

That simply wasn't true. Of course we wanted to freshen things up, but you never make change for its own sake. We hadn't been good enough in 2001 so we had to re-evaluate exactly where we stood and how best to deploy the talent at our disposal. Most of it would be from the existing panel but others would have to get their chance, too, if we were to progress. If we weren't good enough in 2001 we wouldn't be good enough in 2002, unless we made some adjustments.

We reached the 2002 League final against Cork in a game which was great for us as it kept us hurling at a very high level into early May. Besides, we had new lads aboard such as Derek Lyng, Pat Tennyson and Martin Comerford, and a League final against Cork in Semple Stadium was the ideal way to test them out in a competitive game which came close to the Championship environment. We would have a good idea where we stood after playing Cork.

It turned into a cracking contest, one which we won by a point. It was another example of how valuable the League can be in terms of moulding a team together. We led by ten points at one stage in the first half but Cork battled back with a ferocious burst and actually took the lead late on, but points from the Dowling brothers, Sean and Brian, edged us home in a thrilling finish. As a preparation for the Championship, it couldn't have gone better. Had we won easily, as seemed possible in the first half, it wouldn't have tested the squad or told them anything about themselves, but they really had to dig deep when Cork came back with such vigour in the second half.

We were without DJ Carey that day so it was most encouraging to score 2-15 in what really was an excellent game. We were back in Semple Stadium five weeks later for the start of what would, in many ways, be a defining Championship for us. Croke Park was unavailable early that summer because of redevelopment work so the Leinster semi-finals were switched to Thurles where we played Offaly.

Even after winning the League, there was a degree of uncertainty in the Kilkenny air about exactly where we were headed that year. Personally, I was quite comfortable with our position, not just because we had found some new talent and won the League, but also because there was an edge to what we were doing that wasn't there the year before. We had learned a hard lesson and weren't going to be caught again.

It was claimed afterwards that my attitude changed dramatically after the 2001 defeat by Galway but I think too much was made of that. Yes, I took that defeat badly because I blamed myself for not presenting the Kilkenny team in a manner that gave them the very best chance of winning. I wasn't going to do the same again because, if I had, it would have been a betrayal of all my principles and indeed a betrayal of Kilkenny hurling. But to claim that I became hard and cold after 2001 – as has been suggested in some quarters – is to completely miss the point. All I did was to re-assert the values I took into the job in the first place and place them in the different context of a team that had won an All-Ireland Championship and lost it the following year.

There really was mighty incentive to win the 2002 All-Ireland but, after beating Offaly fairly comfortably in Thurles, we came very close to being re-routed to the All-Ireland qualifiers when Wexford turned in an excellent performance in the Leinster final.

This was Wexford at their defiant best on one of those days that, however hard we tried to shake them off, they hung on in there. It was point for point most of the way and we scraped home by two in the end. Having come so close, Wexford were devastated by the defeat, especially as they felt that the sending-off of Liam Dunne near the end made the crucial difference. They could have been right because this really was a game of inches where every advantage had to be exploited.

That defeat seemed to take an awful lot out of Wexford who didn't perform nearly as well when losing to Clare in the qualifiers a week later. The Leinster final left us with plenty to think about as we looked ahead to the All-Ireland semi-final against Tipperary.

On the plus side, we had displayed real steel under pressure but we also knew that a repeat of that performance wouldn't be nearly good enough against Tipperary. They were the reigning All-Ireland champions but had surrendered the Munster title to Waterford in a smashing game in Páirc Ui Chaoimh.

Tipp were always going to re-group for a second coming, which they duly did to set up an All-Ireland semi-final with us. For two counties that had enjoyed so much success over the years, Championship clashes between Tipperary and Kilkenny had been pretty rare over the previous twenty years. In fact, rather surprisingly, this was the first time since the 1991 All-Ireland final that the counties had met so it generated huge hype.

Kilkenny-Tipperary rivalry has always been very intense although it was not something I ever experienced as a player as our paths didn't cross in the Championship during my career. Tipperary didn't win any Munster titles – in fact they won very few Championship games – in that period, so I never experienced the thrill of playing against them on the All-Ireland stage. It was different for Tipperary manager, Nicky English. He had been on the team which beat Kilkenny in the 1991 final so he was looking for the big player-manager double. Sorry Nicky, but we were in no mood to oblige.

Quite often a game that offers high expectations doesn't quite deliver but this one certainly did. It was a ferocious contest between two teams who drove on to the absolute peak of their powers. We won by four points but the margin in no way reflected how tough, tense and really tight this game was. Tipperary were only a point down with a few minutes remaining but we finished that bit stronger and added three more points. The difference between our performance that day and a year earlier against Galway was so marked that it was as if we had a completely different team. Actually, we didn't.

In fact, eleven of the team that started in 2001 played in the 2002 semi-final while a twelfth, Charlie Carter came on as a sub. Derek Lyng and Martin Comerford were new to the team and made quite an impact but the big difference was that we were more in tune with what was required. The old order had been restored after the mistakes of 2001.

We were back in the All-Ireland final for the fourth time in five years against a Clare side that had re-grouped most impressively under Cyril Lyons after losing to Tipperary in the first round of the Munster Championship. Clare still had a great swagger and confidence about them as a legacy from the glory period in the second half of the '90s and built up an impressive momentum as they made their way to the All-Ireland final. Among their victims were Wexford, Galway and Waterford so it was pretty clear how much they had improved since losing narrowly to Tipperary in May. Still, we beat them by seven points after getting a great start when a piece of DJ magic got us an early goal. We led by six points at half-time but, typical of Clare, they battled back with great heart and we had to dig deep again when they cut our lead back to three points in the third quarter.

People have often said since then, that, had we got it right against Galway in 2001, we would have won the All-Ireland and clinched the treble a year later. That's not necessarily the case. In fact, far from it. If we had won in 2001, who knows how we would have reacted in 2002? Maybe that's the year we wouldn't have been right. As it was, we got the sloppiness out of our system in 2001 and were back on track the following season. Who knows, maybe things happen for a reason after all?

Mind you, I wouldn't have believed that on the evening of August 19, 2001, as we returned home to Kilkenny after a miserable Croke Park experience. Still, it taught us valuable lessons so some good did come out of it.

CHAPTER 13

NOTHING PERSONAL, JUST BUSINESS

***Competitions are there for those who want to** play in them. If the Cork 2008 squad felt that they wouldn't or couldn't be part of the 2009 League until internal difficulties were sorted out, that was their prerogative However, that doesn't mean that the rest of us should consider it a lesser competition for that. It's like saying that Padraig Harrington's major wins last year were tainted by Tiger Woods' absence. No, they weren't.*

Monday, April 6, 2009: *So, here's what supposedly happened yesterday. We beat Cork by twenty-seven points in the National League in Nowlan Park because we wanted to punish them for messing up the competition. All the better if we could humiliate them in the process. We wanted to really bury them once and for all. We had become the GAA's moral police force, dispensing justice on behalf of outraged hurling citizens.*

Also, we were allegedly annoyed by suggestions from within the Cork camp that we wouldn't have won the 2007 and 2008 All-Ireland finals if they had been properly tuned up. I'm not even sure whether that was ever said but it was reported as having happened. Apparently, we were furious over that perceived slight and we now wanted to teach Cork a painful lesson in front of our own people. We were, it seems, on some sort of vengeful mission where squashing Cork wasn't just a target – it was an absolute priority.

Here's what actually happened. We needed to win to ensure we stayed in line for a place in the League final. Playing Cork would always be big for Kilkenny anyway, so there's never any need for a manager to drive them on. There's an in-built sense of rivalry between Kilkenny and Cork that gives every game – whether it's Championship, League or challenge – a special edge. It's a healthy edge too, honed from years of battling it out at all levels.

The idea that we would somehow take it on ourselves to punish Cork for what had gone on there earlier in the year is ridiculous. We mind our own business in Kilkenny and let others take care of theirs, although in this case the Cork strike impacted on the whole of Division One.

Their absence from the early rounds of the League distorted the competition in that they had played weaker teams in some games before getting the 2008 squad back. It was put to me at a press conference before the start of the League that Cork's weakened state would devalue the campaign and I have to say I greatly resented that suggestion.

What happened in Cork wasn't good for anybody, least of all the Cork players and the County Board. It was damaging all-round for the GAA, however the suggestion that a national competition would be demeaned or devalued by one team fielding a weakened side is an insult to everybody else.

Just as teams are bigger than any one individual, competitions are also more important than the individual participants. Nobody took any pleasure out of the Cork situation, but it was solely of their making and only they could resolve it. As for the rest of us, we were far too busy getting on with our own lives and jobs to worry about Cork. I certainly don't think any of us were conscious that we were playing in a League irreparably damaged by the Cork strike.

Competitions are there for those who want to play in them. If the Cork 2008 squad felt that they wouldn't or couldn't be part of the 2009 League until internal difficulties were sorted out, that was their prerogative However, that doesn't mean that the rest of us should consider it a lesser competition for that. It's like saying that Padraig Harrington's major wins last year were tainted by Tiger Woods' absence. No, they weren't.

We all hated what was going on in Cork because it wasn't doing anybody any good but that was as far as it went for everybody outside of Cork.

I stopped reading about the Cork row after a while because it was more of the same being trotted out day after day, week after week. As I said: their row, their problem, their responsibility. All I knew was that, when the dispute was eventually settled and Cork got their 2008 players back, they beat Clare and Limerick in successive games. In fairness, that was quite an achievement because Clare and Limerick had been up and running for weeks.

While there was always going to be a major focus on our game with Cork because of how the season had developed for them, I saw it purely in terms of another League outing that we had to win if we wanted to stay in control of our own destiny.

Cork had made a clear statement of intent with their wins over Clare and Limerick. We were lucky to beat Limerick in our first game and weren't all that impressive against Clare either, despite having a decent margin to spare at the end, so we genuinely saw Cork as a big challenge.

We felt that if they could come up to Nowlan Park and beat us after having had very little formal training up to then, it would have been a fairly damning reflection on what we were at. Obviously, the Kilkenny public saw it as an important day too as a crowd of nearly 15,000 turned out, which added to the atmosphere and the sense of occasion. It was a day where we had to deliver. We were really concentrated for that game and played very well, whereas Cork didn't.

In fairness, they had a new set-up with Denis Walsh taking over as manager for the first time. He had very little time to get to know the players, let alone work with them. Besides, many of them were inexperienced, so once we got a run on them, they were in trouble. We won by 4-26 to 0-11 which further fuelled the rumour machine which was full of stories about our determination to wallop Cork by as big a margin as possible.

The real desire was to play well, which we did. With competition for places so intense, our lads had their own private motivation which had nothing to with Cork and everything to do with themselves. Why on earth would the Kilkenny players or management have any other agenda? What happened in Cork was a great pity but it was none of our business.

Besides, it would be awfully foolish to be judgemental about Cork or to get smug about your own situation because the potential for trouble exists in every county. If you begin to believe that things will look after themselves rather than making sure they're absolutely right, you'll invite problems. And once that invitation is issued the replies come in thick and fast.

County Boards, management and players all have a role to play in ensuring that standards are set, met and re-evaluated all the time, otherwise little things can start to go wrong. And once that happens, it can be difficult to control them.

So, no, you can take it that Kilkenny had no extra motivation to beat Cork other than to take the League points. The day we start becoming judge and jury of how others approach their business off-field is the day we lose the plot. Frankly, it's not a day I envisage arriving any time soon. Or at all for that matter.

The win over Cork, and Tipperary's win over Galway, has produced an unusual situation with one round of games to go. We're both three points clear of Dublin who are in third place so it's going to be a Kilkenny-Tipperary League final. Obviously it would be better for the League if the finalists weren't decided until the final round, but that's not our concern. Unusually, ten points was enough to clinch a place in the final.

So, it's a Kilkenny v Tipp final then! And, guess what? Our big win over them a few weeks ago won't count for anything. They will be a completely different proposition next time.

CHAPTER 14

GOD IN KILKENNY HEAVEN

McEvoy and Carter quit in mid-season 2003. Carter would later go public on his reasons, blaming Cody for not playing him more often and alleging that the manager wanted him out of the panel. The end came after he played no part in Kilkenny's win over Dublin in the Leinster semi-final. Carter, who had been nominated as team captain by his club, Young Ireland, left the panel a few days afterwards.

Martin Breheny writes: If God were choosing a location for hurling heaven at the end of 2002, Kilkenny would have been the obvious destination. The All-Ireland senior and minor titles – plus the National League – had been safely secured. Seven All-Star awards had been banked, bringing to twenty-two the number won during Brian Cody's four years in charge – three times more than the total of the previous five years.

DJ Carey had won his ninth award, extending to two his lead over Noel Skehan at the top of the leader board. Not that Skehan would have minded. He was in his first year as a selector and a key part of the management set-up.

Kilkenny hurling was now in a much happier place than the uncertain world it had occupied in the 1994-98 period. The team had matured through the disappointments and successes of previous seasons and clearly still had plenty of room for further expansion. The average age of the thirty-strong squad for the All-Ireland final was just over twenty-four years. The starting fifteen (including Carey, aged thirty-two) averaged just over twenty-three years and included midfielder, Derek Lyng and full-forward, Martin Comerford who had been the two big finds of the season.

The subs were a mixture of youth and vast experience, the latter cohort led by John Power (thirty-six), Charlie Carter (thirty-one), Stephen Grehan (thirty) and Brian McEvoy (twenty-eight). Included in the younger brigade were twenty-one-old James Ryall from Graigue-Ballycallan and a nineteen-year-old from Tullaroan, named Tommy Walsh, who wore No.29. It would be the last time he was handed such a high-numbered jersey.

Carter, McEvoy and Power all came on as subs against Clare in the final, but none of them would wear the Kilkenny jersey again in the Championship. Power, who had epitomised the very essence of honesty and commitment during his long career, retired after the final, ending a sixteen-year career which had been interrupted in 1998 when he was left off the panel. However, one of Cody's first decisions when choosing his new squad a year later was to recall Power, who contributed as much in his second coming as he had in his earlier days.

McEvoy and Carter quit in mid-season 2003. Carter would later go public on his reasons, blaming Cody for not playing him more often and alleging that the manager wanted him out of the panel. The end came after he played no part in Kilkenny's win over Dublin in the Leinster semi-final. Carter, who had been nominated as team captain by his club, Young Ireland, left the panel a few days afterwards.

The hurling landscape was changing noticeably towards the end of 2002. Waterford had won their first Munster title since 1963 and were about to embark on a new phase where they were consistently regarded as serious All-Ireland contenders. Clare had used the 'back door' to reach the All-Ireland final but were clearly heading for a transitional period.

Tipperary had run Kilkenny closer than the four-point margin in the

Double tops. *Noel Skehan and I prepare to bring the Liam McCarthy and* Irish Press *Cups back home after Kilkenny win the All-Ireland senior and minor titles in 1972. Ten years later I captained the senior team to an All-Ireland win from full-back with Noel, still an outstanding goalkeeper, behind me. He later worked with me as a selector.*

Those were the days.
First year in St Kieran's College, that famous hurling nursery (back row, second from right).

Big boys now.
A shot of my days as a 5th year in St Kieran's (back row, on the left).

Learning the trade as part of a St Kieran's juvenile team in 1968 (back row, second from right).

On a 13-a-side St Kieran's team in 1970 (front row, first on left). The 13-a-side game was tried at colleges level for a period. Future GAA President, Nickey Brennan, is second from the right, front row.

We have the cup.
I'm a happy camper (far right, back row) after an U-14 success.

Captaining Kilkenny to victory in the 1972 All-Ireland minor final was one of the proudest days of my career.

That winning feeling.
Hoisting the Irish Press *Cup after the 1972 All-Ireland minor win.*

Back home after winning the 1972 All-Ireland minor title. Ger Henderson (far left) and I progressed up the ranks quite quickly.

Away from it all on an All Star tour.
I take in the Grand Canyon with Elsie.

Proud Parents.
With our son, Diarmuid, in St Kieran's colours, after an U-14 final.

Family Ties. *With Elsie, my mother, Annie and father, Bill, and the two lads, Diarmuid and Donncha in 2000. Not forgetting our welcome visitors, Bob O'Keeffe and Liam McCarthy.*

Well done. *With Donncha after The Village won the 2004 AIB Leinster club final with a win over UCD.*

'Cody & Sons'. *Donncha, Diarmuid and me with some silverware.*

Look after our guest. *Diarmuid keeps a close watch on the Liam McCarthy Cup.*

Start them young. *I get in some practise with Donncha in my sister's garden in 1991.*

Bright Blue Yonder. *With Elsie, Diarmuid, Ned Quinn (then County Chairman) and his wife, Lucy, during a team holiday in New Zealand.*

Key Personnel. *Elsie and I with former selector, Johnny Walsh and his wife Breda relaxing in Key West, Florida during another team holiday.*

Up, up and away. *Diarmuid, Elsie and I avail of the local taxi service on a mountain top in New Zealand.*

No slip-ups. *Skiing in Vermont, USA. We have seen the world through our involvement in hurling.*

A great honour. *Mayor Pat Crotty confers me with the Freedom of Kilkenny City in 2008.*

Behind the Scenes. *I have always had a great back-up team including (l-r), Tadhg Crowley (team doctor), Robbie Lodge (physio), Michael Dempsey (team trainer and selector), Martin Fogarty (selector) and Claire Lodge (physio).*

Family values. *With Elsie, Donncha, Diarmuid and our regular guest, Liam McCarthy.*

In The Village clubhouse in 2003 with Donncha who was on the minor team that won the All-Ireland final on the day the seniors completed a two-in-a-row.

James Stephens, the man after whom our great club is called. (Courtesy of James Stephens Club.)

THE

Police  Gazette,

OR

HUE-AND-CRY.

Published for Ireland on every Tuesday and Friday.

☞ All Notices intended for insertion in the Hue-and Cry, are to be transmitted under cover addressed to the Inspector-General of Constabulary (the words Hue-and-Cry to be written on the left hand corner of the Envelope). No Description can be inserted unless an Information shall have been Sworn; but it is not necessary to forward the Informations to the Inspector-General.

As the Law (48 Geo. 3, c. 140, s. 44.) only permits the insertion of Notices respecting Felonies, no other description of Notice can be inserted in the Hue-and-Cry.

DUBLIN, TUESDAY, MARCH 26, 1867.

By the Lord Lieutenant-General and General Governor of Ireland.

A PROCLAMATION.

WODEHOUSE.

WHEREAS, *James Stephens* has been an active Member of a Treasonable Conspiracy against the Queen's authority in *Ireland*, and escaped from the *Richmond Prison* on the *Twenty-fourth* day of *November* last.

NOW WE, being determined to bring the said *James Stephens* to Justice, Do hereby offer a Reward of

ONE THOUSAND POUNDS

to any person or persons who shall **give such Information as shall lead to the Arrest** of the said *James Stephens*; and a further Reward of

One Thousand Pounds

to any person or persons **WHO SHALL ARREST** the said *James Stephens*.

AND WE do hereby offer a further Reward of

THREE HUNDRED POUNDS

to any Person or Persons who shall give such information as shall lead to the Arrest of any one whomsoever who has knowingly harboured or received, or concealed, or assisted or aided in any way whatsoever in his Escape from Arrest, the said *James Stephens*.

And We do also hereby offer a FREE PARDON, in addition to the above-mentioned REWARD, to any Person or Persons concerned in the Escape of the said JAMES STEPHENS who shall give such Information as shall lead to his Arrest as aforesaid.

Given at Her Majesty's Castle of *Dublin*, this *Twenty-sixth* day of *January*, 1866.

By His Excellency's Command,

THOS. A. LARCOM.

Description of the above-named JAMES STEPHENS:—

JAMES STEPHENS is about 42 years of age; 5 feet 7 inches high; stout make; broad high shoulders very tight active appearance; fair hair, bald all round top of head, wore all his beard, which is sandy, slightly tinged with grey, rather long under the chin, but slight round the jaw approaching the ears; broad forehead; tender eyes, which defect seems to be constitutional, and has a peculiar habit of closing the left eye when speaking; high cheek bones, and rather good looking countenance; hands and feet remarkably small and well formed, and he generally dressed in black clothes.

WFTZ

Wanted! *James Stephens was much in demand back is 1867, with a large bounty on his head, courtesy of Her Majesty's Lord Lieutenant-General in Ireland. (Courtesy of James Stephens Club.)*

Enjoy it now, lads, because we'll soon be back training. Some of the Kilkenny boys enjoying themselves in Australia during a team holiday.

All-Ireland semi-final suggested, but Nicky English quit as manager afterwards and, as often happens when an All-Ireland winning manager departs, there was a period of upheaval. It lasted quite some time for Tipperary, who wouldn't win another Munster title until 2008.

Wexford came within two points of Kilkenny in the 2002 Leinster final, but the long-range forecast was for bleak times. Galway – the great enigma of hurling – were to remain just that. The manner of their victory over Kilkenny in the 2001 All-Ireland semi-final suggested they were the best equipped of all to trouble the black-and-amber over a sustained period but, not for the first time, it didn't work out like that.

And then there was Cork. Their success in 1999 was achieved with a very young team so there seemed no apparent reason why they couldn't improve and become the dominant force in Munster into the new Millennium. They retained the Munster title in 2000 before losing to Offaly in the All-Ireland semi-final, after which Jimmy Barry-Murphy resigned as manager.

What followed was to be the start of a remarkable period for Cork hurling: one in which strike, division and unrest were replaced by one of the most driven forces ever to emerge from the county.

A week after Kilkenny won the 2002 Leinster title, Cork were well beaten by Galway in the All-Ireland qualifiers, having earlier lost to Waterford by one point in the Munster semi-final. The season had gone from bad to worse to awful for Cork. Some of the players later admitted that the day they played Galway was the lowest point of their careers. It showed. They were beaten all over the pitch and eventually lost by nine points when it could just as easily have been nineteen points.

Morale was at an all-time low over what the squad regarded as a total breakdown between themselves and the County Board. The players felt their needs and expectations were a secondary consideration to an out-dated tradition which operated on the basis that, what was good enough for Cork teams of the past, was good enough for the new generation.

The row led to a players' strike which changed the GAA landscape forever. While the Cork squad spent weeks in the run-up to Christmas in a lonely position on the strike plinth, their Kilkenny counterparts were enjoying the fruits of their All-Ireland success, including planning for a lavish holiday in South Africa in January.

Peace was eventually restored in Cork. Players were happy the strike had served its purpose in creating an environment in which they believed they could return to being real All-Ireland contenders. Besides, the players knew that having taken the ultimate sanction of strike action they would be under enormous pressure to deliver once they got back on the hurling fields in 2003. Otherwise, they would be portrayed as self-absorbed megalomaniacs who had lost touch with reality and whose appreciation of their own worth didn't quite tally with reality.

Their response to the challenge was as brave and genuine as Cork supporters hoped it would be. Donal O'Grady and his ambitious squad were about to embark on an epic battle for supremacy against Brian Cody and Kilkenny which would define the next two seasons.

By a curious coincidence, Kilkenny had won All-Ireland doubles in 1982-1983, and 1992-1993. Could they now maintain that sequence in the next decade?

CHAPTER 15

DOUBLES AND TROUBLES

Brian McEvoy also left the panel shortly afterwards, presumably because he thought he should have been starting too. I made no attempt to contact either of them. They had made their decisions and, as far as I was concerned, that was the end of it. The media whipped things up as much as they could, but my focus – and that of the entire panel – remained solely on winning the All-Ireland which, happily, was achieved a few months later.

My sole and abiding objective, since the day I agreed to take on the Kilkenny job, is to put together the best squad, prepare them as well as possible and then select the team which gives us maximum chance of achieving success. To me, the squad is everything. It's made up of individuals, but the overriding and consistent theme is the common good, the common goal, the common endeavour. In fact, there is no other theme.

What's good for Kilkenny hurling is good for the individual. What's good for Kilkenny hurling is good for me. What's good for Kilkenny hurling is good for everybody in the county. The idea that I might, in some way, have favourites or work against somebody is so far off the mark as to be laughable. However, like every other manager, I do have to make choices. If those who don't agree – or perhaps are effected by those choices – interpret them in a certain way, that's understandable. There's nothing I can do about it.

I have never shied away from making decisions. Tough or easy, popular or unpopular, they have to be made honestly, dispassionately and, above all, in the best interests of Kilkenny hurling. That's my brief and my responsibility, and it is one I take very seriously. Any judgement regarding the make-up of the team or the panel is arrived at purely on its merits, using one simple criterion: will it advance our chances of success?

How could it make sense to do anything other than what's right for everybody? It wouldn't, and I have never allowed a personal issue to interfere with decision-making. And, if I were to bring sentiment into it, I would be diluting my ability to do the job with which I have been entrusted.

No manager likes telling a player that he's not on the panel, no more than he enjoys leaving somebody off the team. But, quite often, it has to be done. After all, only fifteen players can start a game.

I would always contact a player who was being omitted from the panel and explain why it was happening. It's the least he deserves. There isn't a player alive who will agree with the decision to leave him out of the team or panel and it's natural that he will think the manager is the greatest fool on earth, or that he has a personal agenda. Sometimes he might even believe that it's a combination of both. That's management for you. It's not a popularity contest. It brings with it responsibilities that have to be discharged as honestly and as honourably as possible.

There was a degree of controversy in 2003 when Charlie Carter left the panel the week after we beat Dublin in the Leinster semi-final. It was fuelled, to some degree, by the fact that he had been nominated as team captain for the year. We have always operated the system in Kilkenny where the county champions nominate the captain and, despite what people might say, it has served us well. It's the way we do things in Kilkenny and I certainly have no problem with it. Indeed, I benefited from it myself when I was appointed captain in 1982. However, being put forward as captain never guarantees a player his place on the team. Nor should it.

Charlie obviously felt he should have been on the team for the 2003

Championship and, when he didn't play against Dublin, he left the panel. That created a bit of a stir in the media, but it had no impact on the panel or on what we were trying to achieve. It was his choice.

Brian McEvoy also left the panel shortly afterwards, presumably because he thought he should have been starting too. I made no attempt to contact either of them. They had made their decisions and, as far as I was concerned, that was the end of it. The media whipped things up as much as they could, but my focus – and that of the entire panel – remained solely on winning the All-Ireland title which, happily, was achieved a few months later.

I would probably have been criticised for not trying to get the two lads back if we had been beaten somewhere along the line that summer, and I would have taken that criticism. You can't live your life worrying about what others are going to say about you if things turn out in a certain way.

I have never been one to have my opinion formed by conventional wisdom or influenced by anything other than what I know and understand. My priority has always been to get the best team on the pitch, which is not necessarily the same thing as getting the best individuals out there. In fact, it isn't the same thing at all. Teams win games, individuals don't.

Individuals fit into the team but they're secondary to it. Reputation, or what has gone before, counts for very little in my mind. When we brought Derek Lyng and Martin Comerford into the panel, they hadn't any pedigree at minor or Under-21 level but they could hurl and they had a great attitude. I was never interested in fellas who were supposed to be stars or who saw themselves as stars. However, I was – and still am – very interested in fellas who are absolute team players, lads with massive character who will see every challenge through to the very end.

From my perspective, I'll do whatever it takes to give them the best chance of being successful which does, of course, involve making hard calls from time to time. I would always do what I thought was right for the team irrespective of the personal consequences. I can live with criticism but I couldn't live with myself if I lacked the courage to make the right calls as I saw them.

Players can react in different ways when things aren't going their way, as they perceive it. The tough ones hang on in there and try to work their way through it because they know that – here in Kilkenny anyway – the team is always picked on merit and that whether a player is on the first fifteen or the panel is down to him, not the manager or selectors. In effect, the team selects itself, based on who is playing best at any given time. That applies as much for an All-Ireland final as for the first round of the League. The lads know that, which is why they have always remained so focused in how they go about their business. It's the sort of attitude I love and one which I have been lucky enough to come across in the vast majority of Kilkenny players.

I recall one year coming up to an All-Ireland final when JJ Delaney was carrying a niggling injury and we felt he shouldn't even be training. So I walked over to him one evening and suggested that he ease off for a few sessions. His response was typical of a man on a mission. He paused for a second, glanced back at me and said, "If I don't train tonight, one of the boys will step in and what happens then?"

"How do you mean?"

"Someone comes in, does well and he'll be playing in the final. So, if you don't mind, I'll train away – I want my place on the team."

I turned and walked away contented. "Good man, JJ," I thought. "That's a savage attitude, exactly what we want." I hadn't asked him to ease up just to see what reaction I'd get but I was delighted with his response.

That's the sort of hunger it takes to drive things on. If anybody ever loses sight of that and walks away, so be it.

It's the same during a game. It doesn't matter how well or how badly it's going there's serious work to be done, every second of every minute. We've been lucky enough to have enjoyed some great times but it's the days when things are going against you that you really learn about your players.

The 2003 National League final against Tipperary certainly told me what I wanted to know about how we were shaping up for that year's

Championship. The public largely ignored the game, probably because they weren't enamoured by the thought of travelling to Croke Park on a May Bank Holiday Monday, but those who made the journey were treated to a remarkable game.

Tipperary led by eight points after an hour and seemed to be on their way comfortably to the title. There's very little a manager can do in a situation like that except hope that his players have the spirit and determination to retrieve the situation. I needn't have worried. Others may disregard the League but we don't, and it showed that particular day.

We scored three goals in an amazing burst to take the lead before Tipperary retaliated with one of their own to go back in front again. Henry Shefflin equalised and, just as it looked like the game would finish level, he struck again, booting the ball over the bar for the winning point. Kilkenny 5-14, Tipperary 5-13. Only one point between the teams from a total of thirty-seven scores. Truly, an amazing game. Indeed, had it been in an All-Ireland final it would have gone down as one of the most exciting in history.

It was fantastic to win it, but the manner in which the lads dug in when they fell so far behind was even more pleasing than the actual result. It showed that the attitude was perfect for the Championship.

Subsequent results suggest that we reached the 2003 final fairly easily – beating Dublin, Wexford and Tipperary by big margins – but figures can sometimes be misleading. Tipperary actually led by two points at half-time in the All-Ireland semi-final after hurling very well. There was very little in it going into the third quarter, but we got on top from there on and won by twelve points, which wasn't a true reflection of the overall game. Little things can change the trend and we got the breaks when we needed them most that day.

Cork were waiting for us in the final, having got their season well and truly back on track after the controversies of the previous winter. Now, I'm not sure if it's possible to add an incentive to win an All-Ireland final but, if it were, then Cork certainly managed it in 2003. The players' strike and the subsequent fall-out seemed to have a hugely unifying effect on the squad. It showed in Munster where they destroyed Clare, who had hammered Tipperary, before dethroning reigning champions, Waterford in the final.

Cork got a real fright in the All-Ireland semi-final when Wexford came back at them to snatch a very late draw with a marvellous goal by Rory McCarthy, but it was a much different story in the replay which they won by a mile.

Cork had racked up big returns in every game but then so had we, so all the pointers were towards a very high-scoring final. Quite often, though, what has gone before counts for little and this was one such occasion.

We took a six-point lead into half-time and increased it just into the second half but, even then, I had a sense that Cork would come back at us. They were too good a team not to put together a spell in which they would dominate so, the question was, how much damage would they do in that period?

Quite a lot, actually! We went seven points clear just after half-time but were then hit for 1-6 as Cork entered their golden patch. All we got back was a point, leaving us one down early in the final quarter. Cork would have been conscious of the strong finish that won them the 1999 final, but so were we and this time we had the mental firmness to counteract it. Martin Comerford's goal around five minutes from the finish eventually proved the difference and we edged home by three points, 1-14 to 1-11.

DJ Carey was captain, which was entirely appropriate given how much he had contributed to Kilkenny for so long.

I make no apologies for saying that I was delighted DJ got a chance to captain the team to an All-Ireland win, because he deserved it. There were lads on the team in 2003 who were only seven or eight years of age when DJ won his first All-Ireland back in 1992. He would have been a hero to them, so it was nice that they were in a position to help him realise his dream of captaining Kilkenny to an All-Ireland win.

Besides, he had been at the heart of Kilkenny hurling for so long and had brought so much honour to himself, his family, his club and his county that I think everybody in the county and, indeed, beyond (with the exception of Cork!) were happy to see him get his hands on the Liam McCarthy Cup. It crowned the remarkable career of a remarkable hurling man.

No sooner had we won the final than talk of a three-in-a-row started. Not among the team – and, I can assure you, very definitely not among the management – but it became a big thing for the media and the general public. It was inevitable I suppose and, while it wasn't something I particularly worried about, I was aware that if we had a good run in 2004 it would be difficult for the players to keep the treble out of their thinking.

It's not that a player would wake up in the morning thinking, "We're going for the three-in-a-row this year," but they were living and working among the supporters and were bound to be touched by the excitement and anticipation of it all.

I knew damn well just how tough it would be to win the 2004 All-Ireland title. I always say that you never know what a new year will bring – either for your own team or the opposition – and that applies however well you might have done in the previous season. While we tried to divert all talk of the three-in-a-row there's no doubt that preventing us from winning it became a big issue among the opposition, starting with our old rivals in Wexford.

They would always take great delight in beating Kilkenny, especially in a year like 2004 when we were chasing something special. I was part of the supposedly unbeatable Kilkenny team that had our three-in-a-row hopes dashed by Wexford in 1976 when they thrashed us in the Leinster final, so I needed no reminding just how dangerous they could be.

And, yes, they did it again in 2004, albeit by a much smaller margin than 1976. I can still see Adrian Fenlon lining up a sideline cut underneath the Cusack Stand well into injury time in the Leinster semi-final. We were a point up in a game where neither side ever got far enough ahead to take control. It was one of those days where a draw would probably have been a fair result. DJ had given us the lead a minute earlier and it looked as if it might be enough, but Wexford just weren't going to be denied this time. In fairness, it would have been tough on them if they had lost. There was every chance that Fenlon, who was deadly accurate with line balls, would slice it over for the equaliser but the ball didn't quite make it that far. It fell short and the rest is history.

The ball broke loose and Mick Jacob stuck it in the net for the winning goal. One second we're leading and on our way to the Leinster final, the next the ball is in our net and we're out of the provincial race and facing into new territory.

We had no complaints and no excuses. There was absolutely no question of being over-confident or anything like that – in fact, I was very happy with the attitude in the dressing room coming up to that game. It was just one of those days where Wexford matched us all the way and got the crucial break right at the end which they exploited to the full.

I was just glad that we had another chance to rescue the season. Some years earlier that would have been the end of the line so, while the 'back door' might have its critics, you wouldn't have found them in our camp as we packed our bags in Croke Park and headed home that evening. Losing to Wexford completely changed the dynamic of our season. Had we beaten them, we could have reached the All-Ireland final with two more games, but now it would take a minimum of four. As it happened it took five, as we drew the quarter-final with Clare.

It was the first time since 1996 that Kilkenny had failed to reach the Leinster final and the first time that we would embark on the All-Ireland qualifier route. This was definitely not a year when we wanted a long journey but we were mighty thankful that the opening was still available to us. We had less than two weeks to get ready for the qualifiers and, for the first time, we had to get our heads around the fresh challenge which awaited us. We were still All-Ireland champions and back chasing the three-in-a-row, but were coming at it from a different and more awkward angle than we would have liked.

We beat Dublin well in the first qualifier to set up a massive test against Galway in Thurles. I had no doubt that the determination and ambition was still there, but it's only when you face a really tough examination that you can be absolutely sure of where you stand and Galway looked well primed to provide us with it.

They had, after all, beaten us convincingly in the 2001 All-Ireland semi-final. While that was three years previously, it was still a fresh and pleasing memory for them. They had received another boost in early 2004 when they beat us in a National League game up in Pearse Stadium before going on to win the title, so their confidence levels were high. Conor Hayes had them motoring nicely that year so we knew we would be really up against it if we gave them any leeway whatsoever.

The mood in our camp was brilliant going into that game. Losing by a last-second goal to Wexford had left everybody feeling so frustrated that they couldn't wait to get back out again. There really was a savage determination to return to the All-Ireland track, and I could sense from the squad that they weren't going to let Galway get in their way. They were still hurting deeply from the Wexford game and realised that another defeat so soon would change the whole perception of Kilkenny hurling. One year All-Ireland heroes, failures the next. That's how fickle and cruel sport can be.

The Galway game was always going to be a defining test of our resolve, and I'm sure they saw it in much the same way which added to the sense of anticipation heading into Thurles.

We had the edge throughout most of the first half and led by five points at half-time. We pressed on early in the second half too and led by six, but Damien Hayes landed a Galway goal to bring them within three points of us. They hadn't been that close since the quarter-hour mark so now we were being asked the big question all over again. How intact was our spirit? And how much did Galway have left in the tank?

I would have to say that what happened afterwards was quite remarkable. It was as if Hayes' goal was the red rag our lads needed to stir them. They tore into Galway with unbelievable momentum and ferocity, and ripped them apart from there to the finish. Galway managed just two more points while we hit 3-9 and ended up nineteen-point winners, 4-20 to 1-10. Quite an evening in Semple Stadium. Henry Shefflin scored more on his own than the entire Galway team put together. We could never have anticipated such a dazzling performance or such a comprehensive win over the reigning League champions, but it was as if the lads were desperate to purge the memory of the Wexford defeat in a very public way.

Some days later, I was informed by our County Board that the boys in Croke Park wanted a little chat with me. For reasons that I could never figure out, sections of the media had a right go at me after the Galway game claiming, among other things, that I had spent half my time on the pitch and that I had tried to intimidate referee Diarmuid Kirwan as he headed for the dressing rooms at half-time.

It would appear that the media hadn't much to write about that week so I was fair game for a wild raft of accusations. Yes, I was animated on the sideline because this was the most important game of the year for us up to then. Yes, I drove my players on as best I could but I certainly didn't try to intimidate the referee. I greatly resented that claim because it's not the way I do business and everybody in the game knows that. Neither Conor Hayes nor anybody else from Galway had a problem with me either but, for some odd reason, some people in the media decided to act aggrieved on Galway's and the GAA's behalf.

I'm not sure whether the Games Administration Committee's decision to summon me for a hearing was based on what they saw or what they read, although I suspect the latter was an influencing factor. There were suggestions in the papers that I would be banned from the sideline for eight weeks, which would effectively be for the remainder of the Championship assuming, of course, that we got to the final.

I was annoyed by what appeared to be something of a media witch-hunt over what was really a non-event. I had always been fair to the media on the basis that they have a job to do, but now some elements in their midst were acting as prosecutor, judge and jury over a case they themselves had trumped up.

Still, I was quite confident that the GAC would view the whole thing in a reasonable manner, which they did. I gave them my side of the story honestly and sincerely and would have been very disappointed if they had taken action against me. They accepted my explanation and that was the end of the matter, except in certain media quarters where individuals appeared to be upset because I wasn't banned. Why that was the case I still don't know, nor do I know why the media made such a big deal of it in the first place. Was it a case of somebody setting the agenda and others following in a sheepish line? You'd think they would have more interesting things to write about at the height of the Championships.

Looking back on 2004, the game against Galway was as close as it came for us in terms of getting things right. For whatever reason, the spark wasn't there by the time we played Clare in the All-Ireland quarter-final in Croke Park two weeks later. Clare set themselves up with an extra defender but I don't think that was as significant as was claimed when the game finished level. Yes, it made life more difficult for our forwards but it wasn't the first, or indeed the last, time that we had to cope with unorthodox formations. Far more relevant to how the game developed was the dismissal of Tommy Walsh on a second yellow card early in the second half. We were leading by four points at the time but it was always going to be difficult after that. Sensing there was something to be had, Clare dug in and got a draw in the end.

We did better in the replay in Thurles six days later, but there were still signs of staleness. We won by five points despite scoring just 1-11, not exactly an impressive strike rate but our defence did extremely well. We were back in action a week later, this time in the All-Ireland semi-final against Waterford who, after winning a brilliant Munster final against Cork, were itching for a crack at us. Three hard games on successive weekends definitely took its toll. Indeed, there were times against Waterford when we seemed to be hurling on pure instinct. Henry Shefflin scored two first-half goals for us, which was quite an achievement because a week earlier we were all extremely concerned when he sustained a nasty eye injury in the replay against Clare.

An eye injury is always very scary, so it was with considerable relief that we learned that not only would Henry make a full recovery but that he would also be available for the semi-final. It was a frightening experience for him but, typical of his attitude, he just got on with preparing for the game once he got the all-clear from the medics. Just as well, because if it weren't for his two goals the three-in-a-row bid would have ended against Waterford.

There are those who would say that might have been no bad thing, given what happened us in the final! We hung on in the closing stages against Waterford and just about got home safely, but it was very evident that we weren't playing with the fluency of the previous two years.

That's certainly not what you want going into any All-Ireland final, let alone against Cork who had layer upon layer of motivation, topped by the burning desire to prevent us from winning the treble. Naturally, it was claimed afterwards that the three-in-a-row factor contributed to our poor second-half performance in the final, but I don't believe that was the case at all.

No, this was one of those days where we found nothing in the tank when Cork raised the tempo and intensity in the second half. We started well enough, certainly in terms of winning possession, and actually led by three points after twenty-two minutes. However, there were warning signs that couldn't be ignored. We were shooting far too many wides and, as the tally mounted, I sensed it would come back to haunt us. Boy, did it do just that!

The second half was a disaster for us. We scored just two points in thirty-five minutes – both from Henry Shefflin from a free and a '65' – and none for the last twenty-three minutes. It was a world of which we had no experience and one we never want to re-visit. Those figures told their own depressing story of how the season ultimately came crashing down all around us. We scored 3-9 in a relatively short space of time in the second half against Galway, and now we couldn't manage a single point from play in a full thirty-five minutes. How strange was that?

I felt very sorry for the players because whatever they tried it just didn't come off, whereas every break went Cork's way, but that's what happens on a day like that. Our lads were as brave and committed as ever, but Cork were rampant as they notched up point after point. It was a shattering experience for us but there was nothing we could have done about it. With the exception of the Galway game, we hadn't reached the standards we set for ourselves and, while we got to the final through the back door, we were obviously living on borrowed time. The signs were there against both Clare and Waterford. Actually, if you looked deep enough, they were there against Wexford, too.

The strange thing about the Cork defeat was that, when I reflected on it afterwards, I had no regrets or second thoughts about how we might have approached the final differently. Everything that could be done had been done and, unlike 2001 when I blamed myself for the defeat by Galway, this was different. We had prepared as well as possible but something was missing throughout that campaign, and we just couldn't find it.

That can happen and, when it does, there's no way out. Still, we could never have expected to be so comprehensively beaten in the All-Ireland final. We lost by eight points which, apparently, was the biggest defeat suffered by Kilkenny in an All-Ireland final since 1964.

That's hurling for you. You go into Croke Park chasing an All-Ireland treble and leave with the biggest trimming for forty years. Crazy game, this.

CHAPTER 16

RED CARD FOR YELLOW

***I don't believe for one second that hurling is** any way dangerous or in need of a discipline crackdown, so I wish it were left alone. There are more than enough rules – and more than enough officials to implement them – to cater for all aspects of the game without meddling any further. And when rules are being re-examined it should be done in isolation and not as part of a double act with football which has totally different needs.*

Monday, April 20, 2009: *The experimental rules are on their way out, and good riddance. They got a good run at Congress over the weekend but failed to reach a two-thirds majority so they won't be used in the championships. Hopefully, we won't hear any more about them either.*

I'm delighted that they will end on League final day, not because I feared that they would impact on Kilkenny any more than any other county, but because I believe they would damage hurling. These changes were designed for football, yet for some reason they were also attached to hurling.

The thing is, they are wrong for hurling. There's no logical reason whatsoever why the same rules should apply to hurling and football because they're two very different and distinct games. And there's definitely no reason why, if experiments are being tried out, they should come in a 'fits one, fits all' format.

I said at the start of the League that I would wait for a few rounds before forming a judgement on the new rules. I wasn't a fan of them from the start but was prepared to give them a chance. The more I saw of them, however, the more I reckoned they were as unfair as they were unnecessary.

We had Eddie Brennan sent off against Waterford on a straight red card last month, but it was later rescinded. Jackie Tyrrell and Seamus Prendergast were sent off on yellow cards but they too were rescinded. Rightly so, because they should never have been given them in the first place.

My record shows that I'm not a man who criticises referees. Even when we lose, you won't find me blaming the referee. They have a tough job and need every support they can get but bringing in silly rules certainly isn't the way to go about helping them. As well as applying the rules consistently, referees have to be allowed to use common sense and, when they do, they generally get it right.

Sometimes you get the impression that referees feel forced into making decisions in case the assessor up in the stand makes a note of something and the ref finds himself answering questions at some future meeting. Of course rules have to be applied, but common sense and instinct aren't bad assets to take onto the field either, provided a referee is confident enough to use them.

I don't believe for one second that hurling is any way dangerous or in need of a discipline crackdown, so I wish it were left alone. There are more than enough rules – and more than enough officials to implement them – to cater for all aspects of the game without meddling any further. And when rules are being re-examined it should be done in isolation and not as part of a double act with football which has totally different needs.

It was mostly the strong hurling counties who opposed bringing in the experimental rules on a permanent basis at Congress, so surely there's a lesson there. It's possible that the new rules were appropriate for football but the hurling world wasn't going to have them foisted on them. And thank God for that.

I also found it interesting that there's already talk of re-visiting the experimental rules, tinkering around with them and giving them another go in some format. It's being mooted on the basis that a majority at Congress was in favour of retaining them for the Championship although it didn't quite reach the two-thirds required.

Surely though, if they were rejected that should be the end of it. They needed a two-thirds majority and didn't get it, so leave them be.

Anyway, we'll be back to the old rules for this year's Championship which will be a relief to everybody who enjoys the game as it is.

We beat Dublin in our final group League game last Sunday, but only after a great struggle. We were probably a bit lucky to take both points as it was only right at the end that we kicked on. It was the second time in three months we'd played Dublin and I have to say I'm very impressed by their rate of progress.

But then I'm not surprised. They have some super hurlers who have come through good underage teams and look ready to press on now. Anthony Daly's arrival has brought new enthusiasm to the Dublin scene and he also comes with plenty experience. He did a fine job when he was in charge of Clare and, while they didn't win anything in that period, he got the maximum out of them.

Managers shouldn't always be judged on what their teams win because they can only work with the resources at their disposal. I have been very lucky with the number and the quality of players available in Kilkenny but, obviously, it's not the same everywhere so I appreciate how lucky I am to be working with so much talent.

That Daly was prepared to commit himself to travelling from Clare to Dublin a few times a week was a real vote of confidence in the Dublin squad and they have certainly responded in this League. They finished in fourth place eventually which was a bit disappointing as they had very close calls against Limerick, Tipperary and us. Still, they beat Galway, Cork and Waterford, and drew with Clare, so they'll be happy enough heading into the Leinster Championship.

The odd thing is, though, that while they did quite well in Division

One they will need to be very careful against Antrim in the first round. This is a very good Antrim squad, well managed by 'Sambo' McNaughton and Dominic McKinley, and they won't have the slightest fears about taking on Dublin in Croke Park.

As for us, we're back in the League final, which was the first target for the season. We never, ever take anything for granted so it's nice to be back in a national final. That's what lads hurl for and every time you reach a final it should be savoured because you don't know when – or indeed if – there will be another. People will claim that chasing the All-Ireland four-in-a-row is all that concerns us now, but that's just not the case.

We're still two months away from starting the Championship so that's all very much in the future. For now, all our attention is on the League final against Tipperary in two weeks' time. I'm happy enough with the way our League has gone so far. Losing to Waterford early on certainly concentrated our minds because another defeat would usually rule you out of a top-two finish. As it turned out, we could have afforded to lose again but, after the Waterford setback, the target was clear – win all the remaining games.

We have had seven very competitive matches, which is what every team wants at this time of year and we can now look forward to the added bonus of a League final. We've got what we wanted from the campaign so far, which is encouraging given that we haven't been able to come anywhere close to calling on all our players at any stage. In fact, we've probably never had any more than ten of last year's All-Ireland final team, but then this is a new year so it's a clean sheet for everybody. And with lads pushing for places it has kept the intensity levels at just the right pitch.

It has been suggested that we're peaking too early in the season, but I'm happy to ignore that because it's not true. On days when we get things right, we're capable of playing very well at any time of year. As for peaking too early, myself and my management team have been around this particular block often enough to know how to structure the preparations, both for the short and long term.

The close call against Dublin on Sunday might bring a bit of reality to the scene after the big wins over Tipperary and Cork. You'd think we had done something strange and wonderful in those two games when, in fact, all that happened was we got a great start against Tipperary and beat a Cork team that clearly was behind us in terms of training and preparation.

Still, you'll hear daft talk about how a second Kilkenny team would fare against other counties. There seems to be a suggestion that Kilkenny have two teams capable of performing at the very highest level. No, we don't. Nobody is prouder than me of the quality of hurler we have in Kilkenny, but to suggest that we could field a second team which would match the other top counties is simply not true.

Say, for instance, that we have a fully fit panel of thirty-five players and we ignore the top fifteen and pick from the remaining twenty. How would we do? We'd be blown away!

I'm always amazed when I hear claims that we could field two teams and be competitive with both. The truth is that we have a solid base of players working to a pattern. I'd never be afraid to slot any of the squad into the actual team – either before or during a game – because they know the drill, the pattern and what's expected of them. They're with lads who have been exposed to all sorts of demands, tests and pressures so it's relatively easy to integrate into the overall system. It would be altogether different if you chose a team which didn't include any of the experienced guys.

Anyway, we're heading towards the end of April and we're in pretty good shape. We have lads like Noel Hickey and Derek Lyng who are in recuperation mode, but they're coming along nicely. Noel is ahead of Derek in the recovery stakes but both are on schedule.

'Cha' Fitzpatrick is on his way back too. He got a bout of the mumps, which was a serious blow to Ballyhale Shamrocks as he wasn't anywhere near his best against Portumna in the All-Ireland club semi-final, and he has since contracted a post-viral infection. What's important is that he comes right for the Championship.

Do I know the Championship team now, assuming of course that everybody is fit and raring to go by June? Absolutely not. I have never operated on the basis of looking at the previous year's team – irrespective of how successful it was – and regarding each of them as No.1 in his position. He may well be, but he's got to prove it all over again.

Current form always counts for more than what happened in the past. It's a policy which has served us well and is one which I think the players appreciate too because they know that we have no preconceived notions about which team to send out. Lads understand, and they know that everybody gets a fair chance all the time. If you're a regular, you realise that you're there only as long as you keep performing. On the other hand, if you're trying to force your way into the team you know that if you keep working away there's a decent chance your turn will come.

I would never have players on the panel who were happy just to make up the numbers. If a player is lacking ambition, being a squad member can be a comfortable place to be. You get the perks without the responsibilities. However, if that's your mentality, you're not for me! I want everybody pushing and driving all the time to force themselves as high up the ranks as they can go. So, if you're down in the lower end of the subs you have to strive to move up, and if you're higher up you must put pressure for a place on the first fifteen.

As for those not on the panel, I want them doing exactly the same thing as they try to force their way in. Being a member of a county panel should always be a great honour. We regard it as the ultimate privilege in Kilkenny, but with privilege comes responsibility, not just to your county but also to your club, your family and yourself.

You live your life as a Kilkenny hurler and all that entails because, if you don't, somebody else will. We have been fortunate that the players at all levels buy into that culture. They know it's the only way they have a chance of making progress. It's all about the next challenge, wherever you're at or wherever you're striving to go.

CHAPTER 17

HANGOVER HILL

What nobody realised at the time was that events off the field would probably have a bigger bearing on Kilkenny's destiny than anything that happened on it. Shortly after the Leinster final, full-back Noel Hickey was ruled out for the season after a heart scare.

Martin Breheny writes: The 2004/2005 winter loomed long and dark for Kilkenny as they reflected on what had been a strange season which had started out with such high hopes of completing the All-Ireland three-in-a-row, and ended in crumpled failure.

The defeat by Cork in the final provided a fertile feeding ground for statisticians as they delved into figures from an unfathomable game. Who could possibly have envisaged that Kilkenny wouldn't score a single goal or a score of any kind in the final twenty-three minutes? Or that they wouldn't score from play in the second half? Or that only four players would get on the scoresheet, or that DJ Carey wouldn't score at all and Henry Shefflin would manage just one point from play? It was just all so untypical of Kilkenny.

Their final return of 0-9 was the lowest in an All-Ireland final since 1987 when, coincidentally, Kilkenny managed the same score when losing to Galway. And, if all that wasn't disappointing enough, the 2004 defeat was the heaviest inflicted on Kilkenny in an All-Ireland final since

Tipperary beat them by fourteen points in 1964.

Truly, 2004 was a strange, frustrating year for Kilkenny. It had started as it ended, with a sound thrashing. They lost the Walsh Cup final to UCD by sixteen points (2-16 to 0-5) in February and, while it was largely a second-string team, it still came as quite a shock to the system to be so comprehensively out-scored.

Kilkenny have always prided themselves on being on the favourable side of history but, on this occasion, they were forced to endure a painful afternoon as UCD became the first non-county side to win the Walsh Cup. Kilkenny would later have their National League treble ambitions wrecked, early on, when they lost to Waterford and Galway.

Kilkenny actually found themselves in the relegation section (the top three in the two Division One groups played off against each other to decide the finalists, while the bottom three from either section played off to decide relegation). While escaping that ignominy was a mere formality, it still wasn't where Kilkenny wanted to be in April.

Two months later, they found themselves in another situation they would have preferred to avoid, as Wexford forced them off the Leinster highway and onto the back roads of the All-Ireland qualifiers. They re-discovered their bearings and reached the final, only to be taken apart by Cork – a defeat which left them without any titles for the first time since 1997.

It was quite a comedown, made all the more unpalatable by the impact of Cork's success on the All-Ireland table. It hoisted them back to the top with twenty-nine titles, one ahead of Kilkenny. It was a double hit for Cork who not only regained the top spot, but prevented Kilkenny winning the three-in-a-row.

The difference between first and second manifested itself in other ways, too. Cork won seven All Stars in 2004 while Tommy Walsh, JJ Delaney and Henry Shefflin were Kilkenny's only representatives, five fewer than in 2003.

By the start of 2005, things had changed in Kilkenny. Mick Flynn continued as trainer but Under-21 manager, Martin Fogarty, and former Laois football manager, Michael Dempsey, had replaced Noel Skehan and Johnny Walsh as selectors. It was regarded as a freshening-up exercise and a re-jigged panel made a quick impact, too, when they won the Walsh Cup, beating all three main Leinster rivals – Dublin, Offaly and Wexford – in quick succession.

The effect of the changes gathered momentum in the National League where Kilkenny won seven of eight games to qualify for the final against Clare. A surprising eight-point defeat by Clare in the early rounds was the only blemish on Kilkenny's chart, otherwise, it had been wins all the way – several by very large margins against Waterford, Galway, Laois, Dublin, Cork, Wexford and Tipperary. And, when they blitzed Clare by fourteen points in the League final, it left Limerick as the only top-tier team that Kilkenny hadn't beaten in Walsh Cup and League.

Unlike 2004 – when Kilkenny never really fired on all cylinders in the League – this was altogether different and created the perfect backdrop for the approaching Championship. Nevertheless, the hurling markets had their doubts as to whether Kilkenny could supplant Cork as All-Ireland champions. Kilkenny were installed as marginal favourites in the pre-Championship betting, largely because the Leinster Championship was deemed not to be as competitive as Munster.

However, much of the expert view which appeared in the media in early May reckoned that Cork offered the most complete package and that, if it came down to another shoot-out with Kilkenny, they would prevail again – albeit, by a much smaller margin than in the previous year's final.

The Kilkenny team which set out on the 2005 adventure included five changes from the 2004 final – Jackie Tyrrell for Michael Kavanagh at corner-back, Bryan Barry for Ken Coogan at midfield, Eoin Larkin for John Hoyne at centre-forward, Richie Power for 'Cha' Fitzpatrick at corner-forward and Richie Mullally for Eddie Brennan. Tommy Walsh moved from defence to attack with Mullally coming in at right half-back.

The Leinster semi-final against Offaly provided Kilkenny with no extra insights as to where they stood. In fact, they learned nothing about themselves as they hit Offaly with a scoring avalanche which buried the hapless underdogs. Henry Shefflin scored 2-11 – two points more than the entire Offaly return – as Kilkenny powered to a ridiculously easy win, 6-28 to 0-15.

Even allowing for Offaly's poor showing, the manner of Kilkenny's triumph was hugely impressive. So much so, that they were the hottest of favourites to beat Wexford in the Leinster final. Wexford had beaten them a year earlier but Kilkenny had avenged that defeat with relentless ferocity in a thirty-point destruction of the Model men in the League.

Despite that, there was a quiet sense of confidence in Wexford. They believed that the 2004 Leinster semi-final win over Kilkenny was no fluke and that, provided they hurled at full capacity and kept respect for their greatest rivals to a minimum, they could make a big impact. They certainly did that in the first twenty minutes of the Leinster final, scorching into a seven-point lead which actually should have been higher.

The memory of the 2004 All-Ireland final mauling by Cork couldn't have been far from Kilkenny's consciousness as they faced a real crisis, but this time it elicited an effective response. They were back level by half-time before dipping again early in the second half, when they fell three points behind.

However, they recovered a second time and followed the points route to success. They were still only a point clear with five minutes remaining before adding two more to win by 0-22 to 1-16. It was difficult to assess the Kilkenny performance on the basis that their battles with Wexford often take on a life of their own and don't adhere to any particular pattern.

However, when Clare trimmed Wexford by eleven points in the All-Ireland quarter-final three weeks later, it raised doubts about Kilkenny's well-being for the big tests ahead.

This was the first year of the four All-Ireland quarter-final Championship format which presented the Leinster and Munster champions with an extra fence. Kilkenny were drawn against Limerick, who had shown decent form in Munster where they lost to Tipperary by a point in extra-time before losing to Galway – also by a point – in the All-Ireland qualifiers. However, they beat Antrim and Laois to book a quarter-final date.

Kilkenny beat Limerick by five points in a mid-range performance which divided analysts into two camps. One camp claimed that the wins over Wexford and Limerick – while not exactly inspiring – pointed to a team who were getting ready to peak at exactly the right time, while the other side suggested that Kilkenny were still suffering from the psychological hangover of the defeat by Cork in the previous year's final. What nobody realised at the time was that events off the field would probably have a bigger bearing on Kilkenny's destiny than anything that happened on it. Shortly after the Leinster final, full-back Noel Hickey was ruled out for the season after a heart scare.

A virus attached itself to the muscle around the wall of Hickey's heart, leaving him with a condition, which was extremely worrying for a period. Thankfully, the good news eventually emerged that he would make a complete recovery and be able to return to hurling. Meantime, there was a sense of shock in the hurling community all around the country that a young, ultra-fit athlete could contract such a condition. John Tennyson, a strapping twenty-year-old from Carrickshock, was summoned as a replacement full-back and did well against Limerick. The game was played as the second leg of a double-header which also featured Galway v Tipperary, so the Kilkenny players and management would have seen little of that dramatic encounter.

Tipperary were well fancied to reach the semi-final having beaten Limerick and Clare before losing to All-Ireland champions, Cork, in the Munster final. They looked to be cruising comfortably in the right direction when they led Galway by six points with twelve minutes remaining. Then, in an explosive finish – which hinted at the capacity of the Galway attack to do serious damage if the opportunities arose – Tipperary were hit for 1-6 and could only manage a point in response, eventually losing by 2-20 to 2-18. It was an impressive flourish, but then Kilkenny would have known from the previous spring that, when the mood took Galway, they were well capable of racking up a big score.

Galway scored 1-21 (Ger Farragher bagged 0-15) in a League game in Nowlan Park, but leaked more heavily at the other end conceding 4-16 to end up four points short. Still, it was a decent performance by Galway which suggested that they had put the horror of the 2004 Championship thrashing by Kilkenny well behind them.

The big question heading into the semi-final was, which Galway team would turn up? The 2004 version was no match for Kilkenny in any department but, clearly, Conor Hayes had them firing much better a year later. The spirited revival against Tipperary suggested they were on an upward swing and, if it were maintained, Kilkenny would be confronted with a sustained and dangerous challenge.

It was a tie that offered all sorts of exciting possibilities – although nobody could have anticipated what was to unfold on Sunday, August 21 as referee, Seamus Roche from Tipperary, tossed in the ball between Fergal Healy and David Tierney, and Derek Lyng and Tommy Walsh.

CHAPTER 18

IN SEARCH OF THE TREBLE

The more I thought about it the more I wanted to come back stronger than ever. Talk of Kilkenny being a finished force caught in a time-warp made me all the more determined to get things back on track. I swore that, by Christ, we'd prove Kilkenny weren't gone. And if people think we are, we'll bloody show them. And quite soon too! If I had any doubts about continuing, the suggestions that we were beaten dockets about to be dumped in the bin helped me make up my mind to carry on.

Every manager in every sport knows what it's like. You're standing on the sideline, surveying what's unfolding in front of you and knowing that there isn't a damn thing you can do about it.

It's right there within touching distance, yet you might as well be watching on television and trying to influence the play with the remote control. When a game takes on a tempo and texture of its own it can become a wild, uncontrollable force, totally immune to interference.

You can tinker around the edges, make some adjustments here and there but it usually won't make the slightest difference. The 2005 Kilkenny-Galway All-Ireland semi-final fell neatly into that category. The end result was the same as 2001 in that Galway won but, other than that, there were no comparisons whatsoever.

In 2001, we weren't able to withstand the sheer intensity which Galway brought to their game. We weren't ready for it which was my fault but I never felt the same about the 2005 semi-final because we were totally focussed and well prepared. The season had gone well up to then. We won the National League after losing just one game all through and then beat Offaly and Wexford to regain the Leinster title. With their confidence levels high after beating us in 2004, Wexford were well primed for the Leinster final and turned in a brilliant opening twenty minutes, after which they led be seven points. They had landed some glorious points and embellished their free-flowing game with a goal from Des Mythen which left us facing our first real crisis since Cork overwhelmed us ten months earlier.

Our response was very heartening and the forwards finally found their range. They fired over a string of points and we were back level by half-time. Wexford had plenty more to give and went three points ahead early in the second half but, once again, we pegged them back and eventually won by three points, two of which came in stoppage time.

We lost Noel Hickey before the All-Ireland quarter-final against Limerick and, while we didn't hurl particularly well, we did enough to win. Hickey was always going to be a big loss but, in terms of preparation for an All-Ireland semi-final, the games against Wexford and Limerick were ideal in that they tested us in every department.

People would claim when we lost to Galway that complacency had set in after beating them so comprehensively in Thurles a year earlier, but that's just not true.

We keep complacency detectors on constant alert just to be on the safe side but, in fairness, it's not a problem we have had to deal with. And it certainly wasn't an issue in 2005. Anyway, how on earth could we take anything for granted against Galway after what had happened in 2001? Besides, they had hurled very well in the 2005 All-Ireland quarter-final against Tipperary, where they had staged a great recovery so their confidence was high and we knew exactly what to expect. Also, just as we were incredibly determined to get things right against them in 2004, they were equally driven to gain revenge a year later.

All the ingredients were there for a high-quality contest, but what nobody could have predicted was that the game would develop into the highest scoring All-Ireland semi-final in GAA history, producing a total of 9-36. That's close enough to the average score for two games, yet it came cascading down in Croke Park on one warm August afternoon. In the end, we lost out by one score – 5-18 to 4-18 – in a game which refused to be confined by any of the usual norms. It was enthralling and enjoyable too, unless, of course, you were from Kilkenny and left wondering how you lost a game where you scored 4-18! It was talked of afterwards as one of the classics, but try telling that to those of us who were at the receiving end. Games you win are classics, games you lose are disasters – it's as simple as that.

Having lost to Cork in the previous year's final, it was disappointing not to get another shot at them in 2005, but it wasn't to be. Galway deserved to beat us – end of story.

We could have offered the excuse that Noel Hickey's absence loosened the bolts in our defence and that Galway removed them completely, but I didn't go down that route for the simple reason that I have always believed that the team which scores the most deserves to win. Also, I believe firmly in the power of the panel. There are days when you'll be without certain players but you just get on with it. You'll miss them, but that's life. It happens to you, it happens to your opponents, it happens to every team. Unfortunately, it was our turn to be on the receiving end that year but that's the luck (or, perhaps more accurately, the bad luck) of the draw.

I don't know how we would have fared if Hickey had been playing and it's pointless to even surmise. We had fifteen players on duty and brought in four subs but we still came up short, which was all that mattered. It was Galway's day and good luck to them. They exploited their chances – especially when goal openings presented themselves – and set us a target which we couldn't reach despite a valiant effort over the final stretch.

It really was a strange, unpredictable game. We had 3-12 on the scoreboard at the three-quarter stage, which would quite often be enough to win a game. But to have it in the bank with more than a quarter of an hour to go and still lose was – to say the least – most unusual, especially when you add a further 1-6 as we did in the closing stages. The trouble was that, by the time we had scored 3-12 Galway had chalked up 5-17 after hitting us with a three-goal blitz in a wild, whirling twelve-minute spell earlier in the second half. Niall Healy scored all three in one of those golden spells that a player will always remember. By the way, so too do the opposition.

I looked up at the scoreboard and tried to imagine how it might look at the finish. "At this rate," I thought, "Galway will win by twenty points and we will have conceded a record score! When last did Kilkenny lose a game by twenty points? How will I explain that? Where the hell has this tornado come from? Galway aren't just beating us, they're pulverising us".

The memory of the second-half wipe-out against Cork in the All-Ireland final eleven months earlier was still fresh in Kilkenny people's minds as they watched Galway pile up the scores. Hell, if this keeps up the eight-point defeat suffered against Cork last year will look like a close call. At 5-17 to 3-12 the only question on everybody's mind was how much more damage Galway were going to inflict. We had tried this, that and the other, but to no avail. It was as if the ball had become attracted to Galway hands and hurleys by a magnetic force. A flick here, a flick there and into a Galway hand. And when the ball broke into open space it veered in the direction of a Galway player every time. At least, that's the way it looked.

Of course, what was really happening was that, because Galway were playing so fluently, they were making great things happen for themselves. Like, for instance, rattling in five goals and tossing over points for fun from all angles and distances. Our lads were left facing a stark choice – take a right hammering and write the day off as a very bad job or dig in and see what could be salvaged. It was down to them because there was very little I could do to help them.

What happened from there on was quite remarkable and made me prouder of the squad than I had ever been over the previous six seasons, a period which brought us three All-Ireland wins. I could see lads looking at each other as if to say, "We can't let this happen, we're buried in a big hole here, we've got to find a way out. We can't go back to Kilkenny having suffered a humiliating defeat like this".

It's not easy to summon the spirit to begin a revival when you're facing such a desperate situation. Your mind is racing, your power levels are down, the breaks aren't going your way while the opposition believe they could hurl on 'til nightfall and still not make a mistake or lose an ounce of energy.

That's why I was so proud of how our lads somehow managed to not only devour large chunks of Galway's lead but come tantalisingly close to clearing it out altogether. We out-scored them by 1-6 to 0-1 over the final eleven or twelve minutes, having finally retrieved the sort of rhythm that normally comes so naturally. Indeed, if we had had another two minutes more, there's every chance that we would have at least earned a draw, or maybe even won. I'm sure that with the exception of Galway people, everyone else would have been delighted by the prospect of a replay. We certainly would!

Galway held on but, boy, were they pleased to reach the finish line as we were closing in on them step by step. The strange thing was that, having produced such an excellent performance against us, Galway didn't play nearly as well against Cork in the final. It's easy to say that you play as well as you're let and that Cork did a much better job on them than we had done, but in that particular final Galway's overall game came nowhere close to being as high-tempo as it had been against us. I remember watching that final and thinking, "Why the hell do Galway reserve those special days for us and then don't repeat it next time?" Mind you, it was more frustrating for them than for anybody.

I had very mixed emotions walking off the pitch after that semi-final. Naturally, it was hugely disappointing to have lost but the way the lads had fought back so bravely proved one thing – their spirit and resolve were still very much intact. They had lost but they would be back, stronger and more determined than before. It also proved to me that I still had the dressing room.

It would have been easy for the players to see out the game from a long way back and casually dump responsibility for a second major Croke Park defeat in a year at my door, but that wasn't their way. They took responsibility, individually and collectively, and made it clear that we were all united, on and off the pitch. It was a really manly reaction to what had happened, but then that's what you'd expect from that group.

Still, I had reservations about what the future held for me. Whatever the circumstances, we had lost two big Championship games in eleven months so it was obviously time to re-assess. I spoke to the players in the dressing room afterwards and told them that the Kilkenny public could never thank them enough for what they had done. It might have appeared like a farewell speech and, to be honest, I was happy to let it sound like that, just to test the mood among the squad because I had to have them firmly behind me if I was going to stay on. I got my answer a few hours later.

After getting off the team bus at the Newpark Hotel I was walking across to my car when three players followed me over. I won't identify them because I have always respected the privacy of the camp: that's sacrosanct to me, always was, always will be. Anyway, the three lads wanted to clear something up and felt this was as good a time as any.

"Hope you weren't saying anything in the dressing room."

"How do you mean, lads?"

"Sounded like you might be thinking of walking away."

"Look lads, I have no idea what I'm doing at this stage. I've only had a few hours for this to sink in. I'll have to think about things."

"You can't go. Everyone wants you to continue. You know that."

"Thanks, lads. Appreciate that. But I won't be making any quick decisions. I've got to think things through."

I sat into my car, knowing that even if I wanted to leave it would be very difficult after what had just happened. What the three lads had done meant an awful lot to me and, to be honest, I felt they were probably speaking for the rest too. I wasn't looking for reassurance, but it showed that I still had the dressing room and that the players were already thinking of the future rather than wallowing in the pain they had endured earlier on. Their hurt was being channelled in the right direction which is so important after a defeat.

It was satisfying to know that I still had the support of the players but it didn't alter the fact that we had conceded 5-18, lost the All-Ireland semi-final and left Croke Park in a state of misery for the second time in eleven months. Someone told me afterwards that Kilkenny hadn't given away as many goals in an All-Ireland semi-final since the 1920s. Here we were just five years into the new Millennium and we had already conceded more in a semi-final than at any time in the previous seven decades only a year after suffering our worst All-Ireland defeat for forty years.

We had also won three of the previous five All-Ireland titles but, what do you think the Kilkenny supporters were discussing on their way home from the semi-final? They wouldn't have been happy with how things had gone and I've no doubt my popularity rating wasn't exactly high as Kilkenny cars sped down the N7 and N9 that evening. When a team loses, the manager naturally becomes the centre of attention among supporters who tend of have short memories.

That's the nature of management and you've got to live with it. I'd be very much a man to keep my own counsel in good or bad times. I don't seek outside approval and have always followed my own instincts. I'm lucky that my wife Elsie has been immersed in the GAA all her life, both as a successful player and coach with Buffers Alley and Wexford camogie teams. She has great knowledge of how it all works and, when it comes to hurling matters, I would very much respect her opinions. She was of the view that I should continue but only, of course, if I really wanted to.

I had some serious thinking to do. Did I want to take this on again and, if I did, how would I go about refreshing the scene? Would we be successful? Could we take it on again?

The reaction to the defeat by Galway surprised me. We had lost by a goal in a freakish sort of game, yet if you listened to some people you would think we hadn't done a thing right all year.

How's this for contradiction? There was lots of media coverage given to the semi-final in the context of where it stood in the catalogue of best all-time games. Frankly, I consider comparing teams, players and games from different eras as nonsense because you're never evaluating on a like-for-like basis. Still, some people are fascinated by it, so let them have their harmless fun. What I found more interesting was the assessment of where Kilkenny stood as a result of losing to Galway.

It seemed the general view was that, while the game was one of the all-time Championship classics to which Kilkenny had contributed enormously en route to a narrow defeat, we were now heading rapidly for the downward slopes and facing an uncertain future. It was a baseless argument but it gathered momentum very quickly.

Even some of our own were at it. Enda McEvoy wrote in *The Sunday Tribune* that we wouldn't have lived with Cork in the All-Ireland final. We had, according to Enda, staggered across the finish line in the 2003 All-Ireland final while Cork strolled across it two years later. He seemed to think that we were living in the past whereas Cork had changed the face of hurling in much the same way as Clare had done in the 1990s. Nobody changes the face of hurling, but never mind! Most of all, he didn't expect Liam McCarthy to be coming to Kilkenny any time soon and probably not at all this decade.

So there we were, beaten, old-fashioned, lacking finesse and about to head into a dip while Cork would, at the very least, pick up the three in-a-row with casual ease in 2006. And that was coming from a Kilkenny man – so what did the rest think?

I also seem to recall Donal O'Grady suggesting on Today FM that Kilkenny might struggle for a while and I thought to myself, "Really Donal? Where's the evidence that we have slipped so badly?" It just wasn't there.

The more I thought about it the more I wanted to come back stronger than ever. Talk of Kilkenny being a finished force caught in a time-warp made me all the more determined to get things back on track. I swore that, by Christ, we'd prove Kilkenny weren't gone. And if people think we are, we'll bloody show them. And quite soon too! If I had any doubts about continuing, the suggestions that we were beaten dockets about to be dumped in the bin helped me make up my mind to carry on.

Still, if everybody reckoned we were about to drop into a deep, lonely trough, then I was happy to let them believe it. So, I kept talking about how we were heading into a transition phase and how it would take time to re-build the team. Deep down, I never believed a word of it. Depicting us as a county in decline because of what had happened against Wexford and Cork in 2004 and Galway in 2005 was miles off the mark, but it was very strong currency at the time. In fact, I felt that with a few adjustments we were in with a right good chance of picking up the pace quite quickly and making a major drive for honours in 2006.

Change is inevitable as part of the natural evolution of a squad, but I wasn't going to make sweeping alterations just for the sake of it. Besides, it wasn't necessary. By their own choice, Peter Barry and DJ Carey didn't play for us after 2005, but most of the others did. Indeed, if you look at the nineteen players we used against Galway in 2005, fourteen played against Cork in the 2006 final. And since Noel Hickey was unavailable for the Galway game but, happily, was back in 2006 it would have been fifteen in normal circumstances. Scarcely a sweeping transition, now was it?

Peter, a fine captain in 2005 and a player who had given so much to Kilkenny, had opted out, as had DJ. The only real difference, I suppose, was in the sense that Kilkenny, post-DJ, represented transition in itself. He had been around for so long and was such an institution in hurling that it was difficult to visualise a Kilkenny squad without him. However, all careers, no matter how illustrious, come to an end sometime. Unfortunately for DJ, it ended in defeat in 2005 although, obviously, that in no way detracted from what he had achieved during the previous fifteen years. Nobody in Kilkenny, or outside either, could be in any doubt as to the contribution he made to hurling in a golden career.

With DJ and Peter gone, we had to find replacements and move on. That's exactly what we did, quietly and without fuss while all the time being happy to let everybody believe we were deep in transition and looking beyond 2006.

I had no doubt whatsoever that we would be hugely competitive in

2006. That guaranteed nothing, of course, but I also knew we were good enough to be in with a right good chance of winning the All-Ireland if we got everything right. The process of getting it right involved another good run in the League which we won again before retaining the Leinster title.

Any year you win an All-Ireland is a good year, but I'd have to say that beating Cork in the 2006 final made it all the sweeter. There isn't a healthier rivalry in hurling than between Kilkenny and Cork and we also have a huge respect for each other. It's natural, though, that we want to keep each other down and, when it comes to reaching a milestone such as the three-in-a-row, then we'll both do whatever it takes to stop the other achieving it.

Not that it always works, as Kilkenny knew from 1978 when we failed to prevent Cork landing the three-in-a-row. I had painful memories of that particular final as a player which I didn't want to experience again as manager.

We were on the wrong side against Cork again in 2004, only this time it was they who were trying (and succeeding) to stop us winning the treble. Understandably, they got huge satisfaction from that, especially since they were in a position to savour it from quite some way out in the final. Two years later, the ball was back in our court as we were presented with a chance to wreck their treble ambitions. They had lived fairly dangerously en route to the final, especially in the All-Ireland quarter- and semi-finals where they had a point to spare over Limerick and Waterford respectively. In many ways it was the ideal way to reach the final. They had done just enough to get there and would have felt that they were conserving the best for the biggest day of all. It's irrelevant how a team gets to a final – all that matters is that they reach it and then make it count.

Our path had been fairly straightforward. After winning Leinster, where we beat Westmeath and Wexford, we were pitted against Galway for the third year in a row. As ever, we didn't know what to expect from them, but we were fiercely determined that there would be no re-run of 2005. In fact, it turned out to be one of our very good days. We had them under pressure from fairly early on, and opened up a big lead before having Derek Lyng sent off on a second yellow card in the second half. He didn't deserve it but it happened anyway. It might have proved very significant on another day, but we were defending a big lead at the time so there was room for manoeuvre in the likely event of a Galway revival.

They rallied over the closing stages and cut the gap to five points but couldn't get any closer. To be honest, I felt there was more in our lads if they came under real pressure. We had eight points to spare over Clare in the semi-final, but Cork had beaten them fairly comfortably in the first round of the Munster Championship so you could read nothing into our relatively easy win.

So then, the scene was set for the big showdown between the two teams that had shared the previous four All-Ireland titles between them. It was portrayed as the ultimate shoot-out between the two best teams in the country. Cork were fancied to win on the basis that they were a more complete team who got everything right for so long. Also, it was assumed that their big win over us two years earlier would give them a significant psychological edge.

Personally, I didn't believe a word of it. Kilkenny would never be spooked by Cork in an All-Ireland final and, anyway, we had beaten them in 2003, so it wasn't as if we didn't know how to handle them. You certainly don't need artificial motivations for an All-Ireland final but I suppose that, deep down, everybody in our camp remembered 2004 and how Cork had taken great glee in stopping us winning the treble. It would be just as sweet for us if we could now do the same, but we knew damn well that simply wishing alone wouldn't be much good once the war began. No, we would have to be ready for everything and anything Cork threw at us.

The game went very much to plan for us. It was absolutely vital that we closed Cork down, stopped them playing their running game and did not allow them to deliver those telling hand passes which they used so effectively to create space. The only antidote to that type of game is hard work and total concentration. When a Cork player got the ball, I wanted two men converging on him. If he got his pass away, I wanted two men converging on the intended recipient.

We had to be in their faces, behind their backs and coming in from either side too. I wanted the black-and-amber to be a blur in front of their eyes all the time. I wanted it to look big, powerful and utterly confident. Wherever Cork players turned, they were to see a Kilkenny man approaching. And if they turned the other way, another Kilkenny man was to be steaming in. There would be no let-up, no hesitation, no compromise. Wherever Donal Og Cusack tried to place his puck-outs, I wanted our lads on top of the would-be receiver. Get there, whatever it takes. This was to be the test of everything we stood for. There was one chance to get it right so let there be no regrets afterwards.

Playing that type of game for a full seventy minutes demands incredible energy and commitment. More than that, it calls for a mental energy which can never be allowed to drop for the full seventy minutes, and into stoppage time too. The mood in our camp in the build-up to the final was terrific. It was as if the entire panel felt they were putting their very identity as people and hurlers on the line.

We suffered a double injury blow in the weeks before the final when JJ Delaney and Donncha (Cody) both sustained knee injuries which ruled them out. We were lucky enough to have such an experienced campaigner as Michael Kavanagh to take over from JJ at corner-back. It's at times like this that the importance of a big squad becomes vital.

Five or six of the team had won All-Ireland medals in 2000 and several more were aboard in 2002-2003 but, although this was only a few years later, it looked as if it were from a different world. Those successes would be savoured some time long into the future but, for now, all that mattered was beating Cork and stopping them winning the treble.

Cork put in a mighty effort in that final, but our lads hurled with such intensity that they were never going to take no for an answer. The greater the challenge, the more they responded. From my perspective, it was a joy to watch. They had applied everything we had talked of down to the last detail and never, ever relented. We won by three points after Cork pulled back a goal five minutes from the end but it was one of those days that I never felt would go against us. It didn't matter what Cork offered we had an answer, but, then, the mood in the dressing room was so good coming up to the game that I would have been very surprised if the lads hadn't delivered. This was completely different to 2004. The sharpness was back and this time we never allowed Cork to inflict their running game on us. We stopped it at source and then went back to wind up again to repel the next wave. It took unbelievable concentration and massive will, but we had both.

An awful lot had been said and written about us over the previous two years, not all of it flattering either so I suppose this was a day to show exactly what Kilkenny hurling was all about.

I would regard our 2006 clash with Cork as one of the truly great finals. There was an honesty about it that brought real credit to both sides and, while we came out on top in the end Cork had made a heroic attempt to join the elite band who had won the treble. On another day they might have succeeded but, we smothered them, all over the field and never allowed them to set the agenda. Still, they deserve enormous credit for the manner in which they set about retaining the title. I have no doubt that there have been years when the Cork performance of 2006 would have won the final, but it just wasn't good enough this time.

The sense of relief at the end was unbelievable. And, if stopping Cork winning the treble wasn't satisfying enough, the Liam McCarthy Cup would be brought back to Kilkenny by another Village man. Jackie Tyrrell was the first from our club to captain Kilkenny to the senior hurling title since I was lucky enough to do it twenty-four years earlier but, then, we had only two county titles in the intervening years. What was that about, Village men being unlucky captains? Not any more.

Returning home the following day, I couldn't help thinking how much had changed in a short space of time. A year earlier, Kilkenny were portrayed as yesterday's men who would have to wait an awfully long time for a new dawn, if indeed one came at all.

Our preparations were supposed to be out-dated, lacking in method and finesse. By comparison with Cork and their sophisticated ways, we were pre-historic. Yet, a year later, we were All-Ireland,

Leinster, National League and Walsh Cup champions and had remained unbeaten in all competitions throughout the year. Not bad for a squad in transition. Not bad either for a squad which was written off just because they had narrowly lost one game to a rampant Galway team.

It was especially rewarding for the lads who had been on the teams that lost in 2004 and 2005 as it showed that, despite the depiction of them as yesterday's men, they were still powerful hurlers with lots to offer and years of hurling ahead of them.

We wouldn't encounter Cork in the Championship for almost another two years, but there would be other big challenges out there – though some would have held a different opinion. We beat Offaly by big margins in 2007 and 2008 which fed into the perception that, on each occasion, we merely had to turn up to reach the Leinster final. That wasn't the case. We prepared for those games as honestly and as diligently as we did for any All-Ireland final because, if we hadn't, we would have been beaten.

In 2008, in particular, Offaly pushed us to the limit for half an hour. They hit hard, but legitimately, and contested every ball with real intensity so, if we hadn't been ready for them, we would have been in trouble. We pulled away in the second half and racked up a big score but if we had taken any chances going into that game, it would have been very different.

The idea that we amble through the early rounds and pace ourselves to peak later in the season has no basis whatsoever in fact. We treat every game and every opponent with the utmost respect because, if you don't, you'll be punished, and rightly so. Besides, Kilkenny certainly don't need a reminder of what Offaly can do when they get a run on the opposition.

We would never take a chance in the early rounds because, as we discovered when we lost to Wexford in the 2004 Leinster final, the qualifier route can be very draining. The route through the Championship which involves the least number of games is always the best option, provided you can avail of it.

We beat Wexford twice in the 2007 Championship and, while we had plenty to spare in both games, some daft conclusions were drawn.

Principally that, apart from Kilkenny, Leinster hurling was a wasteland. So how then did Wexford reach the All-Ireland semi-final? By beating Tipperary in the quarter-final!

Wexford got little enough credit for that performance with most of the media spotlight focusing on Tipperary and how they allegedly blew it. That was very unfair on Wexford who hurled very well and fully deserved to win. They didn't repeat the same level of performance against us in the semi-final, but they had every right to be there after their performance against Tipperary.

Our 2007 quarter-final clash with Galway was played after the Tipp-Wexford game and had generated huge hype ever since results from Galway's qualifier group set up the pairing. With Ger Loughnane in his first season in charge of Galway the media turned it into a Loughnane v Cody battle which, of course, it was never going to be, certainly not from my perspective anyway. Games are won by the players on the field, not by the men walking the sideline.

Sadly, there was a tragic backdrop to that game as the entire hurling world was plunged into deep sadness following the death in a road accident of James McGarry's wife, Vanessa. The accident also claimed the life of Mary Lonergan, another woman from a great hurling family. Truly, an awful day which left everybody in Kilkenny in a state of shock.

It's amazing how circumstances can change perspectives in a matter of seconds. The moment we heard the dreadful news on the Thursday before we were due to play Galway, all thoughts of the game disappeared immediately and were replaced by an overwhelming sense of sadness and sympathy for James, his son Darragh and the two families who were so severely traumatised by Mary and Vanessa's deaths.

Playing the game the following Sunday was never an option and the decision to defer it was made very quickly with the full backing of all the counties who were due to play the quarter-finals. It was a very difficult time for everybody. All we could do was offer as much support as possible to James and Darragh as they faced up to the unspeakably sad circumstances in which they found themselves.

The quarter-finals were put back until the following Saturday and, when we returned to preparing for the game early in the week, we all knew that the biggest tribute that could be paid to James and Darragh, and to Vanessa's memory, was to win and take the season on for as long as possible.

We all wanted to win so badly for the McGarrys but, on the other hand, it wasn't easy for the players to concentrate on hurling at a time when their close colleague and friend had had his life so cruelly turned upside down. It wasn't exactly the easiest quarter-final we could have drawn at any time, but it was made all the more difficult by the circumstances.

Galway would be hugely driven to beat us and, with many people convinced that Loughnane's arrival was the catalyst they needed to win the All-Ireland after a long wait, there was massive interest in the game. Loughnane's presence in the Galway camp meant nothing to me. With or without him I had recent, first-hand experience – not once, but twice – of how dangerous Galway could be.

Noel Lane had been in charge when they beat us in 2001, while Conor Hayes was manager for that 2005 epic struggle where they squeezed us out, so it was pretty obvious that, on any given day, Galway were capable of producing something special.

The 2007 quarter-final was a cracking contest, the closeness of which was not reflected in the final result which showed us winning by ten points. We were level nine or ten times through the first hour in a game that looked as if it couldn't quite make up its mind which way to turn.

In the end, it veered in our direction thanks to two goals by Eddie Brennan, embellished by some points which saw us home. It wasn't the first time that Eddie had popped up for crucial goals, but they were never more welcome than on that particular afternoon. There were times in his younger days when some critics claimed that Eddie would never make it as a constant presence in our attack. They were wrong and I always knew they would be.

Yes, he had to work very hard to become such a great player, but his attitude was always sound. If he was replaced he took it the right way and just worked and worked to make sure that he got better and that he got the most out of his talents. There was no sulking or whining or walking out if things weren't going his way, which is a lesson for players everywhere. Keep the head down and work hard because, ultimately, that will achieve results. Feeling sorry for yourself most definitely will not. It never has and it never will.

There was a degree of surprise in hurling circles when Limerick qualified for the 2007 All-Ireland final as Cork and Waterford were seen as more likely Munster candidates. Indeed, after winning the Munster title, Waterford were well-fancied to reach the All-Ireland final but were hit by a Limerick tornado in the semi-final. It left us facing a team that had showed real steel in resurrecting their season. We were resounding favourites to beat them. As always, we didn't pay the slightest attention.

Games are won on the pitch and not in the bookie's shop, where people who think they know more than they actually do bet on the outcome, so there was no danger of over-confidence going in against Limerick. They had beaten the Munster champions and deserved their place in the final: as far as we were concerned we had to approach the game in exactly the same frame of mind we brought to the clash with Cork a year earlier.

The circumstances were different because Limerick hadn't been in the final for a long time, but Richie Bennis and Co had them very well tuned. We didn't know what to expect of them, whereas we could always gauge Cork because they had been in so many recent finals.

As things turned out, the final flowed very much our way from the off. We hit Limerick for 2-3 in the first ten minutes and kept them at bay from there on, but it wasn't as easy as it might have looked. Bear in mind, we lost Noel Hickey with a hamstring injury well before half-time while Henry Shefflin couldn't come out for the second half, having damaged his cruciate ligament. Losing that pair was a huge blow, so it was just as well we took a comfortable lead into the break.

It was claimed afterwards that we had targeted an early blitz as the way to beat Limerick, and that they stood off too far and paid the price in the opening ten minutes. I'm always amused by reports of the tactics we're supposed to have drummed up for various games.

So we wanted to start well against Limerick? As opposed to what? Not starting well? Every team tries to hit a game at full pace from the throw-in because it makes life an awful lot easier. Sometimes it happens for you, sometimes it doesn't. Either way, you have to be ready because there's absolutely no way of knowing how any game will evolve. We had no specific plans to blow Limerick away in the opening stages because if we based everything on that and it didn't work out, where would it leave us? Besides, a manager has to trust his players to work their way through whatever problems they encounter. They won't always be able to do that because they're up against a better team, but the one thing you can't do is fill their heads with complicated theories. Hurling is a simple game and should be treated as such.

No sooner had Henry Shefflin received the Liam McCarthy Cup after the win over Limerick than we were being asked about the three-in-a-row. We knew it would continue non-stop from there on, and most especially once the 2008 season got underway.

There's very little you can do in a situation like that except to think in terms of one game at a time. Neither management nor players can stop the media or the general public highlighting landmarks like the pursuit of a three-in-a-row, but they can control how they react to it within the confines of the camp.

Ours was a simple policy – don't talk about the treble, focus on what we had always done and get on with preparing as best we could. Losing to Tipperary in the League semi-final in Nowlan Park certainly wasn't in our plans, but it brought a positive spin-off as it made it very easy to get through to the players that, however much praise and adulation they were receiving from various quarters, there was high-class opposition out there who would do just about anything to become the team to wreck our treble ambitions.

As it happened, Offaly, Wexford and Cork all failed in their attempts, leaving us facing Waterford in the final. In terms of PR for hurling, it could hardly have been much better. Kilkenny bidding for the three-in-a-row against their close neighbours who hadn't even been in the final for forty-five years, and who hadn't won one for forty-nine years. Still, this particular team weren't exactly big day novices, having been in the top three or four since 2002.

To add to the edge, Waterford had re-built their challenge after changing manager in mid-season. With Davy Fitzgerald in charge, they re-launched their All-Ireland bid via the qualifiers and went on to show just how formidable they were by inflicting a first defeat of the year on Munster champions, Tipperary.

Mind you, I wasn't all that surprised that Waterford beat Tipperary in the semi-final. In a way, it was set up for Waterford. They had built momentum with every game and were poised for a big surge against Tipp. The managerial changeover between Justin McCarthy and Fitzgerald had gone smoothly, even if the circumstances which led to it were unfortunate.

No, despite the tips and the tipsters, we regarded Waterford as very tough opponents.

They had beaten us in the 2007 League final and would have taken a lot of encouragement from the manner of their victory. We led them by three points at the three-quarter stage and by one with five minutes to go, but they out-scored us 0-4 to 0-1 from there on. They would rightly have regarded that win as a major positive when it came to playing us in the All-Ireland final.

I had no fears that the three-in-a-row angle would inhibit us in any way. I never put the 2004 defeat to Cork down to it, and was certain it wouldn't be relevant this time either. Players are only conscious of the actual game when they're playing an All-Ireland final. When their careers are over and they look back on what they achieved they might think more about the significance of a particular final, but when you're wrapped up in it, all that counts is now.

We were expecting Waterford to take us with a ferocious intensity but, one thing was for certain, we weren't going to be bullied. I was a bit surprised by the antics of a few Waterford players before the game started. They made their presence felt, to our forwards in particular, in ways which had the opposite effect to what they had intended. Did they think players who had been around the circuit for years and who knew exactly what it took to win an All-Ireland were going to be knocked off their stride by a few kicks and sly digs? If they did, they were mistaken.

As events transpired it was an incredibly easy win for us. We had it well wrapped up by half-time and went on to complete a victory by a margin we could never have anticipated. Waterford didn't do themselves justice, but then we never let them. Having said that, who would have predicted a Kilkenny win on a 3-30 to 1-13 scoreline?

We brought James McGarry in as a sub late on in what was an emotional occasion for everybody. It was fantastic that he was still on the panel after the personal devastation he had suffered fourteen months earlier, so giving him a chance to play a part in another All-Ireland final was the least I might have done for a man who had given so much to Kilkenny hurling. I might have a reputation for not making changes simply for change's sake, but this was different. I judge each case on its merits and when it came to bringing James on in the 2007All-Ireland final, I certainly didn't feel I had to explain myself to anybody.

The ovation he got when he came on wasn't just from Kilkenny people. Although, the Waterford fans were knee-deep in dejection on an occasion that had turned out so disappointingly for them, they too, sportingly, acknowledged his introduction. It was a lovely touch which Kilkenny people deeply appreciated.

Being able to bring James on for the final minutes of the successful three-in-a-row attempt was the crowning moment in a marvellous year. It was also his final act as a Kilkenny player after an outstanding career.

As far as I'm concerned, one of the great mysteries in hurling is how James McGarry was never selected as an All Star goalkeeper. How the selectors could justify his omission year after year is beyond me, and they certainly stand indicted for crimes against good judgement.

How many goals did he concede in six All-Ireland finals between 1999 and 2006? Three. That's one goal every 140 minutes, which is some record. He was incredibly consistent right throughout his career, and I have no hesitation in saying he was as good a goalkeeper as I have ever seen. Perhaps, when it came to the All Stars, his problem was that he made things look too simple. I've heard it suggested that the reason he was never selected was because he had such outstanding defenders in front of him that his workload was lighter than his rivals in other counties. Rubbish.

McGarry made many outstanding saves over the years but, equally importantly, he was a brilliant organiser. The defence always had complete faith in him. He was never hurried or fussed and always knew exactly what he was doing. He made the goalkeeping art look so simple. The way he'd kill the ball, control it and clear downfield was brilliant. It wasn't flash but it was so efficient that every Kilkenny defender loved playing in front of him. And he had a good effect on the manager's nerves too.

Shame on the All Star selectors, they have done the scheme a great disservice by not honouring one of the truly great goalkeepers of all time. By continually overlooking him, they demeaned themselves and the scheme. Still, Kilkenny people know the truth about James McGarry and that's more important than recognition by people who got this one so badly wrong.

There's no doubt that winning the 2008 All-Ireland title will always be regarded as extremely special in Kilkenny as it was actually the first time the county had won the three-in-a-row on the pitch (it seems one leg of the only previous treble in 1911-12-13 was won on a walkover).

This time, it was all done in the heated cauldron of battle over three memorable seasons where we didn't lose any Championship games. There's no doubt that added to the sense of satisfaction. Had we won the treble after losing in Leinster, it might be argued that it didn't match previous three-in-a-row achievements by Cork or Tipperary, which were gained in pre-All-Ireland qualifier days where there was no safety net for teams beaten in the provincial championships. As it was, nobody could question the merit of our treble. It was a time to savour and enjoy it because you never know what the future holds.

CHAPTER 19

THE SCENT OF SUMMER

***All the lads know where I stand when they're** playing against The Village. I want Noel Hickey back to his very best – hopefully, even tomorrow night – but I still want to see him cleaned out. Kilkenny is one thing the club is another and, whatever happens, I'm a Village man first, Kilkenny manager second.*

Friday, April 24, 2009: *I love this time of year. The long bright evenings are here, the club scene is taking off, there's a whiff of summer in the air and you can sense the rising excitement among everybody. And we're back in Nowlan Park.*

We do a lot of the early season work in St Kieran's College but we're in Nowlan Park now, and that's where we'll stay for as long as the season lasts. The players are always glad to get back here. This is where you judge how you're going, it's where lads queue up to take each other on and it's where they sharpen themselves against one another.

We're out in the National League final against Tipperary on Sunday week, but there are club games this weekend. The Village are playing Dunnamaggin in Callan tomorrow night and I'll be up on the bank shouting our lads on. The only time I'll think like Kilkenny manager is to check how Noel Hickey is coming along.

Noel has been out all season after having a second Gilmore's Groin operation, but he's on his way back now. He'll be playing for Dunnamaggin tomorrow, so we'll see how he goes. Noel has had a tough few years with injuries plus, of course, the heart muscle virus scare which was of great concern for a while in 2005. Thankfully, he made a complete recovery from that and has also kept battling back after injury problems.

We were all very worried when we heard of the heart scare, but it turned out to be a virus problem which came right with the proper treatment. It meant, of course, that we were without Noel for that famous All-Ireland semi-final against Galway. Would it have been different if he were playing? You can never tell, but let's put it this way – the Galway forwards might not have found it as easy if he had been in among them.

He has been through a lot but he's very strong mentally, which has been a great help in getting him through all the setbacks he has suffered. Nobody is keener than me to see Noel back to full fitness and bursting to regain the full-back jersey for Kilkenny but, tomorrow night, I'm a Village man and that's all that counts.

All the lads know where I stand when they're playing against The Village. I want Noel Hickey back to his very best – hopefully, even tomorrow night – but I still want to see him cleaned out. Kilkenny is one thing the club is another and, whatever happens, I'm a Village man first, Kilkenny manager second.

That's when I'm following the club scene but, of course, it changes the minute I'm back with the county squad. They come first then and they know that. I don't see them as clubmen any more. Now they're Kilkenny men, united in a single drive towards doing the very best they can for themselves, their clubs and the county. I don't think anybody can accuse me of being biased towards Village men in all the years I've managed Kilkenny.

I love when the club scene begins to warm up. I watch as many games as I possibly can, and not just those involving the Kilkenny senior panel either. You never know who you might spot in an intermediate or junior game and anyway, from a pure enjoyment viewpoint, they are just as attractive.

The clubs are important and we have no problem with the county players going back to them to train and play as often as possible. In fact, it's good for the players to return to their clubs and take on the responsibility that befits them as county men. If you forget who you are or where you came from, then you're losing something that you will never get back. You'll be the loser, not those around you.

We've managed to maintain a good balance between club and county over the years. It's important to get it right because the smoother the relationship the better it will be for everybody both in terms of games and training for club and county.

From my perspective, I'm lucky to have such a fantastic trainer as Michael Dempsey. The last few months have been his time as he put in the foundations for the fitness regime. He'll take it through from here too so that, when we head into the championship, everything will be spot on.

I have the utmost confidence in everything he does and would never interfere in his programme. He decides what he wants to do and how much time he needs to do it. He'll always be looking ahead, conscious not just of the up-coming games, but also of the longer-term strategy. The most sensible thing I can do as a manager is to trust him fully and let him bring his excellence to bear on his job. It would be silly to have such a proven expert on board and then interfere with what he wants to do. Naturally, we talk everything through all the time, but it's very much a team effort, as indeed it is with the many fine people involved in our backroom team.

Michael always seems to manage to keep the players fresh and you'll never hear us offering the excuse that we were in the middle of heavy training if we lose a League game. We train so that we'll be at our best in games, so to blame a poor performance on training makes no sense to me. The schedule of games is known well in advance, so the trick is to work the training around them rather than allowing the training to dictate and then blame it if you lose a match.

Michael's experience both as a Laois footballer and trainer has been a huge help and, I have to say, there's isn't a single aspect of how he goes about his work that I'd question.

Martin Fogarty brings an awful lot to the scene too. He has a wonderful hurling brain, and is a fantastic judge of players and teams – whether it's our own or the opposition. Having successfully managed Kilkenny Under-21 teams, he understands and appreciates exactly what's required. As well as knowing the scene inside out, he brings huge energy to everything he does. He's very much his own man which is a vital quality for anybody involved in team management.

Martin and Michael are key members of a superb backroom team which also includes physical trainer Noel Richardson, Dr Tadhg Crowley, physiotherapists Robby Lodge and Clare Lodge, dietician Noreen Roche, sports rehabilitator Roisin Young, and team assistant Denis Coady who has been involved with the team for years. Denis has a huge workload which he takes on with great enthusiasm, down to every last detail.

Martin and Michael came in at the start of the 2005 season, replacing Johnny Walsh and Noel Skehan. Johnny had been with me since the start while Noel came in when Ger Henderson left at the end of 2001. It was my decision to change selectors after 2004. I did it for no other reason than I felt the scene needed to be freshened up.

Johnny, who had been there since I came in, and Noel were excellent selectors and brought an awful lot of knowledge and expertise to the scene, but I felt that it was time to make a change. If either of them were manager, they might well have felt the same way and decided to replace me, which I would have fully understood.

Still, it wasn't an easy call to make because the lads had done everything that would have been expected of them. I still meet them from time to time and am always interested in their opinions because they are serious hurling men who know the game inside out. The same goes for Ger Henderson who was with me for a few years at the start. These guys gave incredible service to Kilkenny and, on a personal level, I am especially thankful for the help they gave me.

Mick O'Flynn was with me for years as team trainer, but he filled that role with distinction long before I arrived. I'd have known from my playing days as he trained The Village around the time won the 1982 All-Ireland club final. A great trainer and a great character who exerted a very positive impact wherever he went!

I have been exceptionally lucky with all the people I've worked with right from the start. I can't overstate how important that has been in the entire 'Team Kilkenny' project. As manager I'm out front, but many others have done so much to make everything work so well. They probably don't get the credit they deserve among the general public, but I certainly know how much they have all done.

John Healy was County Chairman when I was appointed and was clearly a big influence on the decision, but Ned Quinn took over at the end of 1998 and was there for many years before taking over from Pat Dunphy as Secretary a season or two back. I have a great relationship with all of them and also with current Chairman, Paul Kinsella who is, of course, principal of St Patrick's, where I teach. He's always extremely supportive of what I do which is very much appreciated.

It's all about team work on and off the field because, unless everybody is pulling their weight all the time, problems arise. After all, a chain is only as strong as its weakest link so it's crucial to ensure that every link, is resilient enough to take whatever strain comes its way. It's also important to keep stress testing the strongest links to make sure they're not beginning to weaken in any way.

APTER 20

STICKS, STONES BUT NO BROKEN BONES

I don't recall Loughnane mentioning anything about us 'flicking and belting across the wrists' when he was an RTÉ 'Sunday Game' analyst prior to taking over in Galway, so where did it come from in 2007? Wasn't it amazing that no other manager had spotted our monstrous crimes against hands? They hadn't, because there were none.

It's not in my nature to allow things outside my control to annoy me because, if you can't do anything about it, there's no point in wasting time or energy. Once the season starts, I'm like all managers and have more than enough to deal with without worrying what anybody else is saying or doing. Anyway, that's their business, not mine.

The only exception is when something happens that directly impacts on my team. Then, it becomes personal. That's why I took grave exception to comments by Ger Loughnane in the run-up to the 2007 All-Ireland final against Limerick where he implied that Kilkenny's use of the hurley on opponents was, to say the least, questionable. Actually, that's putting his views mildly.

He had come out with the same rubbish before we played Galway in the quarter-final some weeks earlier referring to how our players allegedly hit opponents across the hands with their hurleys while letting on to be attempting to flick the ball away.

I ignored it at the time because I saw it as gamesmanship. He was obviously trying to get the message out there that we used illegal tactics, an allegation which would, of course, be picked up and dissected by the media. And once it's out there people who never thought about it before suddenly begin to wonder, is this right? That's when it becomes damaging.

Given the extensive media coverage of Loughnane's comments in the run-up to the Galway game, I assume that Loughnane reckoned that it just might register with referee, Dickie Murphy. Referees are only human and if somebody effectively accuses a team of skulduggery there's always the chance they will take notice. Luckily, on this occasion, Murphy was the man in charge. He has been around the circuit far too long to take any notice of wild accusations which were made with a specific agenda in mind.

Throwing out derogatory comments about the opposition isn't something I have ever indulged in but, despite disapproving of his tactics, I decided to say nothing about Loughnane's comments at the time. I didn't want the build-up to the game to be dominated by a slanging match between the managers, which is the way it would have been interpreted if I had taken him on.

I can see the headlines now: 'CODY BITES BACK AT LOUGHNANE', '"CATS" BOSS SHOWS HIS CLAWS', 'KILKENNY RATTLED BY LOUGHNANE CHARGES'. Sorry folks, I wasn't going to be snared into a row which I hadn't started.

I wanted to respond because it wasn't right that our players should be depicted as sneaky hitmen who would pull down on an opponent's wrist, which is just about as mean a foul as you will ever see, but I reckoned this was one time when silence was indeed golden.

If I had hit back at Loughnane, he would probably have come back at me and suddenly the whole thing would have been blown out of all proportion.

Besides, when you're explaining, you're losing! Ger was up to his old tricks, so it was best to let him get on with it and see how things turned out on match day. As it happened, we won a great contest with a late-scoring burst and I thought that was the end of the matter, until he came out with much the same thing before the All-Ireland final.

Now that was different. At least I knew why he did it in the run-up to the quarter-final. It was an attempt – however clumsy and indefensible – to gain an advantage for his team. A bit low, perhaps, but at least he was doing it with a specific purpose in mind. However, repeating it before the final was way out of order as he had no direct involvement. Everybody is entitled to their opinions, but when allegations of such a serious nature are being made against players clear evidence is required, which Ger didn't have. But then he couldn't have because it didn't exist.

I don't recall Loughnane mentioning anything about us 'flicking and belting across the wrists' when he was an RTÉ 'Sunday Game' analyst prior to taking over in Galway, so where did it come from in 2007? Wasn't it amazing that no other manager had spotted our monstrous crimes against hands? They hadn't, because there were none.

If we had indeed been guilty of something as nasty as that I'm sure others would have supported Loughnane – or even come up with it before he did – but there wasn't a single word of support for him which was hardly surprising, for the simple reason that it wasn't true.

I was disappointed in Ger. I have known him since our teacher training days in St Pat's, Drumcondra, where we hurled on the same half-back line – he on the right, and I in the centre. We won a Dublin Under-21 title together on what was a very good team drawn from lads from all over the country.

He went on to enjoy an excellent playing career with Clare and what he did as manager was outstanding and was recognised by everybody in hurling as something special. He had plenty of hardy boys on that team, but they were great hurlers too, and I would have huge admiration for them. But then there's usually a huge respect for each other among hurling people which was why I was disappointed by Ger's rubbish in 2007.

It would have done damage if referees had allowed themselves to be influenced but, fair play to them, they didn't. Neither Dickie Murphy nor Diarmuid Kirwan, who refereed the All-Ireland final, fell for it but then they judged what they saw not what anybody else – including Loughnane – told them they should have seen.

The only time I'd pay any attention to what anybody else says about us is when there's a danger it could do damage, as in the Loughnane instance. Otherwise, I largely ignore pundits and punditry. Good luck to the people involved – it's a thriving business nowadays, but when you're on the other side of the fence it's best to ignore what's said and written.

Punditry is easy because it's not accountable. You don't have to justify what you said two years, two months, two weeks or even two hours ago. In fact, you can say one thing before a game and then completely change your mind at half-time, and again at the end if you wish. That's how it works and I have no problem whatsoever with it, but you wouldn't want to take it too seriously. In fact, you wouldn't want to take it at all seriously. It is, after all, one man's opinion and can be changed, amended and adjusted to suit whatever circumstances have unfolded over the previous thirty-five minutes. The privilege of hindsight and all that – you can't beat it if you're a pundit but, for rest of us, it's just something that's out there and you'd be very silly indeed to take any notice of it.

What I do object to is when players are put down by people who are paid to sit and watch them playing and then feel entitled to be smart-assed about them. I'm talking about all players here, not just the lads from Kilkenny. Our players haven't got much criticism because they've been so successful, but others have had to listen to some awful stuff. It's easy to be a smart Alec in front of an open microphone or a lap-top, but surely standards and fairness come into it too. Players are judged all the time by how they perform, but what inspection do the people who judge them face?

The amount of scrutiny to which players are subjected nowadays is unprecedented in GAA history. It's new territory for everybody and has to be handled carefully. From a management viewpoint, dealing with the media is very much part of the job which is something I've always accepted. Media coverage has grown enormously over the years and, while that's good for the games, there are limits. TV feels it has to dissect every incident, every tackle, every foul and sometimes the truth gets distorted in the search for the sensational. What makes it all the more unfair is that, in a lot of cases, the criticisms are coming from former players and managers who were through it all themselves and who know what's involved.

I'm actually very comfortable with the media, although I wouldn't have much tolerance for daft questions. But then, who would? Win or lose, I have never refused to face journalists after a game, even if I mightn't always give them the answers they want. In fact, I quite enjoy putting my back to the wall outside a dressing room and engaging with the media posse.

That's why I don't particularly like the new set-up in Croke Park where we're brought into this large theatre under the Hogan Stand, plonked at a top-table with the journalists lined up on banks of tiered seats. It's modern and functional and probably suits most people, including the majority of managers and players, but I'd still prefer to meet the press outside in the corridor with my back to the wall where I can see exactly who's asking the questions. It makes it easier to weed out the silly ones!

I'm not remotely anti-press. They have a job to do and I understand that. Everybody who covers hurling has my mobile phone number and I talk to anybody who rings me. I regard it as part of the job. Nor do I lay down any rules regarding how players deal with the media. Any player who's comfortable doing an interview is quite free to talk away. Naturally, I'd advise a young player who's new to the scene to be very careful because we live in an age where the headline seems to be everything. Most journalists are fair in how they present things and as for those who aren't, they get exposed very quickly. Or at least they should.

There's no doubt about it, the media is a changed world nowadays. In hurling terms it's good that there's more coverage, but quantity and quality are totally different fish which don't always fry well together.

Kilkenny's got the odd lash from time to time in recent years for not announcing our team until the Friday night before games. It's amazing how people can read something into a situation that doesn't actually exist. There's a very simple reason why we wait until Friday to name the team for Sunday games. We get together on the Wednesday and Friday nights on the week of Sunday games for two reasons – it suits players and it stops the week from dragging too much. Injuries permitting, we usually pick the team on Wednesday night after the players have left training and since we won't be seeing them again until Friday we're obviously not going to release the selection. I could e-mail or phone the players but I believe they should hear it in person, which is why we wait until Friday night.

If it's a Saturday game we release the team on Thursday night. There's no other reason why we wait that long other than it suits everybody. Ultimately, it's all about the players and what's right for them. They're happy with how we handle the announcement so why should we change it?

The media have a job to do but so have we and, ultimately, what's right for the players and all of us as a group takes precedence. I don't see how anybody could disagree with that.

CHAPTER 21

PANEL POWER

We had Martin Comerford, Henry Shefflin and *Michael Kavanagh sent off on yellow cards which, in my opinion, didn't quite tally with what was going on. Henry isn't the sort of fella who gets involved with opponents – unless, of course, he gets roughed up, which he did yesterday. He took a wallop to the groin area at one stage, but the culprit went unpunished. Henry was later sent off for mistiming a pull while Kavanagh also saw yellow.*

Monday, May 5, 2009: *Mixed emotions today. We won the National League title in Thurles yesterday but we've lost Brian Hogan for between eight and ten weeks. It's one hell of a loss because he has been in the form of his life over the past few months.*

His collar bone is broken and there's no real cure for that, except time. He lasted just ten minutes in yesterday's clash with Tipperary. I suspected straight away, when he went down, that it was bad because you could see he was in real pain and he's not the sort to over-dramatise things. It's tough on him because he was really flying and looking forward to going into the Championship at the top of his game.

Despite playing well, it's not a League campaign he will look back on with any great fondness as it started and finished with injury. We thought we'd lost him for the season in the first game of the campaign against Limerick in Nowlan Park after a nasty collision with Limerick full-forward, David Breen. It was a hell of a bang and both lads were down for quite some time. Initially, it looked as if Brian might have broken his leg but, thankfully, it turned out to be no more than heavy bruising. David looked bad too but, again, it wasn't as serious as was first thought.

Brian might have thought that scare was to be his only close call for the year but, sadly, that's not the case. The collar bone is broken and now he must be patient. It's frustrating for Brian and a setback for us all, but it's at times like this you appreciate the importance of having strength and depth. Yesterday, I sent Martin Comerford in for Hogan and re-jigged the team but 'Gorta' – as we call Martin – must have created some sort of record by being sent off on one of those ridiculous yellow card fouls within seconds of running onto the pitch. He was dismissed with Tipperary's Declan Fanning – who clearly wanted to let 'Gorta' know just how tough a game it was. Both were sent off by referee, John Sexton, so I had to go back to the subs' bench and send on Michael Grace. It was already turning into quite a battle, and there was more to come.

We had Martin Comerford, Henry Shefflin and Michael Kavanagh sent off on yellow cards which, in my opinion, didn't quite tally with what was going on. Henry isn't the sort of fella who gets involved with opponents – unless, of course, he gets roughed up, which he did yesterday. He took a wallop to the groin area at one stage, but the culprit went unpunished. Henry was later sent off for mistiming a pull while Kavanagh also saw yellow.

It meant that we lost Hogan, Shefflin, Comerford and Kavanagh in the course of the game, while Michael Fennelly had to pull out that morning due to mumps. We're still without Richie Power – who is recovering from a hamstring injury, 'Cha' Fitzpatrick is on his way back after mumps while Noel Hickey isn't fully match fit yet. That's a lot of talent on the absent list so, in the circumstances, it was great to chisel out a win in extra-time.

Tipperary were wired for yesterday's game, just as I thought they would be. They took a lot of stick from their supporters after we beat them easily in Nowlan Park in March, and they seemed determined it wouldn't be the same again. It was never going to be, anyway, because what happened in Nowlan Park wasn't a fair reflection of Tipperary. The game ran away from them at one hell of a pace in the first half, which can happen. When it does, there's little that can be done to retrieve it. It was always going to be different on our return to Thurles some weeks later.

Tipperary were fiercely motivated to stand up and be counted, which is exactly what they did. In fact, they ripped into us from the start and although we tacked on a few early points they hit back with two goals in the first ten minutes. They led by five points at half-time but we felt that, with the wind behind us in the second half, we were well placed to peg them back.

However, we got a right shock two minutes into the second half when Seamus Callanan scored Tipp's third goal to put them eight points clear. Okay boys, they're putting it up to you now! It's at a time like this the real character of a team is tested and, I have to say, I was delighted with the response. It came straight away in the form of a Richie Hogan goal, which proved crucial. If we hadn't had the necessary character, and Tipp had added a few more points, we would have been in right trouble. The last thing we wanted to do was sign off from the League with a defeat, let alone a big one.

As it turned out, Richie's goal brought us back within striking distance and, while Tipp were still four points clear with fifteen minutes to go, there was such a sense of spirit in our lads that they weren't going to take no for an answer.

'Taggy' (Aidan Fogarty) hit a great goal and we landed some crucial points to take us into the lead in stoppage time before Tipp got a very soft free which Noel McGrath pointed to send the game into extra time. McGrath scored a goal early in the second period of extra time to put Tipp two points clear, but we dominated from there on and hit six points to their one.

The manner in which we won the game was very satisfying because it showed that the team spirit was very much intact. Little things can make a big difference on a day like that. I certainly could find no fault with the team's application and, once again, lads put up their hands and took responsibility when they had to.

TJ Reid scored a fantastic point from a line ball in injury time while, earlier on, Richie Hogan showed real class when pointing a long-range free from near the sideline to put us into the lead close to the end of normal time. He ended up on 1-10 while 'Taggy' scored 1-5, all from play. That's leadership for you.

In many ways, it was the perfect way to win the League. Had we beaten Tipperary easily it would have fuelled all this nonsense about Kilkenny being unbeatable. There's no such thing as an unbeatable team in any sport but people like to use those labels, however silly they might be.

Tipperary put an awful lot into that League final so it was fiercely important for us that we responded. People might have thought that after winning the All-Ireland three-in-a-row we would have coasted through the League, before putting everything into the Championship. But that's not the way it works.

Lads must have an appetite for every game they play. You can't switch it on and off depending on the mood. What pleased me about yesterday's win was the determination our lads brought to their game when the challenge was really put up to them. It was a great sign of their maturity as a squad and also showed that their desire is still as intense as ever, which is exactly what you like to see coming into the Championship.

So, what did we learn from the League? The panel was tested to the limit because of injury and those damn yellow cards, but it stood up extremely well. That was particularly true in the final where Tipperary put it up to us in every department, from skill to physicality to fitness to attitude to perseverance. We passed all the exams, albeit in a real struggle, but that's the way we like it.

It was our fifth League win this decade and, while I'm not one for statistics, I'm told Kilkenny has never before won so many in a decade. We also reached another final which we lost to Waterford in 2007, so nobody can accuse us of not doing our bit for the League. Others might like to downgrade it – although, I'm convinced that's an excuse when they don't win or have a decent run – but I have always regarded it as being vitally important.

It's the only title on offer at this time of year, so why not do your level best to win it?

So then, the spring chapter is closed. Now it's time to look ahead to the Championship which, thankfully, will be played under normal rules as opposed to those daft yellow card sanctions which took away from the League. Hopefully, that's the end of them and there won't be an attempt to re-cycle and re-package them for next year. Whatever about 'Lisbon Two', we certainly don't need a second vote on those rules. Leave them in the bin where they belong.

Hurling people have tolerated them for the last few weeks since Congress decided that they wouldn't be used in the Championship, but most couldn't wait to see the back of them. They did nothing for the game as a spectacle and, when you see how they distorted yesterday's League final, you realise what a disaster it would be for hurling if they were retained for the Championship. Imagine if players were sent off for the merest of offences (or sometimes no offence at all) in an All-Ireland semi-final or final. It would be unthinkable.

That's it then – the end of the League and the first phase of the year. We have seven weeks to go before we play the Leinster semi-final, so the lads will head back to their clubs for a while now.

We'll cut the panel to thirty-two in due course although, because of injuries, it has to be kept fairly flexible. We always ensure that we have a minimum of thirty players in training so we'll have lads on stand-by. They won't be on the official panel but they will be called in if our numbers are going to drop below thirty on any particular evening. They're quite happy to do that because the training camp is a good place to be.

You learn a lot from working with the squad and, besides, if you're going well you will get a chance to force your way into the panel. That's why nobody refuses an invitation to come in. It might look as if they're only making up numbers for the fifteen-a-side games, but that's not the way it is. They may be just outside the official panel but they're getting closer and, the more exposure they get to the training and other preparations with the squad, the greater their chances of forcing their way in on a permanent basis.

When opportunity knocks it's important to be at home to invite it in. That's how these lads look at it, so they're mad keen to stay as close to the action as they possibly can. Seven weeks to go to the Leinster semi-final. Bring it on.

CHAPTER 22

THE CRADLE OF DREAMS

The man whose capture was so expensively sought answered to the name of James Stephens, co-founder of the Irish Republican Brotherhood in 1863. He was arrested in 1865 but escaped a year later – scaling a prison wall after allegedly receiving assistance from the night watchman and assorted others whose dedication to keeping him incarcerated didn't quite match their desire to allow this free spirit his liberty. Despite the considerable bounties placed on his head, he was never recaptured and later made his way to France and Brussels, before returning to Ireland in 1891.

Martin Breheny writes: In March 1867, a forty-two-year-old Kilkenny man had a very large bounty placed on his head which was described thus: "fair hair, bald all round top of head, wore all his beard, which is sandy, slightly tinged with grey, rather long under the chin but slight round the jaw, approaching the ears; broad forehead, tender eyes which defect seems to be constitutional and has a peculiar habit of closing the left eye when speaking; high cheek bones and rather good looking countenance".

It noted further that his hands and feet were "remarkably small and well formed", and he "generally dressed in black clothes".

The Lord Lieutenant-General and General Governor of Ireland also explained in *The Police Gazette – Hue And Cry* – that the wanted man, who was deemed to be an "active Member of a Treasonable Conspiracy", had escaped from Richmond Prison in Dublin four months earlier and that bringing him to justice was an absolute priority.

The substantial figures they were prepared to pay to anybody who tracked him down showed just how determined they were to apprehend him. A sum of £1,000 was offered for information leading to the arrest of the fugitive, a further £1,000 to anybody who arrested him, and £300 for information about sympathisers who assisted him in any way at any time. Presumably, 'sympathisers' were deemed almost as reprehensible as the fugitive unless, of course, they saw the error of their ways. In which case, they could avail of the £300 reward and a free pardon if the information they provided led to an arrest: in other words they would be rewarded for betraying him.

The man whose capture was so expensively sought answered to the name of James Stephens, co-founder of the Irish Republican Brotherhood in 1863. He was arrested in 1865 but escaped a year later – scaling a prison wall after allegedly receiving assistance from the night watchman and assorted others whose dedication to keeping him incarcerated didn't quite match their desire to allow this free spirit his liberty. Despite the considerable bounties placed on his head, he was never re-captured and later made his way to France and Brussels, before returning to Ireland in 1891.

He died ten years later and was buried in Glasnevin Cemetery, Dublin. Part of the inscription on his tomb reads: "A day, an hour of virtuous liberty, is worth a century in bondage".

When the people of St Patrick's parish in Kilkenny decided, in 1887, to organise themselves as part of the GAA movement which had been founded three years earlier, they deemed it appropriate that the new club should be named in honour of James Stephens, the man from Blackmill Street who acquired the status of a local hero for his brave and relentless pursuit of freedom for his country.

Now, 122 years later, the name lives on and is constantly commemorated through the exploits of one of the best-known GAA clubs in the country. And yet, there are many who never use the club's official name, instead recognising it by the warm, homely title of 'The Village'.

It's unclear as to why the St Patrick's parish area in Kilkenny city became known as The Village. It's believed to have been a local reference to the area outside the City Wall at St Patrick's Gate, but is a name which wasn't mentioned in any old maps. Whatever the origins, the title became – and has remained – very much part of a community where the roots are deeply embedded in the GAA culture and ethos.

The Village won their first Kilkenny senior hurling title in 1935 and added a second two years later, but wouldn't win a third until 1969, when they overpowered The Fenians in the county final. The James Stephens Chairman at the time was Brian Cody's father, Bill. Originally from Thomastown, Bill Cody moved to Sheestown in the St Patrick's Parish in 1951. He worked for the Royal Liver Assurance Company.

He took over as club Chairman in sad circumstance in June 1969, following the death of the then-Chairman, Mick Larkin, who died after taking ill while watching a club game in Nowlan Park. Bill had been Vice-Chairman and was regarded as the obvious man to move up to the No.1 position following Mick's untimely death. Bill answered the call from a club which would benefit enormously from his dedication to the GAA cause.

Bill had played a huge role in reviving the club's fortunes at underage level. He also took his expertise onto the county scene where he served as a Kilkenny minor selector for several seasons. He was a senior selector in 1971: a year in which they reached the All-Ireland final only to lose to Tipperary by three points in a thrilling contest which yielded a total score of 10-31. Unfortunately for Kilkenny, they lost by 5-17 to 5-14.

Bill remained as club chairman until 1985, by which time James Stephens had won another three county senior titles in 1975, 1976 and 1981. The launch of the All-Ireland Club Championships in 1971 enabled county champions to test themselves beyond local boundaries for the first time, a challenge James Stephens embraced with great enthusiasm and efficiency, winning All-Ireland titles in 1976 and 1982. Those successes showcased The Village and its exceptional array of players to the whole country in a way that would never have been achieved in the times when club competition didn't extend to provincial or All-Ireland level.

It was a glorious era for The Village, but then the area produced so many great players of the same generation that, with proper organisation and focus, it was only a matter of time before they reached the highest peaks – which many of them did at both club and county level.

When Bill Cody and his wife Annie moved to Sheestown in 1951, he could have had no idea of the influence the local club would exert on him and his family. But then he made a huge contribution, too, throwing himself into the club and its endeavours with real enthusiasm and expertise. Together with several others, he worked to create an environment in which young, aspiring hurlers could develop and thrive under the careful watch of expert eyes.

Hurling was the lifeblood of The Village people so, inevitably, children were drawn to it virtually from the moment they learned to walk as they listened to tales of great wonder from their elders, watched their heroes play for the club and dreamed their dreams as they set about learning the skills of a game which came as second nature anyway.

Among them was a young lad, born on July 12, 1954. His name was Brian Cody.

CHAPTER 23

FOR THE HONOUR OF THE VILLAGE

County final day is such a special event all over the country, and I certainly always enjoy it in Kilkenny. Naturally, all the more so when The Village is involved. There must have been 15,000 people in Nowlan Park that day, which created such a wonderful sense of occasion. The fact that my son, Donncha, was playing made it extra special so, between that and the return of the county title to The Village, it was as close as it gets to being the perfect day.

I'm regularly asked which success has given me the most satisfaction during the years I have been lucky enough to manage Kilkenny. The answer surprises people, but it's true.

I have had many, many great days with Kilkenny but nothing matches the delight I felt when James Stephens won the Kilkenny county title in 2004 and the All-Ireland title in Croke Park on St Patrick's Day, 2005. The team was managed by Adrian Finan so my role was as an enthusiastic supporter, father of our right corner-back, Donncha, and dedicated Village man. Honestly, I couldn't have felt more pride on those days had I been managing or playing. Or maybe even both put together.

Of course there's a fantastic sense of fulfilment and achievement every time Kilkenny succeed, but club is different. At least to me it is. The

Village, the parish, the people, the hurling – they mean everything to me. They made me what I am as a hurling person and in many other ways too. I had so many great years as a club player at all levels, including winning county and All-Ireland titles, but we then went into a valley period where we didn't win a county senior title for twenty-three years. That's an eternity in a club like ours. I had managed the team through some of those years but to no avail – we never could quite make the breakthrough. We got to a final one year in the mid-'90s, but lost to Young Irelands in a replay.

The longer the years went without winning a county title the more frustrating it became. You begin to wonder if it will ever happen or if you're destined to remain on the outside. So you can imagine the sense of relief and satisfaction which washed across the club in 2004 when we won the title for the first time since 1981. The circumstances couldn't have been any more dramatic as DJ Carey and his Gowran colleagues closed in for a late surge after falling well behind in the final.

Now, the last man you want to present with chances in the closing minutes of a county final – or any other final for that matter – was DJ, and we very nearly paid a heavy price. He smacked in three goals from frees and penalties in the space of a few minutes, but our lads held on for a one-point win.

Waiting for the final whistle was sheer bloody agony, but when it finally came the success was all the sweeter for the manner in which it had been achieved. It has always been my nature to look ahead rather than reflect on the past, but that's a day I will always remember and cherish. The Village was back.

It was fitting that when we finally did emerge from the long drought, the captain should be Peter Barry, an inspirational character who gave so much of himself to club and county.

County final day is such a special event all over the country, and I certainly always enjoy it in Kilkenny. Naturally, all the more so when The Village is involved. There must have been 15,000 people in Nowlan Park that day, which created such a wonderful sense of occasion. The fact that my son, Donncha, was playing made it extra special so, between that and the return of the county title to The Village, it was as close as it gets to being the perfect day.

Coming, as it did, less than two months after Kilkenny's big defeat by Cork in the All-Ireland final, it was the ideal tonic to take into the winter. That's the great thing about sport. It doesn't matter what disappointments you experience, there's always another day, another chance, another goal. And, to my mind, aiming for a county title is a mighty fine ambition, not just for the players involved but for an entire club.

The 2004 win really was a special occasion and there were more to come as the lads set about conquering Leinster and then the rest of the country. The introduction of the provincial and All-Ireland Club Championships back in the early '70s was a fantastic idea as it gave county champions something else to aim for and offered them a chance to test themselves against the best from other counties. That's why the competitions have proved so popular, not only among the players but also with the public.

We beat UCD in the 2004 Leinster final in a game where there was a bit of controversy over a disputed point. It was claimed that we had been awarded a point when the ball had actually gone wide and, since the winning margin was only a point, it was always going to be controversial. There's damn all you can do in those situations – sometimes calls go for you, sometimes against and you have to live with it. It could just as easily have been us who were on the wrong side – this time it went with us and the Leinster trophy was heading back to The Village.

There was another magical spin of the wheel to come on the following St Patrick's Day when we won the All-Ireland title for the third time. We beat a very good Athenry team, which had won three All-Irelands over the previous eight years, so nobody could argue The Village weren't deserving champions. I was lucky enough to win two All-Ireland club medals in my playing days but back then the finals weren't played in Croke Park. Nor were they played as a double-header with football, and they didn't have a St Patrick's Day setting either, so they lacked the sense of occasion which exists nowadays.

We've done it! *You can't beat that winning feeling.*

A full-back's work is never done. *He must keep an eye in all directions.*

Right, Tony, so what next? *Tony Doran was one of the best full-forwards I came across.*

No way through today, Jimmy. *I clashed with Jimmy Barry-Murphy as a player and manager. He was a gentleman on both fronts.*

A rare moment of calm during the 1983 All-Ireland final against Cork.

Every player's dream. *The Liam McCarthy Cup is getting ready for a trip to The Village after the 1982 All-Ireland final.*

What's happening out there? *Keeping a close watch during the 2003 Leinster final against Wexford.*

If the cap fits! *It did during the 2006 League semi-final against Tipperary, which we won.*

We're going well here. *We were on top from the start against Waterford in the 2008 All-Ireland final.*

Nothing personal, just business. *A quick word with Ger Loughnane after Kilkenny beat Galway in the 2007 All-Ireland quarter-final.*

Anthony Daly in comedian mode during an Allianz League press conference.

Facing the media... *It's all part of a modern-day manager's life.*

Small ball, big ball. *I get in some practise with Mickey Harte.*

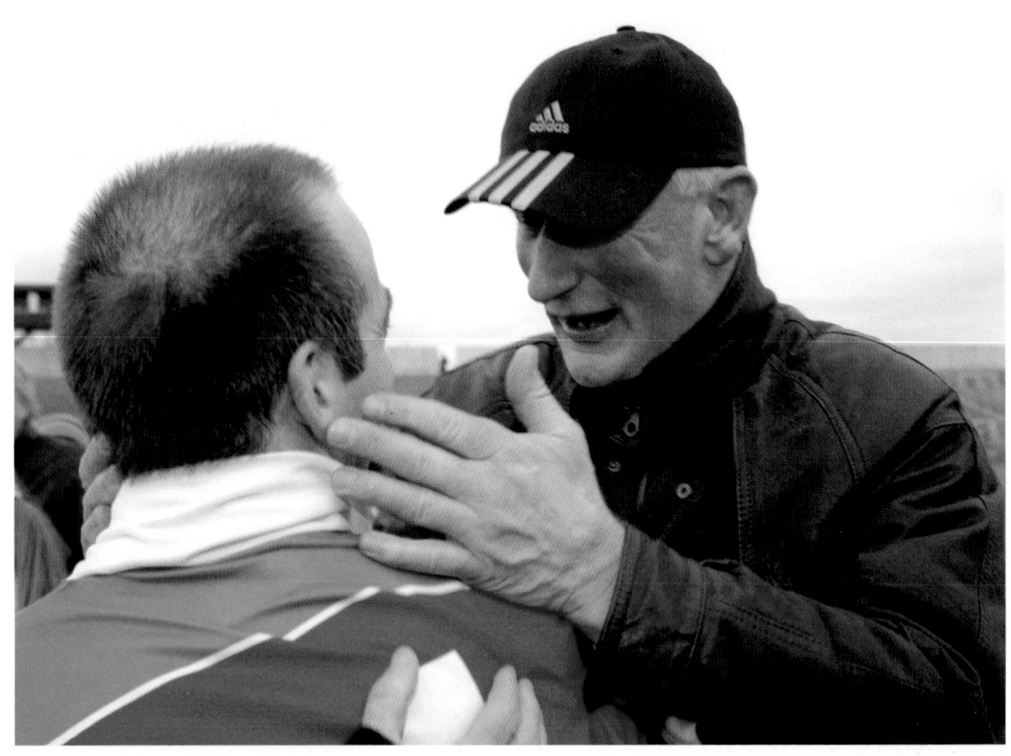

Club is special. *I congratulate Dermot Grogan after The Village wins the 2005 All-Ireland final.*

A word of consolation for one of Waterford's finest, Tony Browne, after the 2004 All-Ireland semi-final.

Not exactly Riverdance, but who cares? *Enjoying an All-Ireland win with Michael Dempsey.*

Henry Shefflin and DJ Carey – what a stroke of luck for Kilkenny that these remarkable talents were born in our county.

Eoin Larkin has his jersey tested for elasticity.

Willie O'Dwyer – he had a great day in the 2007 Leinster final, scoring 2-3 against Wexford.

Tommy Walsh – one of our finest wherever we played him.

Jackie Tyrrell – another Village man who led Kilkenny to an All-Ireland title.

Martin Comerford takes on all-comers from Wexford.

Michael Kavanagh – a model of dependability for well over a decade.

Eddie Brennan – ace goal poacher.

James 'Cha' Fitzpatrick – led Kilkenny to the 2008 All-Ireland title.

Well done, Henry. *As usual, Henry Shefflin was top scorer in the 2005 Leinster final.*

DJ Carey and I celebrate the 2002 All-Ireland final win over Clare.

2000 All-Ireland winning team. *That title ended a seven-year wait for the All-Ireland.*

2002 All-Ireland winning team. *"Not men, but giants", reads the sign behind them. Indeed.*

2003 All-Ireland winning team. *A close call against Cork in the final, but we survived it.*

2006 All-Ireland winning team. *The day we ended Cork's three-in-a-row dream.*

2007 All-Ireland winning team. *A good start against Limerick set us on our way.*

2008 All-Ireland winning team. *The day we landed the treble.*

The winning 2009 Kilkenny team that beat Tipperary and claimed the four-in-a-row.

The start of another campaign. *Keeping tabs on a Walsh Cup game on a rainy January Sunday.*

Our finals in 1976 and 1982 were played in Thurles, which is a fine venue for any game but the crowds weren't nearly as big as you get in Croke Park nowadays. Staging the club finals in Croke Park is a great idea as it gives lads who will never get on a county team a chance to play there. The 2005 final was certainly a wonderful experience for The Village. We had seen other Kilkenny clubs – Glenmore, Ballyhale and St Martin's – win titles in Croke Park over the previous twenty years so it was fantastic to do the same.

After going so long without winning a county title, we were beginning to wonder if it would ever happen again so, when we finally achieved it and then went on to win Leinster and the All-Ireland, it meant so much to so many people. Nothing I had achieved as a manager with Kilkenny could match the feeling I had on those days – in particular, county final day.

Playing for club and county are, of course, completely different. I know it's a cliché to say that club success is achieved with your close neighbours and friends whereas there's a wide spread to the county team, but it's no less true for that. When you're playing for your club you're representing something very personal and, of course, at the back of your mind is the thought that if you do well enough, you'll move on to county level. That is if you haven't done so already. It's every player's ambition to wear a county jersey but it can only be achieved through the club because, quite simply, if you're not doing well there, you're not going to make the county squad.

The club offers the chance to do anything you want as a player. Derek Lyng and Martin Comerford didn't play underage for Kilkenny and weren't star college players either, but they still forced their way into the county senior squad by playing consistently well for their clubs. If you were to believe conventional wisdom about Lyng he 'didn't have the hurling' – a favourite phrase in Kilkenny – but he never believed that. And why should he? He had great ambition, enormous drive and a clear vision of what he wanted to achieve.

His club, Emeralds, helped him along and he eventually became one of the best midfielders of his generation. It was the same with

Comerford in O'Loughlin Gaels. He kept working away with his club and forced his way into the county team without having made a big name at underage level. These lads show exactly what can be achieved by a player if he puts everything in for the club and never loses ambition.

Club culture has always been very close to my heart. As I've written elsewhere, I would have been quite happy to keep working away with the club without ever getting a shot at the county manager's job. I'm a Village man – plain and simple.

It doesn't matter which Village team is playing, I always feel a great sense of pride and emotional involvement. But then, it was always going to be the case as my father was so deeply immersed in the life of the club from as early as I can remember that I couldn't possibly have missed out.

He was very much at the heart of the drive to raise standards, especially at underage level, in the 1960s and continued to be a major influence during the many years he served as Chairman. He loved the whole scene so much and was never happier than when doing something for the club. I suppose that rubbed off on me and, as I've said, the club made me what I was as a player and what I am as a manager. I have always held the view that if you're not passionate about your club, you won't be passionate about your county.

It's the way the GAA is structured, and the day anybody loses sight of that is the day things begin to change, and not for the better either. Prior to our panel breaking up to go back to their clubs, I always tell the players that they are duty-bound to perform at their very best in whatever games lie ahead of them.

I could never understand a county player not putting in maximum effort for his club. You hear about it on occasion, although it's not something that happens in Kilkenny as far as I'm aware. County players have a big responsibility towards their clubs. Apart from having made them what they are, the clubs need them to inspire those around them and what better way to do that than by turning in consistent performances?

Besides, the notion that a county player can somehow switch off when he goes back to his club and then return at full power when he rejoins the county panel is unsustainable. No, as far as I'm concerned, you can't be selective about how and when you perform – there has to be one hundred per cent effort all the time, whether it's for club or county.

That's the basic principle I learned as a youngster and one which I have always regarded as being of the utmost importance.

The Village senior side wasn't going very well when I was learning the hurling trade as a youngster in the 1960s. That's why so much emphasis was placed on the underage scene on the basis that working from the bottom up was the only way to build a solid, sustainable future. It worked.

Rapid progress was made at Under-14 and Under-16 level which inevitably fed through to minor level where The Village reached four successive county finals from 1965 on, with wins in 1966 and 1968, followed by two more in 1970 and 1971. I was at centre-back on the latter two teams and was lucky enough to captain them in 1971.

CHAPTER 24

LET THE GAMES BEGIN

Tyrone won the All-Ireland football title last *year, but they know the exact route they will have to take to win Ulster. Dublin hammered Wexford in the Leinster football final, but nobody came up with the bright idea of leaving them to one side until the first round of this year's Championship was played. Not including us in the draw is isolating us as some sort of super-power in people's heads. That inspires other teams who can use it to fire themselves up. It's not the role of the GAA establishment to inspire people or to portray others – in this case, Kilkenny – as something that they're not.*

Monday, June 8, 2009: *So then, eight months after every other hurling and football team in the country discovered who they were playing in the first round of the 2009 Championship, we finally know who our opponents will be.*

The draw for the Leinster semi-final was made last night: Kilkenny v Galway; Dublin v Wexford. We're out on Saturday week, and the game has been fixed for O'Connor Park, Tullamore. It's not a ground we have much experience of playing in but that's not an issue. Some of the lads would have played minor and Under-21 in Tullamore but that's as far as it goes. Still, a pitch is a pitch and is the same for both sides and, no, we won't be travelling up to have a puck-around. The principles are the same wherever you play. Two sets of goalposts, one of which you try to breach as often as possible, the other which you must defend as stoutly as possible – before you switch ends.

I have to say, though, that I'm curious about one aspect of the draw. Why was it decided to delay the Leinster semi-final draw until after the first-round games? The draw for the provincial Championships in both hurling and football were made as far back as last October and were seen through to the semi-finals everywhere except Leinster hurling.

The addition of Antrim and Galway to Leinster has added greatly to the interest but, for reasons which I certainly don't understand, it was decided to delay the second-round draw until now! Having won the title last year, we received a bye to the semi-finals but were left in limbo while everybody else could focus on their first opponents.

Okay, so it might not look all that important and, frankly, I don't get too excited about things I can't control, but the question arises as to why the Leinster draw wasn't seen through to the end as usual. I have heard suggestions that it was done so that whoever was eventually drawn against Kilkenny wouldn't have to think about it until now. It seems they might lack motivation earlier in the year if they knew that a first-round win would leave them playing us!

What absolute rubbish! As it happens, we've been drawn against Galway, so does anybody seriously believe it would have impacted on them in any way if they had known for months that they would be playing us if they beat Laois? Of course it wouldn't. On the contrary, they would have loved it.

By leaving us out of the draw until last night, it's as if the powers-that-be are acknowledging some form of elitism. It's saying that Kilkenny are something that we're not. We won the Leinster and All-Ireland titles last year but it's all in the past now. This is 2009 and we're in a new campaign. We're back to square one, but the system is saying otherwise. That's dangerous territory.

Tyrone won the All-Ireland football title last year but they know the exact route they will have to take to win Ulster. Dublin hammered Wexford in the Leinster football final but nobody came up with the bright idea of leaving them to one side until the first round of this year's Championship was played. Not including us in the draw is isolating us as some sort of super-power in people's heads. That inspires other teams who can use it to fire themselves up. It's not the role of the GAA establishment to inspire people or to portray others – in this case, Kilkenny – as something that they're not.

I've heard it said that not completing the draw actually breaks the rules in some way. However, it's not an area I'm familiar with, so I'll ignore it. But if that's the case, it's a damn strange way of doing business. If we lose to Galway on Saturday week, people will accuse me of sour grapes, but I don't care. I'm simply making the point that, when it comes to Championship draws, the same rules should apply to every county and I sincerely hope that Leinster goes back to completing its draw when it comes to the 2010 campaign.

Anyway, Galway it is, and I'm really looking forward to getting our campaign underway. It's over five weeks since we won the League final and things have gone well in training. We still have some injury problems but there's nothing we can do about that, except leave the lads concerned in the expert hands of our medics.

Oddly enough, there doesn't seem to be as much mention of us chasing the four-in-a-row as there was for the three-in-a-row last year. Either that, or it just hasn't started yet. It's not something we're even thinking of right now but, obviously, it would be a phenomenal achievement if we could do it.

People might think the last thing we wanted was to have such big contenders as Galway arrive in Leinster at a time like this, but that's not the case at all. Two good Kilkenny men, Nickey Brennan and Ned Quinn, have been serious drivers in manoeuvring a situation whereby Galway and Antrim came into Leinster and I totally support them. If it's good for hurling – which I believe it is – then I'm behind it.

Antrim probably need it more than Galway because they're a bit isolated in hurling terms, and I have no doubt that playing in Leinster will benefit both of them. I know lots of Antrim hurling people and would have to say that their dedication to the game is outstanding. I often wonder if those of us in strong, successful hurling counties down south swapped places with them would we have the same appetite and passion.

Right through The Troubles, the people of Antrim, Down and Derry did great work to keep the game as strong as possible, even if they were a long way from the rest of the hurling world. I'd have special links with Dungiven in Derry through the Hinpheys from Kilkenny who are really inspiring hurling people. But then, there's so many like them. The hurling spirit in the Glens of Antrim has always been something to admire, but there's a lot more to it than passion alone. Technically, Antrim are very good but they're a bit isolated even when it comes to something like organising a challenge game, which counties in the south take for granted. It's almost as easy for Antrim to go to Scotland than travel down to the really strong hurling areas here.

Antrim lost to Dublin quite heavily in the Leinster quarter-final yesterday, which was a bit surprising as they would have fancied themselves to be in contention right up to the end. Then again, it's probably another sign of how much Dublin have advanced this year.

Galway are much closer to the Leinster/Munster power bases, but it has been unsatisfactory for them to have no provincial Championship so joining Leinster is a great chance for them to compete on the same terms as everybody else. It will be good for them, I have no doubt. Mind you, we have no intention of marking their arrival in Leinster by letting them straight through to the final! Sorry lads, hospitality is one thing but business is business.

I know that people are claiming we wanted to avoid Galway in the semi-final in case we lose and have to head out on a 'Discover Ireland' qualifier tour, but that's not the case. Yes, we want to avoid the qualifiers, but I have no hang-ups whatsoever about who we meet or where we meet them.

I suppose, in terms of pure atmosphere, a Kilkenny-Wexford clash in Wexford Park would have been best. It would also be one awfully hard game to win as, indeed, will the one with Galway. Still, we have to get on with it and now it's all about getting ourselves right and not thinking about the opposition, the four-in-a-row or anything else.

We have never taken anything for granted heading into the Championship, for the simple reason that the day you do that is the day decay sets in – and you know what follows! Tullamore on a Saturday evening in June might be different to Croke Park on a Sunday afternoon in August or September, but you have to be right for both or else you're gone. That's a simple fact of life, one which we never forget.

Together with the rest of the management team, it's my job to present the team in the best possible shape for that crucial first test. If we're not mentally right, we'll be in serious trouble and, as we know to our cost, Galway will make hay if they get the chance.

They did it against us in 2001 and again in 2005, and will be very determined to make a big impression in their first season in Leinster. We've beaten them twice already this year, in the Walsh Cup and National League, but this is different. The Walsh Cup is a warm-up competition while you can recover from a defeat in the League but, if we lose on Saturday week, the Leinster title is gone and the season takes on a completely different complexion.

It's a huge game for both sides, not least because the winners are guaranteed a place in the All-Ireland quarter-finals at least, whereas the losers must head for the first round of the qualifiers and have to win two games to reach the last six. Guess which bus we want to be on?

CHAPTER 25

SWINGING OUT OF THE SIXTIES

The kids of the 1960s who'd watched so many heroic figures bring honour to Kilkenny were inspired by the sheer splendour of it all and, even if they didn't know it at the time, were about to set out on some great adventures of their own.

Martin Breheny writes: Kilkenny hurling began the 1970s in third place, behind Tipperary and Cork on the All-Ireland senior honours list. Tipperary led the Liam McCarthy Cup table with twenty-one titles: one ahead of Cork and four clear of Kilkenny.

Tipperary had been the dominant force in the 1945-1965 period, during which the Liam McCarthy Cup had wintered nine times in the county. That was quite a haul and included an All-Ireland treble in 1949, 1950 and 1951 and doubles in 1961-1962 and 1964-1965.

Would they have completed the five-in-a-row if they had also landed the 1963 title? Their All-Ireland wins in the two successive years suggest they would have but, then, who knows what impact a treble haul in 1963 might have had?

Waterford scuppered Tipperary's hopes in the 1963 Munster final before losing to Kilkenny in the All-Ireland final, despite scoring six goals. To this day, Tipperary people can never figure out how their highly-rated forward line were held to 0-8 in the Munster final by a Waterford defence that conceded 4-17 against Kilkenny in the All-Ireland final some weeks later. What made it all the more puzzling for Tipperary was that, a year later, their attack resumed normal service as they returned to the summit and would go on to win a fourth All-Ireland in five seasons in 1965.

By the close of the sixties – or, indeed, by the end of 1971 when they were again hosting the McCarthy Cup – there were no signs whatsoever of the deep recession that Tipperary were about to experience, one that lasted eighteen years and which made the riches accumulated in the 1945-65 period seem from an age so long past that only older supporters could recall it.

Cork won four All-Irelands in the 1945-65 era while Kilkenny collected three. The latter's strike rate was about to improve dramatically from then on, although not to the same level of success they have experienced in this amazing decade.

By the end of the 1960s Tipperary were also leading the pack at minor level with twelve All-Ireland titles: three ahead of Cork and five clear of Kilkenny. The Munster pair also led the way in the Under-21 grade which had been introduced in 1964. Cork (three), Tipperary (two) and Wexford (one) shared the first six titles between them.

Kilkenny took quite some time to adapt to the Under-21 grade, failing to even reach the Leinster final in any of the first four years, which were dominated by Wexford and Dublin. Laois and Offaly also reached finals in the first four years. Indeed, it wasn't until 1968 that Kilkenny finally won the Leinster title, but they came up well short against Cork in the All-Ireland final, losing by six points.

Kilkenny didn't win their first All-Ireland Under-21 title until 1974, with a team which included several players who would go on to carve out hugely successful senior careers. Brian Cody, Ger Henderson, Billy Fitzpatrick, Kevin and Ger Fennelly, Nickey Brennan and Tom McCormack were among the star names that helped Kilkenny beat Waterford in the All-Ireland final.

Cody, Brennan and Kevin Fennelly would later become Kilkenny managers, while Brennan also rose to the very top of the administrative ladder, becoming GAA President in 2006.

While Kilkenny trailed their great rivals, Cork and Tipperary, on all the All-Ireland tables at the end of the 1960s, they headed into the 1970s as reigning senior champions, having beaten Cork in the 1969 final with a team captained by Eddie Keher. They had won three senior titles during the decade, making it their most successful since the 1930s.

However, their 1960s senior haul was only marginally ahead of Wexford's who had won two All-Ireland senior titles and four Leinster titles to Kilkenny's three All-Ireland and five Leinsters. Wexford and Kilkenny had each won three All-Ireland minor titles and four Leinster crowns with the other two provincial honours going to Laois in 1964 and Dublin in 1965. It would take Dublin another eighteen years to win their next minor title while Laois haven't won any since.

Wexford held the edge over Kilkenny at Under-21 level where, in addition to winning the All-Ireland crown in 1965, they won four of the first six Leinster titles.

It was a very good time for Wexford, who would have regarded themselves as very much Kilkenny's equals at all levels. True, they were way behind on the All-Ireland lists, but this was the 1960s and Wexford were doing well. In 1968, for instance, they won the All-Ireland senior and minor titles. Wexford were also ahead of Kilkenny on the college scene where, during the 1960s, St Peter's won three All-Ireland and five Leinster titles compared to two All-Ireland and four Leinster titles for St Kieran's, Kilkenny.

That would change dramatically in the 1970s and beyond, as St Kieran's powered ahead while St Peter's lost ground at an alarming rate, bringing with it a dramatic downswing in Wexford's fortunes. Things would change further up the line, too, as Kilkenny seniors went on to enjoy their best ever decade in the '70s. The best, that is, until the current decade where a series of new records have been accumulated.

It's generally regarded in Kilkenny, and beyond, that what moved them on to a higher level in the second half of the 1960s was the All-Ireland final win over Tipperary in 1967. Three years earlier, Tipperary had humiliated Kilkenny in the final, beating the defending champions by double scores, 5-13 to 2-8. This had reinforced Tipperary's psychological grip on Kilkenny, who hadn't beaten their neighbours in their previous four All-Ireland final clashes, and who had to look back as far as 1922 for their last win. The 1967 final had a deep resonance in Tipperary as victory would have hoisted John Doyle onto a special pedestal as the only man to have won nine All-Ireland senior medals up to then.

At the age of thirty-seven, it would also be his last chance to create the record. But Kilkenny were in no mood to accommodate him, or Tipperary, and won by four points in what was one of the most notable victories in the county's history.

It was an exciting decade for Kilkenny, one in which the county's youngsters had plenty of heroes to admire as they played their games and dreamed their dreams around the county's fields, villages and streets.

Kilkenny were, in fact, about to enter a decade which would prove remarkably successful at all levels. They won four All-Ireland senior titles in the 1970s – and might well have added a fifth if they hadn't encountered an injury crisis prior to the 1973 final.

Indeed, that may well have cost Kilkenny the four-in-a-row as it was sandwiched between an epic All-Ireland final victory over Cork in 1972 and an easy win over Limerick in 1974.

The 1970s were good to Kilkenny at underage level too, as they picked up four All-Ireland minor and three Under-21 titles.

The hurling scene was opening up nationally as Galway finally emerged from the horror show that had been their 1960s experience in the Munster Championship, where they won only one game from twelve attempts. Offaly were improving rapidly in Leinster, while Clare would produce their best team for a very long time in the second half of the decade.

The 1970s would prove to be an exciting time right across the hurling spectrum, and nowhere more so than in Kilkenny. There, a team was being assembled that would lay claim to the accolade of best-ever Kilkenny team, to date. In the years that lay ahead, the team's record would provide emphatic proof of why they should be so highly regarded.

The kids of the 1960s who'd watched so many heroic figures bring honour to Kilkenny were inspired by the sheer splendour of it all and, even if they didn't know it at the time, were about to set out on some great adventures of their own.

Among them was a tall youngster from James Stephens, named Brian Cody. His upward graph had been impressively crafted with St Kieran's College and Kilkenny minors – whom he had captained to All-Ireland glory from centre-back on September 3, 1972. Seven weeks later he would be handed the black and amber jersey as a senior player for the first time. It would be the start of a successful career which lasted until 1985.

CHAPTER 26

BROADENING HORIZONS

There isn't a hurler or Gaelic footballer in the country who doesn't dream of lining out for his county from the day he first plays as a kid. In relative terms, very few ever get to achieve the dream but, for those who do, it's something to be cherished and respected. Times change, but the honour of being chosen to play for your county doesn't. And, if it does, then you're in the wrong game.

At the end of September 1972, Kilkenny hurling was bathed in a contented glow. The Liam McCarthy and *Irish Press* Cups had been harvested and, making it all the more satisfactory, we had beaten Cork in both the All-Ireland senior and minor finals. Beating them once in a season is always special for Kilkenny people, but to win two All-Ireland finals against Cork really sweetened it. And on the same day too!

The senior final was a remarkable affair in which Kilkenny trailed by eight points with less than a quarter of an hour remaining before launching a brave recovery which, eventually, won the day. It's still talked of as one of the really great All-Ireland finals, not just by Kilkenny people but among neutrals as well. Cork probably take a different view but that's understandable after what happened.

If it was a memorable day for every Kilkenny person, it had real magic for me as I captained the minors to success. On a local level, it was a joyous day for 'The Village' as we had no fewer than five representatives with 'Fan' Larkin, Eamonn Morrissey, 'Chunky' O'Brien, Mick Crotty and Ned Byrne on the senior team. The O'Brien brothers – Paddy and Seanie – and I flew the green-and-red flag with the minors.

I must have caught the eye of the senior selectors because I was called into the squad in October and promoted straight into the team for a National League game against Limerick in Nowlan Park. For whatever reason, there were only five or six of our All-Ireland team available for that game so it was a chance for the selectors to assess the depth of the talent pool.

I was amazed and delighted to be selected. What's more, I was named at centre-back, deputising for the great Pat Henderson. No pressure then! At the age of eighteen I was too young and inexperienced to realise the enormity of the responsibility I was taking on, but then youth has no fear. What I did recognise was the honour which had been bestowed on me.

There isn't a hurler or Gaelic footballer in the country who doesn't dream of lining out for his county from the day he first plays as a kid. In relative terms, very few ever get to achieve the dream but, for those who do, it's something to be cherished and respected. Times change, but the honour of being chosen to play for your county doesn't. And, if it does, then you're in the wrong game.

It doesn't matter whether you're from a strong or, a so-called weak county, the satisfaction of becoming a county man is the same – even if your chances of winning titles may not be. I know that might sound easy coming from Kilkenny where, if you're good at hurling, there's a real chance that you will enjoy a successful career. That's assuming you put in the effort and never lose sight of the fact that the game and the team are always bigger than the individual.

The same opportunities don't arise in every county, yet look at the effort so many players continue to put in. That's because, ultimately, all players are driven to perform for themselves, trying to extract the very best from deep inside their psyche and personality. It's done as part of a squad which, of course, makes it all the more enjoyable.

That's why the county scene has served the GAA so well for so long and why being chosen for a county team remains one of the most treasured prizes in Irish sport. I recall the pride I felt when I got the call all those years ago. Wearing the black-and-amber as a minor was one thing, but to be picked for the seniors was completely different. This was where the big boys operated and I couldn't wait to get my chance to see how I measured up. Me? A Kilkenny senior at the age of eighteen!

Kilkenny hurling has its own personality traits, not as part of a stereotype but in a wider sense. We're unquestionably influenced by our past and by the success we have been lucky enough to enjoy. It has become part of a deep-rooted tradition where hurling is very close to the hearts and minds of our people. We know that those who went before us left us a rich legacy which, in turn, must be passed on to the next generation. We are, in a sense, guardians of a priceless asset which we nurture before handing it on in as good, if not better, condition than we received it. Kilkenny's many successes over the years have given the county a real sense of confidence and an understanding that there's a heritage here which must be respected and protected.

While the past may have enabled Kilkenny hurling people to feel confident about themselves, it also creates a modesty which has always been retained. It's not a county where you can get carried away with your own sense of achievement because the chances are that there's a fella down the road who is just as good as you, and someone else on the other side of the parish who did a damn sight more during his playing career.

It's not – and never has been – a county of prima donnas, which I believe is central to its continued success. You're only as good as your last game and you don't live very long on reputation in Kilkenny.

It's all of thirty-seven years since I first walked, self-consciously, into the Kilkenny senior dressing room, but I don't believe much has changed in players' attitudes to the wearing of the black-and-amber. Then, as now, everybody was passing through, while feeling deeply privileged to be part of a Kilkenny team.

The opening day of my senior career went well, even if we did concede four goals. Pa Dillon was playing behind me at full-back and he came to me before the game and told me exactly what to expect. He also promised he'd look after me in the event of any Limerick man thinking he could bully a minor making his senior debut. That was nice to hear because Pa wasn't a man to be messed around with. We beat Limerick by 1-16 to 4-2, and I marked my debut by scoring two points. We weren't to know it at the time, but Limerick would go on to figure very prominently in the Kilkenny story over the next two years.

However well I thought I did against Limerick, I wasn't going to hold a place on the team for the more serious tests ahead in 1973. And certainly not at centre-back where the resident incumbent was one Pat Henderson, a man of proven substance who wasn't about to be displaced by a young lad just out of minor level. Pat Lawlor and my club mate, Eamonn Morrissey, were the wing-backs and, since they had hurled so well in the 1972 campaign, I didn't see any chance of dispossessing either of them any time soon either.

Never mind. There was still plenty of hurling to enjoy with 'The Village', Kilkenny Under-21s and St Patrick's, Drumcondra, where I was studying to become a National School teacher. I had always liked the idea of teaching and, when the call to St Pat's arrived, it was an easy decision to make so I headed for Drumcondra to start the next phase of my life.

Shortly after I qualified from St Pat's I got a job back home in my local school and have been there ever since. Having got a taste of the county senior scene I was, quite naturally, ambitious to push my claims for a place on the team but, with so much quality in Kilkenny, it wasn't going to be easy. I would have to work on my game, try and improve on various aspects and bide my time for a few seasons. At least, that's what I thought, but you never know what's around the corner. Suffice to say, the circumstances which led to me making my first appearance in an All-Ireland final were unusual.

Kilkenny retained the Leinster title in 1973, beating Wexford in a high-scoring final. I was on the panel but not on the team for the Leinster Championship. Still, I was quite happy just to be part of such a great scene. I was learning all the time, so it was a question of keeping the head down and hoping that my time would eventually come.

It really was very exciting to be involved with a senior squad which boasted so many star names, men with god-like stature in my eyes, who had already assured themselves of legendary status. It was a different world back then so, after winning Leinster, Kilkenny qualified directly for the All-Ireland final which was a full eight weeks away. It was an awfully long wait, but that was the way of the world for the Leinster and Munster champions on alternate years when they didn't have to play Galway, London or whoever else made it from that side of the draw.

It was nearly always Galway, although not in 1973 because they had been surprisingly beaten by London in the All-Ireland quarter-final. London, in turn, lost to Limerick in the semi-final.

As reigning All-Ireland champions with a team which looked to be moving on towards the peak of its powers, Kilkenny were well-fancied to beat Limerick who had won the Munster title for the first time since the 1950s. In ordinary circumstances, the script might well have run to plan but, this time, the gods decided to spice things up a bit. Actually, they did more than that. They chose to lump some very heavy handicaps onto Kilkenny which took a serious toll.

Since there was such a long gap between the Leinster and All-Ireland finals, players kept busy on the club scene while the Walsh Cup was also played off during those weeks. I couldn't see that happening now, but things were different back then. It also emerged that Eamonn Morrissey wouldn't be available for the All-Ireland final as he was leaving for Australia in mid-August. I have no idea how much – or, indeed, if any – effort was made to re-schedule his departure but, once it was confirmed that he was going, the selectors were left looking for an alternative wing-back. It wasn't their only dilemma. The left corner-back, Jim Treacy, ruptured his Achilles tendon in a tournament game in late July, ruling him out of the final. Now the selectors were faced with repairing the entire left side of the defence.

If that wasn't challenging enough, things got even worse in August when full-forward Kieran Purcell was laid low with appendicitis. And, just when it looked as if no more misfortune could descend on the camp,

Eddie Keher suffered a broken collar bone in the Walsh Cup final against Wexford. Now our top scorer was gone too, which was absolutely devastating as he was the man feared by opposition defenders more than anybody else. This was getting serious. How many more blows could Kilkenny withstand?

It was beginning to look as if the gods hadn't just ordained that Kilkenny should be tested to the limit, but that they should be driven to breaking point. Losing four of your first fifteen would be seriously damaging at any time of year, but it was devastating coming, as it did, in the run-up to an All-Ireland final.

Still, where there are absentees there are opportunities. Once the selectors started looking through their squad for replacements, I was deemed to be going sufficiently well to be considered as a replacement for Morrissey. The management process was very different back then.

We had a five-man selection panel who chose the team before effectively handing it on to Fr Tommy Maher to coach. Only fairly recently, somebody showed me a cutting from a daily newspaper which gave a flavour of how things worked. The article painted the scene as it applied ten days before the All-Ireland final. "Kilkenny senior selectors were in conclave last night, but their discussion was for the purpose of giving team trainer, Fr Tommy Maher, a broad outline of the lines on which they were thinking about as to who they would call in to replace Eddie Keher, Kieran Purcell, Jim Treacy and Eamonn Morrissey."

I can't see that system working nowadays, but it was of its time and had, obviously, served Kilkenny well as the All-Ireland counter kept clicking along nicely – until 1973. I got an inkling that I was in line to replace Morrissey when I was chosen for the Walsh Cup semi-final against Offaly in Birr in early August. We won, and I must have done well enough to convince the selectors that I was worth persisting with for the All-Ireland final. It was a big call by them although I, naturally, viewed it as the only genuine option! Mind you, it taught me one thing which I took through to my managerial days – if a player is good enough, he is old enough.

It was quite something to go from captaining the minors in the 1972

All-Ireland final to playing with the seniors a year later, but it all happened so quickly that I had no time to get uptight about it. At nineteen, I was the youngest player in the final, but I never thought about that or how I might cope against the Limerick half-forwards. I just couldn't believe that my dreams of playing in an All-Ireland final for Kilkenny had come so early. I would be wearing No.7 in the famous black-and-amber on All-Ireland day, and nothing else mattered.

Given the decimation our camp had suffered since the Leinster final, the All-Ireland final was set up for Limerick and they took full advantage on a miserable, wet day. The weather was so bad that the crowd was only 58,000 – the lowest turnout for years. In those days, supporters could pay their way into Hill 16 and the Canal End – even on All-Ireland final days – so people could wait until the morning of the game before deciding if they would travel. And, even if they were all set to head for Croke Park, they could change their minds. Presumably, that's what happened once they saw how wet it was that day. The lure of watching the game on TV rather than getting drenched on the Croke Park terraces proved too much for many people.

I was marking Liam O'Donoghue and felt I did okay. Still, the loss of four top-class performers was an awful handicap for Kilkenny, even if we managed to disguise it until the second half. We led by a point early in the second half but a Limerick goal, driven over the line in a rugby-like scrum, gave them huge momentum and they went on to win by seven points. That goal wouldn't be allowed nowadays, but it was deemed okay back then and turned out to be crucial as Limerick pressed on from there, leaving us trailing in their wake.

Outside of Kilkenny, the hurling world was delighted as it was Limerick's first All-Ireland win since 1940. As it was my first final and I was new to the scene, I probably didn't feel the same sense of loss as the more experienced Kilkenny players. Still, it was fierce disappointing. But, as a county, we accepted that it was one of those occasions when all the decks were stacked against us. The same pairing would be back for the 1974 All-Ireland final and, this time, it was very different as Kilkenny – who had Treacy back at No.4, and Keher and Purcell restored to the full-forward line – won easily. It convinced us that we would have beaten Limerick a year earlier if we'd had a full deck to deal from. Then again, I wouldn't have made my debut if everybody had been available in 1973.

I was back on the subs' bench in 1974, with my club mate, Tom McCormack, taking over at left half-back. Mind you, I was in good company in the subs alongside the likes of Ger Henderson, Ger Fennelly and Nickey Brennan. We were all on the Under-21 team which made its own piece of Kilkenny history that year by winning the All-Ireland title for the first time.

The general view in Kilkenny – and outside, too – was that, if we hadn't been hit with such a serious injury blitz in 1973, the All-Ireland treble would have been secured a year later. And, since we won again in 1975, there's every possibility that a four-timer would have been achieved. Then again, you never know.

Sport is fickle and who knows how the landscape might have changed if Kilkenny had won in 1973? As it was, we were pushed to the very limit by Wexford in the 1974 Leinster final, winning by a point in one of those remarkably high-scoring games where it was difficult to keep track as the goals and points flew in. We eventually won by 6-13 to 2-24. Championship games were played over eighty minutes in the first half of the 70s, so big scores were quite common when two good forward lines got to work.

Games dropped back to seventy minutes in 1975, a year which will go down in Kilkenny and Village history as one of the most special of all. Kilkenny completed a clean sweep of All-Ireland senior, Under-21 and minor titles, while The Village won the county title. I was lucky enough to be on the Kilkenny senior and Under-21 teams and, of course, I was aboard The Village team too. It was the first time since the 1930s that Kilkenny had retained the All-Ireland senior title, which gave the success an added dimension. It was surprising that Kilkenny had gone so long without winning a double but the opposition had been fierce over the years, not just from Wexford in Leinster but from Cork and Tipperary in Munster.

To top it all off, I was chosen at left full-back on the 1975 All Stars team. Strangely enough, given the year we had, I was the only Kilkenny man to get into the All Star back line, but it wouldn't be the last time the selectors reached some strange decisions. Ask James McGarry! He knows more than anybody how All Star selections work, or don't work as the case may be.

There's always something special about winning an All-Ireland medal at any grade but, obviously, the higher up the ladder you go the more it means, so it was a mighty thrilling experience for me to be part of the Kilkenny team that beat Galway in the 1975 final. We won handily enough against what was a very good Galway team. They'd made a major breakthrough earlier in the year whey they won the National League, after many years in the wilderness. They beat the so-called 'Big Three', Cork, Kilkenny and Tipperary, to win the title and showed that it was no fluke when they beat Cork again in the All-Ireland semi-final. They may have been a bit nervous in the final and did not perform as they would have liked. On the other hand, that particular Kilkenny team was probably at its peak. The day went well for me at left corner-back, which probably gave me the inside track towards the All Star award later in the year.

It was the only time I played in an All-Ireland final on the same team as Eddie Keher (he had been out injured in 1973, and I was a sub in 1974) and it's something I always treasured because he was such an iconic figure in Kilkenny hurling. I was only a kid when he played in his first senior All-Ireland in 1959, so to be on the same team as him sixteen years later was an experience worth treasuring.

Some of the current squad would have experienced something similar with DJ Carey in his latter years. They, too, would have been small kids when he first played senior for Kilkenny, but he was still there all those years later when they had grown into senior players. It goes to show how enduring the likes of Keher and Carey really were.

In terms of the amount of success I enjoyed during my playing career, nothing could come close to 1975, but I was out of underage from there on and, anyway, Kilkenny didn't win another senior All-

Ireland for four years. Even then, I wasn't on the panel having broken my ankle in the winter of 1978 and taken quite some time to regain full fitness afterwards.

As I've repeatedly said, the club scene has always been very close to my heart so, while I was walking on air after being part of Kilkenny teams that won All-Ireland senior and Under-21 titles in 1975, I was in a different orbit altogether when The Village won the county title some weeks later. Five of us had been on the Kilkenny senior team so The Village were very well placed to make a bold bid for the county title, which we won by beating Galmoy in the final.

By now, of course, the All-Ireland Club Championships were gathering momentum and, since it was the first time The Village had played in them, it represented a new and exciting challenge which would take us all the way to the final against Blackrock in Thurles the following May. We were lucky enough to get that adventure off to a successful start, having had a really tough battle with Buffers' Alley in a first round game down in Wexford Park.

It was one of my first battles with Tony Doran, who lined out at centre-forward. He was a phenomenal player with the heart of a lion and the strength of an ox. On top of that, he had an amazing capacity to create a chute for high balls to drop into his great big hand. Once he got the ball, his strength and courage took over as he turned and drove towards goal. I had a great battle with him in that particular provincial club game which we won by a few points.

We went on to win Leinster and the All-Ireland, beating Blackrock in the final which was a massive victory, not just for us but for the Kilkenny club scene. The All-Ireland Club Championships had been introduced five years earlier and had been dominated by Munster in general and Cork in particular. Roscrea of Tipperary had won the first one but the next four went to Blackrock (twice), Glen Rovers and St Finbarr's.

Apart from The Fenians – who got to the 1975 All-Ireland final – Kilkenny champions hadn't even won Leinster, so we were fiercely determined to show what The Village could do when we met Blackrock in the 1976 final. Mind you, you wouldn't have thought that in the first quarter when we conceded 2-1 and didn't register a single score. Now, it was a miserable day in Semple Stadium but this was ridiculous. Here we were, the champion club from the home of the All-Ireland champions, hurling like fellas who came together for the first time on the way to Thurles.

In fairness, Blackrock had an outstanding squad, including Dermot McCurtain, John Horgan, Ray Cummins, Eamonn O'Donoghue, Pat Moylan and Frank Norberg. Not to mention our own Frank Cummins who was living in Cork at the time and who had joined up with the Rockies. Still, despite Blackrock's all-round strength, we shouldn't have made such a shocking bad start. No score at all in the first quarter – how much worse could it get?

If we didn't get our act together, we'd be beaten out of sight and The Village wouldn't be a very welcoming place that night, or any other night for that matter. Perhaps such a practical consideration provided the necessary jolt of shock therapy because we clawed our way back before going on to win by six points.

Yet another piece of history for 'The Village', now the first Kilkenny club to win the All-Ireland title.

On a personal level, things couldn't have gone better for me. A brilliant 1975 was followed by an excellent start to 1976. The All-Ireland club title had been secured and Kilkenny were tipping along nicely towards the National League final. We won that too, having been taken to replays by Cork and Clare in the semi-final and final. Significantly, though – or at least we thought so – we won both replays. Clare came very close to beating us in the first game, but it was all very different in the replay where we ran in six goals to win by fifteen points.

It was an unusually late finish – June 20 – to the League, but it looked okay from where we stood as it had kept us hurling competitively until just before the start of the Championship. We were All-Ireland and National League champions, confidence levels were high and everything was in place for a crack at the Championship three-in-a-row.

Sure, what on earth could go wrong?

CHAPTER 27

WE HAVE LIFT-OFF

It was good to see that 'Taggy' and Eddie still *had their poaching skills intact. Galway would have been disappointed to be behind at half-time and came out for the second half very much like a team that was angry with itself and the world. In the space of eight minutes they were five points clear after Canning had sent a free whizzing to the net and Niall Healy poked home their third goal.*

Monday, June 22, 2009: *One down, who knows how many to go? Our 2009 Championship campaign is underway and we've started on the right track. We couldn't have asked for tougher opponents in the first leg of our All-Ireland mission than Galway, and they certainly lived up to their rating in Tullamore on Saturday evening.*

We won by four points in the end but, boy, was it one hell of a struggle. Galway really tore into us, just as we expected they would, and gave themselves every chance of winning – not just once, but twice. They brought a huge intensity to their game right from the off and, if we hadn't been ready for it, we would have been blown away. We didn't hurl as well as we can, but then, you're not going to get it just right every day. Besides, you hurl as well as you're let.

You're not conscious of history or anything like that going into a

Championship game but, on this occasion, there was no escaping that it was different to anything we had experienced before. It was, after all, the first time that we had played an outside team in the Leinster Championship, so it was always going to have a special atmosphere.

Apart from it being the first such Kilkenny-Galway game, the rest of the hurling world were tuned in to see exactly how we would cope, and to make a judgement on Galway who are right up there among the main All-Ireland contenders. We might have won the last three All-Irelands and remained unbeaten in the Championship since Galway beat us in the 2005 All-Ireland semi-final, but it means nothing now.

We're heading into the Championship on the same basis as everybody else and there really is no way of knowing what will happen? All we can do – and this applies to players and management – is to prepare as well as possible and then hope the performance comes. It's not a science, it's not pre-programmed and it's not rehearsed. And while we have lots of experience of getting it right, it doesn't mean it will happen next time.

The longer any sequence goes, the more likely it is to end and, when you're up against one of the top sides in the country – as we were against Galway – you have to be prepared for every eventuality. Like, for instance, conceding an early goal to Joe Canning who scored after just five minutes. Of all teams, Galway are at their most dangerous if they get an early run on the opposition. Heads up, tails up and off they go! If you're not careful, you could be three goals down very quickly.

Canning's goal presented us with the first test of the Championship and the response was most encouraging. Goals by Aidan Fogarty and Eddie Brennan had us in front by two points at half-time. To be honest, we were lucky to be leading because we hadn't played with very much fluency. First night jitters and all that – we hoped.

It was good to see that 'Taggy' and Eddie still had their poaching skills intact. Galway would have been disappointed to be behind at half-time and came out for the second half very much like a team that was angry with itself and the world. In the space of eight minutes they were five points clear after Canning had sent a free whizzing to the net and Niall Healy poked home their third goal.

Forty-three minutes gone and we'd already leaked three goals. That's as many as we'd conceded in our previous six Championship games put together. Pressure time. I wasn't especially worried as there was still an awfully long way to go, and I felt that we hadn't really got our game going yet. Once we did, we would apply the kind of pressure on Galway that they hadn't felt up to then. Besides, a five-point lead is nothing in hurling, even if it's better to have it, than be chasing it.

What happened next reassured me that, wherever else the season takes us, we certainly won't surrender our title due to a lack of appetite or application. We sent Derek Lyng in as a substitute at midfield and he made a huge difference. He missed the entire League through injury but he worked unbelievably hard to get himself right for the Championship and it showed. Indeed he underlined, once again, why he has been such a valuable part of our operation for so long.

It wasn't just his experience that made a big difference, it was the way he drove into and out of tackles. Give a hit, take a hit and plough on regardless. That's Lyng and that's exactly what he did on Saturday. The whole team lifted their game in unison and gradually the points began to fly over. Henry (Shefflin) landed one brilliant long-range effort which lifted the whole team and Eoin (Larkin) hit a golden spell, during which he, too, scored some fantastic points. The defence tightened up with JJ (Delaney) doing an excellent job on Canning, so we made rapid inroads on Galway's lead.

We hit ten points without reply, which was some strike rate, and, while they pressed us again near the end, we had a cushion which we guarded all the way to the finish line. Scoring ten successive points is a very difficult thing to do at any time but even more so against a Galway team whose confidence levels were sky-high after forty-five minutes. You could sense that they felt something big was about to happen but, thankfully, our fellas had the resolve and the know-how to re-direct the game our way. You can't coach that. It's either there or it's not.

I suppose the key thing about our performance was that we never panicked. Even when Galway scored those two early second-half goals, the lads had enough belief in themselves to assess the challenge and work through it. But then, we've been down this road many times before and there's no doubt that experience counts when the pressure really comes on.

We ran up a fine score (2-20) but, obviously, we weren't happy to concede three goals. Overall, I'd describe it as a functional rather than fancy performance and, hopefully, there's a lot more in the tank. There will need to be.

Still, we're up and running in Championship '09. I was in Nowlan Park yesterday where Dublin booked their place in the Leinster final with a two-point win over Wexford. It was fully deserved, too. This is a rapidly improving Dublin team who will offer a new kind of challenge to us in the final. As for Galway, we've beaten them for the third time this year, but we could well be meeting them again. I have no doubt they will make progress in the qualifiers but, for now at least, we can forget about them. There's a new challenge waiting in the Leinster final in the form of a Dublin team that's finally living up to the promise it has shown in recent years.

CHAPTER 28

LOWS, HIGHS. MYTHS AND MAGIC

I did well enough, too. I was Kilkenny's second-highest scorer (2-3) behind 'Chunky' O'Brien in the two Leinster games against Offaly and Wexford and landed another 1-2 in the All-Ireland semi-final against Galway. So, my confidence was high heading into the final against Cork – who were bidding for the three-in-a-row. Cork had taken over after our departure from the scene in 1976, twice beating Wexford in All-Ireland finals.

Where the hell did that come from? One day, you're sailing merrily along without a wave in sight, not a single cloud in the sky and the weather forecast promising more of the same for the foreseeable future, the next you're shipwrecked on jagged rocks in the midst of a howling gale with all your possessions scattered irretrievably.

That's how it felt after the 1976 Leinster final which, according to popular opinion, was supposed to be a tricky but negotiable stepping stone for Kilkenny in our pursuit of the All-Ireland three-in-a-row. Wexford hadn't beaten Kilkenny in the Leinster final for six years and, while there were some intense tussles in the interim – including a draw in 1972 – there was no reason to believe that Wexford would unseat us in 1976. Well none that we had spotted anyway.

We were, after all, unbeaten in the Championship since the 1973 All-

Ireland final, a loss we put down to unfortunate circumstances over which we had little control. Basically, we reckoned that fate rather than form unseated us. Restored to full power from there on, we had won two All-Irelands topped up with a National League title as well. Our confidence couldn't have been higher as we headed for the 1976 Leinster final, even if Kilkenny were always wary of Wexford. Indeed, that's something that hasn't changed to this day, and never will.

Still, maybe we weren't wary enough in 1976. Wexford didn't just beat us in that final – they demolished us and then steamrolled over the debris so that by the end of the day it was as if we never existed on a hurling field. From three-in-a-row favourites to crushed non-entities, and all in the space of one July afternoon in Croke Park. Wexford won by 2-20 to 1-6, which was, apparently, Kilkenny's biggest defeat in a Leinster final since the 1890s. To be honest, we were lucky to escape with a seventeen-point defeat. It said a lot about Wexford's superiority and our inept performance that, only for a string of fine saves by Noel Skehan, we would have been thrashed by an even bigger margin. It sure is bad when you lose by seventeen points and your goalkeeper is your best player!

There was no obvious explanation as to why we were so off-tune that day. Fair play to Wexford, who produced a high-tempo performance, but even they would admit that we were incredibly poor. We would normally expect to score 1-6 in less than half an hour, yet that was our total return for seventy minutes.

So what happened? Maybe we took our eye off the ball after beating Clare in the League final replay. We drew with them in early May but the replay wasn't played for six weeks, during which time we had been to America on an All Star tour. That, followed by a League final replay was a most unusual way to head towards July and may well have contributed to the lethargy which would all but paralyse us against Wexford. Beating Clare so easily looked great at the time, but counted for absolutely nothing a month later.

There were some indications that our form against Clare shouldn't be overvalued when they lost quite heavily to Limerick in the Munster semi-final two weeks after the League final replay, but we felt we were going so well that we didn't take any notice of what was going on in Munster.

Whatever happened, we weren't ready for what Wexford threw at us and, the harder we tried, the more disjointed we became. We always knew that Wexford were well capable of turning it on in the Leinster final but it was still quite a shock to be taken apart so ruthlessly and systematically.

It wasn't a good day for me on a personal level either, certainly not as far as the media was concerned. The match report in the following day's Irish Independent noted that, "Brian Cody was by no means at his best at left-corner back". Perhaps not, but then I wasn't the only one who didn't do himself justice on a bewildering afternoon that still serves as a reminder as to what can happen when a team is better prepared for battle than their opponents. Quite simply, Wexford hurled us off the field and half way up Jones' Road.

If that sort of thing happened now, teams would get a second chance via the All-Ireland quarter-finals but, back then, there was no safety net. And believe me, that was one mighty fall from the high wire. How would we have done if we had been given a second chance? Who knows? It's safe to say that we couldn't be as bad again. At least, I hope we couldn't.

It was back to the club scene immediately after that and, since we were defending Kilkenny, Leinster and All-Ireland champions, there was an added edge for 'The Village' boys. We retained the county title, beating The Rower-Inistioge before going on to reach the Leinster final against Camross of Laois.

It was played in Carlow on a horrible day and, while we were without 'Fan' Larkin, we were fancied to win. We didn't though. Camross beat us a by a point, and deservedly so.

In the space of six months, Kilkenny had gone from being regarded as one of the best teams of their generation to Leinster final flops, while 'The Village' had handed over the Leinster title to Camross and bowed out of the All-Ireland race.

It proved, once again, that you can take nothing for granted in sport.

It's always changing, evolving and challenging which, of course, is a major part of its great appeal.

Things altered fairly dramatically for me in 1978 when the Kilkenny selectors decided that I should be handed a new role at full-forward. Centre-back would probably have been my favourite position but I had also played at corner-back, full-back and wing-back so I had a good all-round feel for how to defend.

Not that I had any problem with playing up front either, and would have moved to the forward line from time to time with the club. Obviously, the Kilkenny selectors felt I could do a decent job at full-forward and, to be honest, I enjoyed much of my spell there in the 1978 Championship.

I did well enough, too. I was Kilkenny's second-highest scorer (2-3) behind 'Chunky' O'Brien in the two Leinster games against Offaly and Wexford and landed another 1-2 in the All-Ireland semi-final against Galway. So, my confidence was high heading into the final against Cork – who were bidding for the three-in-a-row. Cork had taken over after our departure from the scene in 1976, twice beating Wexford in All-Ireland finals.

In fairness to Wexford, they proved they had a very good team at the time, and beat us again in 1977. This time only a few points separated us, but it was more than enough to complete the Leinster final double over Kilkenny, something they hadn't done since the 1950s. We got them back in 1978 and, after beating Galway in the All-Ireland semi-final, there was a good feeling around Kilkenny heading into the final against Cork. For obvious reasons, we wanted to stop them winning the three-in-a-row, but it proved to be beyond us.

We lost by four points after being level at half-time in what was definitely not one of Kilkenny's more auspicious All-Ireland final performances. I was marked by Martin O'Doherty who was in his prime at the time and, while things didn't go my way, I wasn't as poor as some would have you believe.

However, much of the post-match analysis centred on the wisdom or otherwise of turning a defender into a full-forward. The following day's papers reckoned it was a bad move, although few of the critics saw fit to make that point in the course of the season. Hindsight really is a wonderful asset in the land of the pundit. The truth was that, as an entire forward line, we just didn't click that day. We scored a meagre 2-8, which doesn't win many games let alone All-Ireland finals. In fairness, we were up against one of the great Cork teams, but we were still fiercely disappointed because we simply didn't perform. As a converted defender, I was an easy target for the critics.

There were stories afterwards of how I was booed when we arrived home in Kilkenny on the Monday evening, and how this left an indelible mark on me. In fact, you will still read references to what's supposed to have happened that evening, followed by claims that it had a profound impact on me, turning me into some sort of ferocious character.

Sorry to disappoint the conspiracy theorists, but the truth is a lot less colourful. For a start, I have absolutely no recollection of being booed and if it did happen it would have come from a small number of idiots whose views were completely irrelevant.

Some people like to pick scapegoats after a defeat and, if I happened to be a convenient target, so be it. It certainly wasn't something that made any impression on me. As for the claim that the memory of a few idiots booing for the sake of it might have shaped how I came to think and act over the years, it's just plain laughable. But, when a story gets legs it runs and runs and is very hard to stop. And, when it's repeatedly re-hashed, often in a different context, it can become something of a gospel. This one shouldn't, though, because it's baseless.

Even if it were true and a tiny minority had blamed me for the Kilkenny defeat, why on earth should I care? I had played where the selectors had chosen me – end of story. Besides, I was still only twenty-four years old so I reckoned I had several years ahead of me. It would be as a defender, but I still don't think the 1978 experiment of playing me up front was the disaster some would have you believe. It might have lasted for only one Championship campaign but I was glad to have experienced it. Maybe it gave me an insight into attacking play that stood to me as a player and manager later on.

As I recall, I hurled well with the club immediately after the 1978 All-Ireland so, clearly, my confidence wasn't damaged. Something far worse than an indifferent All-Ireland final performance hit me during the following winter. I broke an ankle a setback which, almost certainly, ended up costing me an All-Ireland medal in 1979. I struggled through most of that season, never quite feeling right so it was no great surprise that I wasn't brought into the Kilkenny panel as they motored towards the All-Ireland final. Galway had finally ended Cork's four-in-a-row ambitions in the semi-final but never came close to replicating the same level of performance in the final. Kilkenny won without having to do anything particularly special as Galway conceded some soft goals and didn't really threaten in attack. It wouldn't be the last time that Galway played much better in a semi-final than final.

It was disappointing not to be part of the squad but I felt that, if I got back to full fitness and stayed clear of injury, I had a good chance of forcing my way back onto the scene. Things were beginning to change in Leinster around then as a new and powerful outfit arrived in the form of Offaly who were, of course, trained by one of our own, Diarmuid Healy.

CHAPTER 29

LIVING ON THE EDGE?

> ***The truth is that, far from bullying our way to*** *success, we have played second fiddle in the physicality stakes over the last year. It happened in the early stages of last year's All-Ireland final against Waterford, and also against Tipperary in this year's National League final. Look back at the video of our Leinster Championship games against Galway and Dublin and you'll see that we were second in the physicality stakes there, too. So, it's okay for others to "live on the edge" and bring acceptable aggression to their game but, when we do it, it's a black mark against us. As I say, it all comes down to people being sick of us winning so much.*

Monday, July 6, 2009: *All this talk about Kilkenny's physicality, living on the edge, sailing close to the wind and pushing our luck is getting serious. There's an agenda out there which carries huge risks for us.*

It has been going on for a few years now and seems to be gathering momentum. I suppose in some ways it's inevitable. People are getting fed up with us. They want us to go away for a while and leave the scene to others. It's nothing personal against us, but rather a desire for new teams, new faces and new pairings. It happens to all teams when they are successful over an extended period.

The great Kerry football team of the 1970s and 1980s were accused of ruining the game through hand passing. People wanted shot of them because they dominated for so long. Now, I'm no expert on Gaelic football but, hand pass or no hand pass, that Kerry team would have been phenomenally successful in any era, for the simple reason that they had outstanding footballers who worked very hard at their game. Still, they fell victim to the 'longevity syndrome' which leads to a demand for change purely for its own sake.

Just as Kerry had many superb footballers, I'd like to think that Kilkenny have some handy hurlers around at present, including Tommy Walsh who seems to have become the fall guy in the attempt to portray us as ruthless bullies who physically intimidate the opposition.

I was at a press conference last week and one of the first questions related to an incident involving Tommy in the Leinster semi-final against Galway. Afterwards, a totally disproportionate amount of coverage was given to discussing whether he should have been sent off on a second yellow card.

He had been booked earlier for a minor tap on Damien Hayes and he was later deemed to have fouled Hayes, which led to the Galway supporters baying for a second yellow, followed by red. Referee, Barry Kelly ignored them, but did award a free against Tommy.

I'm absolutely convinced that if that incident had taken place further out the field, it wouldn't even have been a free – indeed, later on, I saw several other similar incidents which weren't penalised. However, judging by the post-match reaction, it seems the opinion was that Kilkenny had got away with it again: Tommy should have "walked", he has, allegedly, been "living on the edge" and really should have gone over the cliff this time.

I'm not quite sure what "living on the edge" means. If it's the definition of being consistently determined and competitive, then that's fine by me. If it's a description of sneaky, underhand tactics, then it's not. I wouldn't tolerate that under any circumstances. Hard?

Yes. Fair? Yes. Committed? Yes. Dangerous? No.

Hurling is a physical game and should be played as such. It's full-blooded, it's manly, it's honest, and it's decent. I have never, ever sent out a team to play beyond the rules. Apart from anything else, it would be stupid because referees spot it very quickly. The vast majority of referees do a fine job – they let players get on with the game in the spirit it should be played and the result is usually a great spectacle.

The danger is there might be others, behind the scenes, urging referees to look for specific things from certain teams, and that's hard for him to ignore. Fair play to Barry Kelly, he called the Walsh-Hayes incident right in the Galway game (he deemed it not to be a yellow card offence, although I would argue it wasn't a foul at all) but he was criticised for his decision later. Still, it can be easy for TV to pick out an incident to make a point, it helps them pass the time.

The danger with labels is that, once they become attached, they're very difficult to remove, irrespective of the incorrect message they may be carrying. So, if the view that Kilkenny lurk somewhere on the edge with mischief on our minds and menace in our hands takes hold, it could have serious implications for us.

Referees are only human and, while I have faith in them, there's always a danger they will be influenced if they're bombarded with a negative emphasis on how we play. I would also be concerned about the people who are monitoring and advising referees. If they start raising doubts about us, God knows what impact it will have.

I totally reject the notion that referees are playing up to Kilkenny because of the notion that it's not advisable to get on the wrong side of a team that's going well: for a start, it's an insult to referees and, secondly, it's not true.

In fairness, some people have come down on Kilkenny's side, pointing out that we most definitely have no case to answer. Cyril Farrell has defended us on several occasions, including after the Walsh-Hayes incident. As a former Galway manager, he might have been expected to look on it with maroon-and-white-tinted glasses, but he didn't! He said that, under no circumstances should Tommy have been yellow-carded a second time.

Others were much harder on Tommy, which I think is most unfair. He's one of the finest hurlers the game has ever seen and to depict him as some sort of sneaky 'hit man' is a disgrace.

The truth is that, far from bullying our way to success, we have played second fiddle in the physicality stakes over the last year. It happened in the early stages of last year's All-Ireland final against Waterford, and also against Tipperary in this year's National League final. Look back at the video of our Leinster Championship games against Galway and Dublin and you'll see that we were second in the physicality stakes there, too. So, it's okay for others to "live on the edge" and bring acceptable aggression to their game but, when we do it, it's a black mark against us. As I say, it all comes down to people being sick of us winning so much.

The trouble is that once the word goes out that a team is up to something, it's very difficult to counteract it. Give a dog a bad name, and all that. We know we're being targeted for unfair criticism, but there's little we can do except urge people to judge us on what they see rather than what they hear.

I'll say this: whatever is alleged, argued or implied, we won't be changing the way we play. We NEVER go out to target any opposition player, and we NEVER go out with a negative approach. Yes, we play hard but so does everybody else and, if they beat us doing that, you won't hear any complaints from our camp.

We know that what we're trying to do this year is unbelievably difficult. We haven't lost a Championship game since August 2005 so, by the law of averages, the day has to come when we hit the wall. We're trying to delay that day as long as possible, which is really all we can do.

We're being analysed left, right and centre, we're being hit with massive physicality, and our forwards are finding it increasingly hard to find room as the opposition pack defences. That's to be expected. So, the challenge for us now is to come up with some variation on what we've been doing, and try something which can't be counteracted by watching videos of how we played in the past.

We reached our first Championship target for the year yesterday when we won the Leinster title for the ninth time this decade. We're extremely proud of that achievement. It hasn't been done in Leinster – or Munster, either – so it's a significant landmark, all the more so since we reached it in a year when Galway and Antrim were playing in Leinster for the first time.

We beat Dublin by two goals in yesterday's final, so we're where we want to be in the first week of July. We're still a long way short of where we need to be if we are to win the All-Ireland. Dublin made it hard for us, as we knew they would. Anthony Daly had them set up in such a way that it was difficult for our forwards to find space. Dublin worked very hard all over the pitch, so we were never going to have it easy. Still, we led from early on and, while Dublin stayed with us, we held the advantage right to the end.

It was by no means a great Kilkenny performance. In fairness to the players, it can be difficult to switch on every day, especially when they keep hearing about how certain they are to win. Obviously, that wasn't the message from inside the camp but the public have taken a different view and, since lads live and work in their local communities, it's impossible to ignore what's being said.

On days like this, you're always looking for someone to step up and take charge of the situation. This time it was Martin Comerford, who led from the front scoring 2-4 from play. That gave us a cushion but, overall, I would have to admit that it was a workmanlike rather than slick performance. You'd like to think there was a fair bit more in the tank if the need arose, but you can never be sure.

For now, I'm just happy to have won the Leinster title. There're just under five weeks to the All-Ireland semi-final and, no, we're not flowing as we would like. Still, it's clear that the genuineness and spirit, which has underpinned everything we have done throughout this decade, is still very much intact which is hugely encouraging. We showed that against Tipperary in the League final and against Galway in the Leinster semi-final. And every time Dublin really threatened yesterday, the right response was there, too.

We'll need lots of quality training between now and the semi-final and, hopefully, our injury count will have dropped by then. Brian Hogan – who has been out since the League final with a broken collar bone – will definitely be available, Noel Hickey is on his way back, too, so we'll see how he goes and 'Cha' Fitzpatrick came on yesterday, so he's getting closer to full power all the time.

We have beaten Galway and Dublin and have seen all of the other teams in action, too. We're in a good place right now but, like everybody, we have had the safety net attached in the event of a fall. It's decommissioned as of yesterday and, once next Sunday's Munster final is out of the way, the same will apply to Tipperary and Waterford, too.

One slip-up from then on and it's the end of the line. That will concentrate minds in every camp and, very definitely, in ours. We know we're in everybody's firing line, on and off the field, so we will have to be ready like never before. Nowlan Park will be a busy place for the next month.

CHAPTER 30

TERMS OF ENGAGEMENT

...anybody who attempts to manage a dressing room through fear is on a loser. Dictatorships don't work. Besides, if you want to be a dictator, team management is not for you because you're ignoring the word 'team', which should be the basis of everything you do. The entire dressing room – players, manager, selectors, coaches, medics, physios, County Board and so on – is a team. Obviously, people have different roles but it's all in a common cause. Get everybody on the same wavelength and the sky is the limit. Within the actual fifteen lads who are playing at any given time there are different responsibilities, depending on their positions. But, at all times, the focus has to be on the same goal. Everybody is equal in their pursuit of it – lose sight of that and decay sets in.

Perceptions can be funny little devils. They might be based on nothing more than a hunch or an impression, yet they can take on a life of their own and, before you know it, they become the gospel according to whoever is preaching them.

The louder and more persuasive the preachers, the more authority they assume, even when their message is built on nothing remotely substantial.

Worse still, they may not even be a distant relation of reality.

Obviously, the media plays a large part in forming perceptions because they're in a position to do so. In fact, to a large extent, that's what they do. I have no problem with that – it's the way of the world and always will be – but I think the public would be wise not to be too trusting of everything that's put before them.

I find it amusing when I read or hear about how I'm supposed to be an intimidating, authoritarian figure ruling the Kilkenny dressing room with an iron fist and a 'no compromise' sign stuck on my forehead. It's not a person I recognise in myself – in fact, it couldn't be further from the truth.

For a start, anybody who attempts to manage a dressing room through fear is on a loser. Dictatorships don't work. Besides, if you want to be a dictator, team management is not for you because you're ignoring the word 'team', which should be the basis of everything you do. The entire dressing room – players, manager, selectors, coaches, medics, physios, County Board and so on – is a team. Obviously, people have different roles but it's all in a common cause. Get everybody on the same wavelength and the sky is the limit. Within the actual fifteen lads who are playing at any given time there are different responsibilities, depending on their positions. But, at all times, the focus has to be on the same goal. Everybody is equal in their pursuit of it – lose sight of that and decay sets in.

I'm Kilkenny team manager but I don't see myself as some sort of supreme guru who makes all the decisions while everybody else jumps to attention. In fact, I don't see myself as any sort of guru. My job is to facilitate the smooth running of the squad in order to give them the very best chance of being successful for themselves and Kilkenny. I'll make decisions where necessary, not in a dictatorial way but as part of a measured, considered approach underpinned by the common good.

Naturally, I bring my own philosophies to bear on how we go about our business but always as part of a team.

I don't, at any time, feel that I have to be the main guy in the set-up. Far from it. I'll do anything and everything that has to be done because

I regard myself as no more important than anybody else in a long chain that's pulling the Kilkenny senior hurling team as quickly as it can. And yes, that includes sweeping the floor.

I remember Martin Fogarty slagging me one night after a training session in St Kieran's College last spring when he saw me busily sweeping the dressing room after the squad had left. "If the rest of the country could see you now, they'd never believe it. You and your little broom sweeping away," he joked.

I considered hitting him with the broom, but thought better of it. Good selectors are worth indulging! Besides, Martin would be the first to grab the broom himself when a sweeping job needed to be done. Sweeping the floor in St Kieran's was the least I might do, especially after all that college has contributed to hurling inside and outside Kilkenny. How could I leave somebody else to tidy up in the morning? That's not my way. And I'll collect cones or do anything else that Michael Dempsey wants when he's training the team.

When he's doing his work, he's the boss and I'm the helper so, if there are cones to be collected, I'm your man. I mention that to illustrate the point that there's no hierarchal system in our dressing room. Some managers might think it's beneath them to sweep dressing rooms or collect cones but I don't. In fact, I believe that being prepared to do just about anything is central to running an effective operation where there are no stars and no egos, only a group of people all on the same wavelength.

If the manager expects the players to go to whatever lengths it takes in training or on match days, then he has to be prepared to do the same. In fact, I would regard it as my greatest achievement as a manager that I succeeded in putting that sort of scene in place. The example comes from the top down and, once players buy into that, it's amazing how it feeds off itself and into the entire system in a very healthy way.

Take, for example, when young players come into the panel for the first time. It's very easy to instil values into them because, from the moment they walk in the door, they see the right example. They might be awestruck to be in the same dressing room as Henry Shefflin and the others who have been around for so long and won so much, but then they see how these lads go about their business. They see the sheer enthusiasm, commitment and effort they bring to everything they do. If a newcomer is any good at all, he'll copy that because he realises it's the way forward.

I don't have to say anything to him. He sees the example and knows that's what he's got to strive to emulate. If he makes it onto the team and establishes himself as a regular, he'll be one of the players new lads look to for example when they come into the panel later on. Lads learn from each other and, once the senior players are setting the right example, it's relatively easy to keep the system and the natural evolution of the squad ticking over.

Of course, it would be different if the senior players were setting the wrong example. That's where problems arise because, very quickly, you create a bad scene. The potential for that is in any county but, once it's managed properly it shouldn't arise. Older players recognise that new talent is coming along all the time with the sole intention of forcing their way onto the team. It's all very friendly but there's a huge rivalry too. That creates an electricity which brings huge energy to the scene and cranks up the competitive charge.

The experienced guy has to fight off competition; the young player wants to replace him and I'm in the middle watching and, indeed, enjoying how both are handling the challenge. They each know that I'm not going to take sides. I won't favour the older player simply because he has been around for a long time and I know what he has contributed. I won't side with the newcomer just because I want to see new faces around. Old or new, it's all the same to me. I'm duty-bound to put the best panel together, which is a responsibility that I take very seriously. Everybody understands that and, in the main, they try to make the best of their time on the scene, including prolonging it for as long as they possibly can. The spark of rivalry between established players and newcomers is great for business and helps keep things fresh and challenging, which is crucial in the dressing room dynamic.

Any player who's invited onto the panel knows that, while he has passed the first test, the real examinations are only beginning. We'll have spotted him because he has been doing well for his club, which is the best exam centre of all. However, once he gets into the county panel he's in a new and even more testing environment and how he reacts to that decides his future. Has he the confidence to drive on and not be in awe of the established players? They have earned their status as leaders by what they have achieved and, while a newcomer must respect that, he also has to show that he's man enough to challenge them as an equal once he gets out on the pitch. Nobody owns a Kilkenny jersey. You have it because you're deemed the best-qualified to wear it at a particular time, but the jersey will out-last every player so the important thing is to make the most of the opportunity while you can.

We're back to respect and honesty again. I've been lucky to have dealt with so many players who understand the culture of what we're trying to achieve as a group that it's now second-nature to everybody, whether they're in the panel for a decade or a day.

Players appreciate the wonderful honour it is to play for Kilkenny. We have all grown up steeped in the traditions of hurling in the county so, when a player reaches a standard where he's good enough to get into the squad, he knows that it's not only a huge privilege but also a massive responsibility. It has always been so. I recall from my own playing days just how honoured I felt to get the chance to pull on the famous black-and-amber. Thankfully, nothing has changed. The current group of Kilkenny players have represented that side of things extremely well and, despite their many successes, have never lost sight of the fact that they're lucky people.

There's no arrogance in Kilkenny hurling. We have enjoyed enormous success down through the years but, as a people, I'd like to think that we have handled it well. It doesn't matter how many All-Ireland medals or All Star awards you have in Kilkenny, you know that you're only a very small part of something so much bigger.

We don't lecture the world on how to play hurling and, irrespective of how successful we have been, you will never find a Kilkenny player showing disrespect to an opponent. That's because the players have a true sense of what playing for Kilkenny is all about.

I'm often asked what guidelines I use in terms of dealing with players, which amuses me because it pre-supposes that there's a manual which carries an extensive list of 'do's and don'ts'. There isn't but, in any event, I have never found it necessary. If I did, I'd consider myself to be getting something seriously wrong.

The players set the rules by their behaviour. They know the standards that must be reached and maintained if they're to get the best out of their careers. Respect, honesty, commitment – they're the only rules that apply.

I get on very well with the players. We celebrate big wins, we go on holidays and All Star trips and I meet them socially at functions towards the end of the year. We'd have a few drinks and a bit of fun together, but we both know we have different roles. There's an invisible line there, which we both instinctively recognise.

I respect them immensely for their skills, their effort and their sheer genuineness, and they know that. I respect them as individual people, too, and I'd like to think the respect is mutual – but then, it has to be a two-way process because, otherwise, it doesn't work.

I suppose that the players would be wary of me in my role as their manager as opposed to as an individual. I'm happy with that. I have my job to do as manager and they know I'll always do it with the best interests of the group at heart. They also accept that I'll make the hard decisions when I have to, but I most certainly don't believe that they regard me as an intimidating character.

I'd be very approachable for any player, morning, noon or night. I'd do anything for them on or off the field. And if a fella can't make training some night, I wouldn't make a big deal of it, provided the reason was genuine as opposed to just an excuse to dodge the session.

Nor would I react if I heard a lad had a few pints some night. Players are ordinary human beings with different personalities and you can't expect them to live a monastic life. You won't find me wandering into bars or sitting in car parks to see who comes out. A county is a small community, so I'd hear things fairly quickly if there was anything unusual going on. Of course, I wouldn't stand for any nonsense. If I discovered that somebody was being stupid or had stepped out of line, I would deal with it very quickly. Any breach of discipline that might cut across what we're trying to do as a group just wouldn't be tolerated. Having said that, we have no rules, only standards which are set by all of us. There's fair flexibility for players because I see what they give and understand that they're all individuals in their own right.

The most effective discipline comes from within the individual and the group. Anyway, at this level, it shouldn't be necessary to force discipline on players If somebody steps out of line the group ethic will bring him back very quickly – unless there's a more serious problem, in which case he's probably of little value to the dressing room anyway. I'm proud to say I have come across very few of those in my years as Kilkenny manager.

Human nature being what it is, I suppose it's natural that certain players might think I'd be closer to some than others, but that's not the case. I would always treat everybody exactly the same way. My loyalty is to the group who, in turn, are loyal to each other. They know that, as individuals, they can achieve nothing unless they're part of a squad that's fuelled by the same ambitions and driven by the same motivations.

As a manager, I have always regarded good communication as a key element of what we're about. Communication extends beyond the panel and onto everybody else who is involved in the project. It involves listening and being sensitive to what's going on in people's lives.

We're not a professional outfit and, when we leave Nowlan Park after training, we all go back to our own lives, our jobs and our families so, from a managerial viewpoint, it's important to be flexible. Having said that, players want to be part of a set-up where serious demands are made of them. They want strong leadership because they know it gives them the best chance of achieving their targets. They might not always agree with the methods used but, as long as they respect them, they will respond in the right way.

Contrary perhaps to popular (if ill-informed) opinion, I'd be very lenient on players. I know the effort they put into their hurling and, once they're doing that, I won't interfere. They set the standards, not me. I ensure that the standards set by the group are adhered to but, since they established them in the first place through their behaviour and performance, it's relatively easy to keep things ticking along.

Looking after players properly is important and, in fairness to the Kilkenny County Board, we have always got everything we looked for. However, it's a two-way street and players have a responsibility, too, in terms of respecting the county they play for and the jersey they wear.

It amuses me when I read articles about the hardship county players are supposedly enduring as part of their commitment to county hurling or football. Of course they put in a huge effort, but aren't they in a very privileged position to be good enough to play for their counties? Playing hurling or football is what they do in their spare time, it demands dedication and hard work, but it's certainly not without its rewards.

Kilkenny hurling has a tradition of success and achievement but, as a county, I don't think we ever take anything for granted. We didn't in my day as a player and we don't now. We have enjoyed a remarkably successful decade but, as a group, there has been no complacency and no smugness.

The next game is always the most important and you've got to be properly prepared for it because you can be damn sure the opposition will be.

CHAPTER 31

ONE GOAL, SHARED RESPONSIBILITY

Quite often I say very little at half-time. I'm not one of those managers who feel they have to be the main speaker on match day. My job is to have everything in order before the game so that the players are ready for any eventuality. That applies at half-time too, so I don't go in for stirring orations! I may suggest they watch out for this or that, but the main thrust always comes from the players. Even in the run-up to a game, I'm not a man for giving long speeches. The last thing you want to do is bore players and, anyway, people react better when you're short and straight to the point. Usually, on the Friday night before a game we have a chat about things. I remind them of the way we play and what we want on Sunday. I may mention certain things about the opposition, if I think it's warranted, but we mostly concentrate on ourselves, and how we're going to get our own game right.

I've heard it said, and seen it written quite a few times over the years, that Kilkenny are robotic. While that's an acknowledgement of how successful we have been there's an implication that we are, in some way, quite boring. It seems we're being chided for ambition – What the hell do those fellas want to win the Walsh Cup for? Have they nothing better to be doing in January? Actually no, we don't. If the desire and drive to win every game makes us boring, then it's a charge we'll gladly own up to time after time.

It's up to every county and every squad to operate as they wish, but I could never countenance a situation where we free-wheeled into any game. We want to win the Walsh Cup because it's a preparation for the National League which is very much worth winning. It sets you up for the provincial Championships which, even in these days of the second chance, are still very much worth winning too.

Again, I've read stories about how Kilkenny toss the Bob O'Keeffe Cup in with the gear on the team bus when we win the Leinster title and lock it away in a dark cupboard when we get back home. The implication is that Kilkenny are blasé about the Leinster Championship, which is most certainly not the case. The Leinster title is there to be won and I feel a great sense of satisfaction each and every time we are successful. That goes as much during my playing career as my managerial days.

It comes back to core values and the simple fact that we play hurling to win the next game and the next competition that's available. Whether that's Walsh Cup, National League, Leinster or All-Ireland Championship, it's all the same. And if there's a tournament game to be won, we'll go for that too. I can't see how that makes us boring or one-dimensional and, if it does, I couldn't care less.

But then labels become attached and, once that happens, they aren't easily removed. Not that it changes one iota of what we do or how we go about it. As I've repeatedly emphasised, it's all about executing the simple things well, keeping a clear focus on our targets and doing our best to hit them.

The ultimate aim in sport is to reach your maximum potential and retain it over an extended period. You have got to put in an enormous effort to achieve that but, when it's done in a group situation, anything is possible. I see one of my main roles as manager as keeping things simple because if you start going down the complicated road you'll meet yourself coming back and, ultimately, everything becomes blurred and confused.

It's far more important to have a clear, uncluttered view of who you are, where you're going and how you plan to get there. I think a lot about hurling away from match days. It's no burden, mind you, because I love the game so much. Even when I'm cutting the grass I could be thinking about the next training session or game, mulling selections around in my head or trying to work out how to get some player who has been going through a bad patch to regain his form and his confidence. Basically, hurling is never too far away from my thoughts.

Having said that, once a game or even a season is over I don't tend to dwell on it. It has always been the same. Don't ask me to go into great detail on games I played or things that happened way back! My memory of even the big days can be sketchy enough. That applies both to my playing and managerial days. For instance, I would struggle to name the Kilkenny team that played in the 1999 All-Ireland final. That might seem strange, but it's the way I am. That's not to say I don't savour the big occasions, I do, at the time, but when they're gone, they're gone. I love the feeling at the final whistle when we win and the few days after an All-Ireland final but, after that, I'm much more inclined to look forward than back.

I encourage players to do the same although, obviously, their perspective is different. They are the ones who are going into battle so it's important that they play the game in their heads well in advance because it helps enormously on match day. So much depends on how mentally prepared a player is for the challenge which lies ahead. We place a big emphasis on getting that right without over-complicating things.

Visualising what way a game will develop is crucial. Say you're a corner-back and, in the week before a game, you're thinking ahead to how it will unfold. In your mind's eye you see the ball coming in and you teach yourself to think, "Go, go, go this is mine! I don't care about the corner-forward, who he is or where he is. The ball is coming my way and I'm going to win it". Do that often enough and, when the game starts, you're instinctively tuned to react just as you've been thinking all week.

If a player has worked out everything in his head well in advance, nothing will surprise him. That's the beauty of our training sessions. Nothing happens on match day that hasn't been practised over and over again in Nowlan Park on the many evenings we've been there. Trust what you've experienced there and you'll be fine – that's our message to the players.

There are many aspects to getting your head right, but most of them are fairly straight-forward. A player may feel a poor decision has gone against him once or twice, or feel the referee isn't giving him a fair deal. It's easy to let these things upset you, but getting upset drains some of your efficiency so, instead, you've got to ignore them. And anyway, things will probably change in a few minutes and your opponent will be the one thinking the referee has it in for him.

It's all about keeping control of your emotions and not allowing anybody to upset them. One or two of our forwards received a few sly digs and kicks at the start of the 2008 All-Ireland final against Waterford, but they didn't react because we had anticipated that it would happen and were ready for it. Had we reacted, Waterford's ploy would have worked. We would have allowed them to set the agenda. Instead, we took it and got on with the game. It wasn't a sign of weakness, on the contrary, it was a sign of how we had the focus right. We weren't in any way intimidated, either physically or psychologically, and very quickly got into a stride which Waterford didn't match.

I could see what was happening at the start but I wasn't worried that it would disrupt our lads because they were ready for it. I'd have great trust in the ability of the team to work their way out of a problem. That's why I'd be pretty relaxed during a game, unless of course there was something distasteful going on.

Once the game is underway, the players are in charge. Okay, so I'm monitoring from the sideline but there's a limit to how much influence a manager can exert, whereas each and every player has the power to make a big difference.

I'm always surprised when I hear about managers making stirring, half-time speeches which provide enough inspiration to keep players going throughout the second half. Matches are not won at half-time and no amount of talk will change that. The standards are set long before that and, ultimately, they are what will get you through.

A manager can make a switch here or there and bring on a sub, but the engine has to be powered by the players. We're lucky to have so many leaders in the squad who have always been prepared to stand up and make their point, whether at half-time or at any other time.

Half-time lasts fifteen minutes – which is actually quite a long time – so it's important to space it out properly, I'd usually have a chat with Mick (Dempsey) and Martin (Fogarty), check for injuries or niggles with the medics and then work out where we stand and how we plan to drive it on. We always go to the warm-up areas as a group before we go back out and I'd make a few points arising from the first half. Some player or other – or maybe even a few – will also step in and have their say. We keep it very controlled, though. If you don't, there's a danger that you wander off course and forget what has been worked on over the previous weeks.

Quite often I say very little at half-time. I'm not one of those managers who feel they have to be the main speaker on match day. My job is to have everything in order before the game so that the players are ready for any eventuality. That applies at half-time too, so I don't go in for stirring orations! I may suggest they watch out for this or that, but the main thrust always comes from the players. Even in the run-up to a game, I'm not a man for giving long speeches. The last thing you want to do is bore players and, anyway, people react better when you're short and straight to the point. Usually, on the Friday night before a game we have a chat about things. I remind them of the way we play and what we want on Sunday. I may mention certain things about the opposition, if I think it's warranted, but we mostly concentrate on ourselves, and how we're going to get our own game right.

At this stage in my career, I have a good idea of what's required, and when, during the season. Obviously, there are times when a few motivational words are needed but I keep it very much off the cuff. I have no set routine on that. I just try to hit on something and work it into what we're trying to do. There are times, after training, that I will ask a particular player to speak. I might tell him in advance or it might be an impromptu call. Everybody has something to contribute, whether his natural style is to be quiet or chatty. Noel Hickey would be a quiet sort of man but he has developed into a terrific leader. James McGarry would also be a naturally quiet sort but he, too, was a great leader down the years and even more so when he was a sub in his final season.

But then we have always had plenty of lads who were prepared to lead, whether in a team talk, training or on match day. It's all about ownership of the project and, ultimately, that's down to the players. They know what they're about and have the will and the ambition to pursue their goals with as much dedication and effort as it takes while, at all times, keeping the basics right.

As I've said, hurling is a simple game where it's all about getting the fundamentals in order. You can talk all you want about tactics or systems but, when it comes right down to it, everything hinges on how a player performs. Take, for instance, half-backs! One of the key elements of their job is to make sure the ball doesn't pass them. When it does, there's pressure on the full-backs and the forwards begin to find their confidence. It's great when a half-back gets a chance to go upfield and score, but his primary role is to lock the front gates and throw away the key. Anything else is a bonus. I would far prefer a half-back to never get a shot on goal, than to end up with two or three points while his opponent hit four points.

As for corner-backs, I'm always hearing about how real pace is absolutely vital if they are to be good at their job. I don't believe that. The ability to defend and to understand the mechanics of defending is far more important than pace. I have seen lots of corner-backs who aren't actually good defenders.

They might be flying machines in sprints, but can they catch a high ball? And how good are they in key aspects of defending such at tackling, shielding the ball, holding their ground and being good under a high ball? Pace is a valuable extra, but only if the other attributes are in place first.

I'm probably influenced in my judgement by the fact I was never described as a fast player but I did have a good instinct for defending. In fact, I still think that I could play inter-county hurling to this very day. The legs wouldn't agree – and aren't going to be put to the test – but, in terms of positioning, cutting angles, and other small things involved in reading the game, I believe I would still get them right.

How many times have you heard, throughout this decade, that the way to beat Kilkenny was to run at their defence – the full-back line in particular? Jackie Tyrrell is reputed to be slow and has regularly been targeted by commentators as somebody who could be exploited by a speedy opponent. But how often has it happened? The thing about Jackie is that he understands defending in all its forms.

Noel Hickey is another who was accused of lacking speed, but he has always been a terrific defender, for the simple reason that he knows the art inside out. That's far more important than being able to out-sprint your opponent.

Besides, defence is a co-operative effort and, if you can get all six working and thinking together then opposition pace is not as big a problem as some would have you believe. I know that because we've come up against plenty of pacy forwards throughout this decade and our defence coped pretty well in most instances. But then, we had – and continue to have – lads who know how to defend and who understand that there's a lot more to it than speed.

They would need to, because the tests come thick and fast in Nowlan Park where, unless you know what you're doing, you'll very quickly be cleaned out by Henry, Eddie, Eoin and the other forwards who love trying to make life a misery for the backs in our training games. Mind you, our backs love to close down the forwards too! It's a real battle of wills and, of course, the ultimate beneficiary is the team as a whole. Just as it should be.

CHAPTER 32

TOWARDS THE FINAL HURDLE

If everybody is fit for the final, there will be *some big decisions to be made. Take midfield: we have four outstanding contenders for two places in Michael Rice, 'Cha' Fitzpatrick, Derek Lyng and Michael Fennelly. It's a good position to be in where we have four top-class midfielders to choose from, but it doesn't make the eventual decision any easier. Nor are we guaranteed to get it right. There are times you have to go with your instincts and hope they work out. The two midfield positions are still up for grabs, so let's see how the lads fare in training over the next few weeks. It should lead to some lively exchanges in Nowlan Park.*

Monday, August 17, 2009: *This is getting serious. What's happening to Tommy Walsh is an absolute disgrace. He's being targeted by opposition who are trying to wind him up in the hope he'll get booked, preferably as early in the game as possible, which leaves him walking a tightrope from there on.*

Why is it happening? For reasons I cannot understand, the media has turned on Tommy and taken to portraying him as a dirty player. Once that starts, it's very difficult to control and, naturally, most opposing teams will play on it.

Tommy is one of the most gifted hurlers ever to play the game. He's the sort of guy who people pay to watch. His skill levels are so incredibly high that there's nothing he can't do with a hurley and a ball. He's also mighty competitive. That's his nature and his instinct. I've played and watched this game long enough to know the difference between honest competitiveness and sneaky, dirty play.

Tommy is very much in the former category. Why should a man with such a delightful touch resort to foul play? He hasn't, but some analysts, with a strong sense of their own importance, have somehow succeeded in creating a perception of him as some sort of hit man.

Other teams are trying to exploit that in the hope of provoking a reaction from him. Take the All-Ireland semi-final against Waterford: right at the start, he was attacked by an opponent. It happened right in front of me and the linesman, who must have seen what went on. It was done to get Tommy embroiled in a row, followed by a booking.

What was Tommy supposed to do? Run away like a coward? He had to defend himself as best he could, but when the referee came over he booked both of them. Crazy stuff. Surely the player who deliberately starts an incident is the guilty party. Those who have snidely used the phrase "living on the edge" to convey the message that Tommy is a dirty player should be ashamed of themselves as, indeed, should others who have jumped aboard the sinister bandwagon.

My phone is quiet today, thank God. The lads were playing important club games over the weekend so, naturally, I'm concerned until I've heard they have all come through okay. A silent phone is a good sign.

We're back in training tonight which will be the first time we have got together since beating Waterford yesterday week. Twenty days to go to the All-Ireland final and now we know who our opponents will be. It certainly hasn't come as a surprise that it's Tipperary, although nobody could have foreseen how easily they would beat Limerick in the semi-final.

Limerick were all over the place and Tipperary took them apart. It was unbelievably one-sided, so we can't draw any real conclusions from Tipperary's performance. However, while they completed the job of reaching the All-Ireland final yesterday, we know that the real platform was laid in the League and Munster Championship.

Tipperary have been an impressive work-in-progress over the last two seasons so it was only a matter of time before they reached the All-Ireland final. They were desperately disappointed when they lost to Waterford in last year's semi-final but reacted in the right way and have been men on a mission ever since.

Given the strength of both counties, it's surprising that Kilkenny and Tipperary haven't met in the All-Ireland final since 1991.

They will be the fourth different county we will have played in four successive finals, following Cork, Limerick and Waterford. It's a game the entire hurling world is really looking forward to, and you can already begin to feel the excitement rising. As neighbouring counties with so many miles of common boundary, the build-up to the final will be something special although, naturally, both sets of players will keep as far away from it as possible.

The media will crank up the four-in-a-row angle, but I honestly believe that it will be overshadowed in Kilkenny by the fact we're playing Tipperary in the final. This is up close and real personal between neighbours. We beat Tipperary twice in semi-finals in 2002 and 2003, but Kilkenny's record in All-Ireland finals against Tipperary is not good. I'm told that 1967 was the only time we beat them in a final in over eighty years.

Not that what happened in the past will occupy one second's thought for us between now and the final. All that counts is getting ourselves as prepared as we possibly can be so that, when the ball is thrown in at 3.30 on Sunday, September 6, we're ready for whatever comes our way. We've known what to expect since the League final in May when Tipperary put us in the shade in terms of intensity and physicality. Even before the ball was thrown in you could sense their intent. They dominated for long periods, but we hung in and dug out a narrow win in extra-time. Many people felt that game was a pre-run of the All-Ireland final, and they were proved right. Still, we won't be concentrating too much on Tipperary in the coming weeks. Naturally, there will be aspects of their play we'll address eventually but, for now, it's all about our own game.

The next two weeks are crucial because that's the period when we've got to do the hard work. Four or five really good sessions, that's all we've got. We'll taper off in the final week so there's no time to waste. This is when having an excellent support team working with me is vital. Everybody knows their own role and what must be done, now it's a matter of getting on with it – which they will, in their highly-professional manner.

As for the players, most of them understand the drill by now. All-Ireland finals are nothing new to them but every final is, in itself, special and different. What happened last year or any other year doesn't count. This is a new challenge and we've got to be right for it. The lads know that there are still places up for grabs. People might not believe it, but I won't know for at least another two weeks what the starting line-up will be.

Noel Hickey still hasn't played for us this year, but he's very close to being right, 'Cha' Fitzpatrick and Derek Lyng have each started only one game, Brian Hogan is just back after breaking his collar bone, PJ Delaney has missed a lot of time too but he's flying in training, James Ryall had a hamstring injury but, hopefully, he's close to being right.

If everybody is fit for the final, there will be some big decisions to be made. Take midfield: we have four outstanding contenders for two places in Michael Rice, 'Cha' Fitzpatrick, Derek Lyng and Michael Fennelly. It's a good position to be in where we have four top-class midfielders to choose from, but it doesn't make the eventual decision any easier. Nor are we guaranteed to get it right. There are times you have to go with your instincts and hope they work out. The two midfield positions are still up for grabs, so let's see how the lads fare in training over the next few weeks. It should lead to some lively exchanges in Nowlan Park.

I'm looking forward to seeing the lads tonight so that we can begin the important work that needs to be done. We didn't even get together for a chat last week because they were back with their clubs, and that was where their focus had to be, so I wasn't going to interfere with them. They cleared their heads of all thoughts of the All-Ireland final and got ready for an important round of club games.

I'm quite happy with that. In fact, I encourage it. They're club players first, Kilkenny players second and, while we have reached the All-Ireland final, they still had responsibilities to discharge for their clubs last weekend. It's up to other counties to run their own affairs as they wish, but I would never dream of trying to get club games cancelled so that we could concentrate fully on the All-Ireland final. Apart from the fact that clubs have to get games, I believe it's good for the inter-county lads to go back to their roots for a round of club games before returning to prepare for the All-Ireland. Of course, there's always a risk of injury, but there's a risk in training, too, and you can't halt that.

We beat Waterford by five points yesterday week, in what was a much truer reflection of the relative strengths of the teams than last year's All-Ireland final where they never functioned to full capacity. Waterford are a serious team and we had to play very well to beat them this time. Not as well as I would have liked, but sport is not a perfect science. Not everyone was buzzing by any means, but enough of them were on their game to provide the sort of leadership required to get us over the line. Henry (Shefflin) was phenomenal, but he has been for a very long time. He was the leader among leaders. People might have been surprised to see John Tennyson at left half-back, but I had no doubts about playing him there because, like so many of our players, he's very flexible. Michael Rice hurled a great second half, in particular and Richie Hogan made an immediate impact when he came on.

And then there was Jackie Tyrrell. Brilliant! He was up against John Mullane, an outstanding corner-forward and, judging by the amount of ball Waterford hurled in his direction, very much a man they saw as a possible match-winner. Jackie played him superbly, marking, covering, blocking, clearing. Mullane was central to

Waterford's game plan so it was crucial for Jackie to do a good job, which he did – without fouling, it must be said.

Again, it showed real leadership. That's the sort of thing that inspires others. It's all about lads taking ownership of what they're doing. I don't have a magic wand on the sideline, ready to wave it as the need arises. The lads have to figure out the solutions themselves which, in fairness, they do very well. To be honest, it's very satisfying watching them do it. It's my job – together, of course, with the rest of the backroom team – to have the squad right going into a game but, once it starts, the players take ownership and drive it on.

Much has been made of the fact that we conceded three goals against Waterford – actually, it could have been more. But, although, we don't want a repetition in the All-Ireland final, it's something I'm not overly concerned about. I don't believe it's part of a trend or anything like that. These things happen. Still, the lads will have taken it personally and will be very determined that to make sure there's no repeat against Tipperary.

I would be far more worried if we weren't creating chances at the other end. We scored 2-23 against Waterford and were only a fraction away from at least two more goals. The problem arises when you're not creating chances and are, instead, trying to survive off scraps, which was not the case against Waterford.

So, then, we're back in the final after a campaign in which we battled through three games without reaching the heights we believe we are capable of. We have had three seriously good games against Galway, Dublin and Waterford, any one of which we would have lost if we hadn't been properly prepared, so any suggestion that we were holding back to allow us to peak in the All-Ireland final is pure nonsense.

Of course we want to peak in the final, but then so do Tipperary. They will be an unbelievably driven team, but we won't be found wanting there either. There's absolutely no question of Tipperary having a greater appetite than us. Nor do I believe, because we've been unbeaten in the Championship for so long, that the day has to come when we hit the wall. Any team can lose but, if it happens to us in the final, it will have nothing to do with hitting the wall or losing appetite.

How could anybody not be properly motivated for an All-Ireland final? If that were to happen to this Kilkenny team then the responsibility would rest, very much, with me. It's my job to get them right and, after that, they take charge of their own destiny.

It's thirty weeks since we set out on the 2009 season in the Walsh Cup game against Dublin in Parnell Park on a raw January day and, so far, we have achieved all our goals. However, the one that really matters is still out there. It's within tantalising reach now. As it is for Tipperary.

After building carefully over the last two years, there's nothing Tipperary would enjoy more than ending the decade as All-Ireland champions. Actually, maybe there is – finishing the decade as All-Ireland champions by beating a Kilkenny team bidding for a fourth, successive title would make it all the sweeter. Tipperary know that and, equally importantly, so do we.

Twenty days and counting...

CHAPTER 33

MIND AND WHAT REALLY MATTERS

Take early morning training sessions ... it might create the impression of mental toughness because you're getting out of bed at the crack of dawn but, personally, I don't see the point of it. A good night's sleep can be important too. Mental toughness doesn't come from gimmicks or trickery. To me, it's all about having players, management and everybody else in the camp thinking the same way, chasing the same goal and sharing a common bond in pursuing it. Each has their own responsibilities, but the sum of the parts is always more important than the individuals.

I'm not big into sports psychology, certainly not in the formal sense anyway. I don't have bookshelves creaking under the weight of mighty tomes all packed with the accumulated wisdom of psychologists, philosophers and various other gurus.

I'm not especially interested, either, in quotations from American coaches which seem to be a growing fascination among the sports-writing community in Ireland. Just because it works in American football, basketball or baseball doesn't make it automatically applicable here. Besides, one-liners, however deep or insightful they might sound, don't do much for me.

You can fill your head with all that stuff and then try to impart it to your players in the hope that it will mean something to them. Good luck to people who do it. If they think it works for them that's fine by me because, frankly, it's none of my business how they go about preparing their teams. Suffice to say that I'm not quite sure how bombarding a hurler with borrowed mumbo-jumbo will do anything to help a forward get around a defender during a National League game on a wet Sunday in March down in Wexford Park, or how it will help a back to close down his opponent in a scorching hot Championship Sunday in Croke Park.

Naturally, you look at everything that's out there in the hope that it will give you an edge but, at all times, you've got to trust your own instincts. As far as I'm concerned, the best part of sports psychology majors on logic and common sense, both of which are pretty basic requirements in management anyway. Without them, you're at nothing.

To that extent, I suppose we all use a degree of psychology but it's certainly not something I have studied or have any great interest in picking up second hand. I feel I have a fair appreciation for what's involved in hurling and in preparing hurlers so that they can deliver to maximum effect with the talents they possess.

I made a conscious decision years ago not to read sports books about managers or coaches because I didn't want to be influenced by anybody else. I had the confidence to do it my way with no influence from outside. That encompasses strengths and weaknesses but, most of all, it embraces honesty.

I didn't want to lean on somebody else's ideas or conclusions because I wouldn't have known the circumstances that led to their formation in the first place. That's one of the dangers of borrowing ideas from other people. What if their philosophy is based on totally different conditions and experiences?

Teams and individuals vary a great deal so what works for one might be completely wrong for the other. That's why, in my opinion, a manager must always apply his own psychology to a situation because he knows his players and their mindset and the circumstances which made them what they are.

Having said that, I have picked up bits and pieces here and there over the years – not because I actively pursued it but because there are always good ideas out there which can be applied to any sport. I have observed how other sports do things but would have no role model whom I regard as the font of all knowledge and wisdom.

Nor would I ever allow myself to get caught into something just because others were doing it. Take early morning training sessions. They have become quite common in the GAA over the years but they're not something that hold any appeal for me. Training in the morning won't make you any fitter or better prepared.

It might create the impression of mental toughness because you're getting out of bed at the crack of dawn but, personally, I don't see the point. A good night's sleep can be important too. Mental toughness doesn't come from gimmicks or trickery. To me, it's all about having players, management and everybody else in the camp thinking the same way, chasing the same goal and sharing a common bond in pursuing it. Each has their own responsibilities, but the sum of the parts is always more important than the individuals.

It amuses me when I hear about how Kilkenny players are supposed to be so tightly controlled that they're afraid to breathe without getting clearance from me. Despite what people might think, there is a huge degree of flexibility within the squad. I always encourage players to express themselves with whatever skills they have. I tell them to play the game as they see it. Do what comes naturally. Be yourself. Do it your way. Express yourself. Don't be afraid to make a mistake. You're in the squad or on the team because you're a damn good hurler – now go out and show how you've reached this level.

We have had a lot of star players on our squad over the years but we didn't – and still don't – have prima donnas. It's the ultimate co-op where everybody is equal. The work ethic is phenomenal and, thankfully, everybody buys into it because they know that's how the squad functions. Of course players' individuality can be easily incorporated within that as long as team values always come first.

I have no problem whatsoever with players who try something that doesn't come off. The modern game is played at a frantic pace and with massive intensity so mistakes will happen. If a forward shoots a wide or two, I won't bawl him out. On the contrary I'd encourage him to keep shooting provided it was the right option and the player is continuing to keep the overall good of the team at the top of his agenda. As with everything else, it all comes down to honesty.

Once players adhere to that, they have plenty of leeway. I don't need to tell our forwards when to switch themselves around in the course of a game. We will have talked things through in advance and, obviously, if I spot the need for a switch during a game I'll act on it. Similarly if the lads believe there's something to be gained by altering positions, I won't interfere with them.

They're on the pitch in the thick of the action and are playing the game as they see it. I like to see them making decisions individually and collectively because it shows they're thinking like leaders and aren't afraid to take responsibility. Of course, leadership can come in many guises. Take Henry Shefflin. People will have their own ideas which were his best games for Kilkenny over the last ten years and, I guarantee you, most of them will be from days where he returned a big score from a mixture of frees and open play.

He has had quite a lot of those, but the game that stands out for me was one where he didn't score even a single point from open play. It was against Galway in the 2007 All-Ireland quarter-final in Croke Park – a game that was in the balance right up to the final few minutes when we pulled away. It was as tight as it possibly could be for over an hour as both sides tore into each other with incredible determination and commitment. There really was nothing in it so it was vital for lads to stand up to the strain.

When we were under most pressure, Shefflin responded in an unbelievable way. He fought for every ball like a dog, drove Galway lads in all directions and led the forward line like a real general. He's one of the most technically gifted players hurling has seen, but he brought so much more to his game that day. There was very hard work to be done and he got on with it. His whole sense of team and his selflessness were immense. He wasn't waiting for others to win the ball or trying to live off breaks. Instead, he ploughed into the thick of the action, took the belts and knocks and got on with it. It was all about the team and nothing about himself. Imagine a young fella looking on, admiring how someone he regards as an absolute legend gets stuck in and does so much dirty work. What an example to everybody.

I make the point about Shefflin because he would be regarded, nationally, as one of the real stars of our team, but he never sees himself that way.

It was the same with DJ Carey. There were people who had the gall to claim that DJ didn't always perform to his best in All-Ireland finals. The implication was that, while he could be brilliant for the rest of the year, he didn't quite deliver in finals. It was often meant in a grudging sort of way: great man, DJ, only not in All-Ireland finals. It was a stupid assessment based purely on his scoring rate. I have no idea how much he scored from open play in finals because I never counted nor cared, either before I became manager or after I took over. The thing about DJ was that he contributed in so many ways, yet he was judged on his scorecard. What about the clever pass, the run that took two defenders with him and left another forward clear? What about the courage and the pace? There was so much to DJ's game that only fools would be critical of him. But then they, too, sometimes get an audience.

If anything, DJ was too much of a team man if, indeed, that's possible. There were times when he passed when he might have had a shot at goal, but his judgement was always based on what he saw as being right for the team. I just love watching team players in action, men who put the communal effort ahead of everything else. It's so central to Kilkenny's mission statement that I just cannot over-emphasise its importance.

If Shefflin's performance against Galway in 2007 serves as an illustration of team ethos at its most refined, another example involving a match against Galway also comes to mind in a slightly different context. The record books show that we beat them by nineteen points in the 2004 All-Ireland qualifiers in Thurles, but the score line gives a misleading impression because it wasn't until the final twenty minutes that we pulled away. Ten minutes into the second half and we were only three points up after Galway got a goal, so the game was still very much in the balance. They were going well at that stage, you could sense their confidence rising so this was definitely a crucial phase of the game.

Shortly afterwards, David Tierney made a burst towards our goal and fired in a shot, which James McGarry blocked. The ball broke and James Ryall was there to pick it up and clear. What made it interesting was that Ryall had tracked back from at least forty yards. Now, if he hadn't chased back with such urgency, Galway would almost certainly have got a goal when the ball broke into space because two of their forwards were closing in. Knowing Galway, if they had got one they would have got three and it might have been a completely different result. It was brilliant team play by Ryall and went largely unnoticed, except by those of us who had spotted where he started from and the effort he made to get back. Had Galway got a goal and Ryall had been well away from the action he wouldn't have been blamed, but his presence of mind and instinct took him right to the action. Brilliant defending!

These are the little things that can make a huge difference. It's all about looking for work wherever and whenever it arises. When that hunger for hard work begins to dissipate it's a sure sign that a player is beginning to wane. Take a half-forward/midfielder/half-back who, in his prime, was always tracking back and trying to be involved in the action as often as possible. When he begins to slip a little, his appetite for work is often the first casualty.

The biggest tell-tale sign that a player is beginning to lose his edge is when he starts to look after his own patch and loses a sense of team. He becomes cagey and plays safe and, essentially, looks out for himself. The corner-back who stays behind his man rather than sweeping out in front of him is a different man altogether from the one he was in his prime. He doesn't have the confidence any more and is hoping to limit the damage by playing goal-side of his man. It's nothing to do with fitness but rather with a fear of making mistakes.

When a forward starts going for his own scores all the time it's another giveaway sign that the edge is going. It might look good when it comes off but it's important to judge things in an overall context. The fella who scores three or four points from play isn't always the best forward, irrespective of how big the headline is the following day. If he's shooting on sight to boost his own return rather than thinking in team terms, it's time to move him on because he won't return to being a selfless team player. A manager will often be criticised for not persisting with someone who still has an eye for goal but, once he's lost the team ethic, it's all over for him. At least, it should be, because he's now on a different wavelength to the others. If that's allowed to creep in, you could soon have everybody playing a different tune and very soon the whole team is off-key.

You don't need to have studied sports psychology in detail, or indeed at all, to know that can't be allowed to happen.

CHAPTER 34

NEARLY THERE

***I certainly never thought it would turn out** anything like this when I agreed to become manager back in late 1998. With Liam McCarthy having by-passed Kilkenny since 1993, one All-Ireland was the target, at that stage – and now we're chasing four-in-a-row, and the seventh since 2000.*

Saturday, September 5, 2009: *Cut the grass today. Very relaxing. Nothing more to be done on the hurling front for now or, if there is, it's not going to happen!*

Everything has been put in place for tomorrow so, now, it's just a question of getting on with our normal routine until we meet tomorrow morning for the journey to Dublin. We've grown used to the early September booking in Croke Park, but the excitement remains the same every year we get there. So it should.

You never know when the good days will end, so it's important to make the most of them while they're here. And, in fairness to the players, they know that and really do appreciate the privileged position they enjoy.

There's a real buzz around the city and county this year, not just because of the four-in-a-row bid but also because we're playing Tipperary in the final.

The stakes couldn't possibly be higher for either county! We're on the verge of doing something really special, while Tipperary see themselves as being in with a right good chance of wrecking our plans. If the boot were on the other foot, we would love to de-rail them too! Tipperary have never won the four-in-a-row, so nothing would please them more than preventing us from reaching a peak they haven't reached.

We announced the team last night and, as usual, tough choices had to be made. 'Cha' (Fitzpatrick) and Martin (Comerford) started the semi-final against Waterford but aren't on the team for tomorrow. I don't think of it in terms of the first fifteen and the others, but the general public do, which is why team changes always make sports headlines.

To me, it's all about panel ... panel ... panel. And I have no doubt that, at various stages tomorrow, substitutes will be called upon, and will be expected to slot into the action as if they were there from the start. That's crucial, because a 'sub' is brought in for a specific reason which needs to be addressed at that particular point and not five or ten minutes later, so he has got to reach the tempo of the game very quickly.

Derek Lyng comes back in at midfield for 'Cha' while Richie Hogan gets his first start of the Championship in attack, having come on as a 'sub' against both Galway and Waterford. He had a brilliant League final against Tipperary last May, scoring 1-10, so, no doubt, people will say that he's being promoted to the starting fifteen on a horses-for-courses basis.

Not so. That was four months ago and has no direct relevance now. He's in because he has been going extremely well in training. So has Derek. You can't hold lads back when they're as ready as this pair are.

It's tough on 'Cha' and Martin to lose out, but they've taken it like the real men they are and will be ready if called in tomorrow. 'Cha' has had a tough year ever since he got the mumps back in the spring. There has been lots of speculation that we were going to start Noel Hickey for what would be his first game with us since last year's All-Ireland final but, unfortunately for him, it just hasn't worked out.

Nobody has put in more effort but he just hasn't had enough competitive hurling. I feel sorry for him – and, indeed, the other lads who haven't made the team – but we're in the fortunate position of having so many excellent players to choose from that some are bound to be disappointed.

The great thing is that they react so maturely. That's what makes this squad work so well. Michael Fennelly hasn't got a start since the Galway game in June, but he has continued to be a terrific captain, driving things on as much as he can. He's going very well at present and will probably get a run tomorrow, depending on our requirements. If he does, I'm sure he'll deliver.

The build-up has gone very much to plan. By now, we know exactly how to pace the weeks to ensure we get the most out of them. It's all about keeping fellas fresh and getting them to the starting line in the best shape possible, both physically and mentally.

It has been a great year so far. We won the Walsh Cup and the National League, and have reached the All-Ireland final after three, straight wins. The only defeat we suffered all year was against Waterford in the League in Walsh Park on the first Sunday in March so, clearly, ambitions have remained very much intact.

We'll need everything working at full power tomorrow because Tipperary are ready to hit us with one mighty effort.

It's incredible to think that we are heading into our eighth All-Ireland final this decade, and chasing our seventh title. If we reach that target, all seven will have been won directly through the Leinster Championship and won't have involved the 'back door'. That makes it all the more special.

I certainly never thought it would turn out anything like this when I agreed to become manager back in late 1998. With Liam McCarthy having by-passed Kilkenny since 1993, one All-Ireland was the target, at that stage – and now we're chasing four-in-a-row, and the seventh since 2000.

Will we do it? I have a good feeling. I haven't seen a single sign among the panel that they have lost anything in terms of drive and ambition. On the contrary, they are more committed than ever. As for talent, we're not short there. Now, we must bring it all together for another big day in Croke Park.

We can't wait.

Diary: Monday, September 7 ...

CHAPTER 35

VIEW FROM THE SUMMIT

It's difficult to take it all in today. There's a *sense of joy and relief among all Kilkenny people as this team has now achieved something none of their predecessors ever did. That such an incredible peak was reached by beating Tipperary, in a high-quality final, adds to the intense satisfaction.*

Monday, September 7, 2009: *This is as good as it gets. Well, for now anyway. We've won another All-Ireland title and, while they're all special, this one is magical beyond words. Four-in-a-row! 2006-2007-2008-2009. Unthinkable!*

We can call it by its name, now, because it's real. All year, we kept hearing and reading about the four-in-a-row, but we didn't mention it or dwell on it among ourselves. All campaigns are built game by game. Walsh Cup, National League, Leinster Championship, All-Ireland Championship.

You don't look beyond the next game, or back to the last one. Others could talk of the historical dimension of what Kilkenny were trying to achieve, but we had to keep our eyes fixed firmly on the next ball rather than on the four-in-a-row. As for the previous successes of this decade, they were gone. The lads might re-visit them in years to come but, for now, the past had to be neatly stored away, because it wasn't relevant to what we were trying to achieve.

The past certainly wasn't going to help us around 4.50 pm yesterday afternoon when the Croke Park scoreboard read: Tipperary 0-20, Kilkenny 0-17. What was that about Kilkenny being at a different level to the rest of the hurling world? We didn't start that daft talk or contribute to it in any way, but it's been out there for some time and had taken on a life of its own after last year's All-Ireland final.

The reality, yesterday, was that when we fell three points behind, around the hour mark, we were facing an unbelievable test of character. This was now a contest between equals, locked in battle and stretching every sinew, in an effort to gain an inch.

We were playing an extremely good Tipperary team, one that had risen magnificently to what was, for most of them, their first senior All-Ireland final. And while they were a man down after Benny Dunne's dismissal, they didn't allow it to disrupt them. On the contrary, it was as if they embraced adversity and set about harnessing it for their own gain.

As happens so often in these circumstances, Tipperary made light of the handicap by working even harder than they had been doing up to then. And, since their work ethic had been phenomenal all day, that was really saying something. The sides had been level on eleven separate occasions, the last being when Henry Shefflin pointed a free after Dunne's dismissal.

Then, in a burst of productivity, Tipperary scored three unanswered points to open up what was the biggest lead up to then. Was this the decisive break? Tipperary people probably felt that it was, and their players would also have been feeling very good about themselves.

Was I concerned? Of course, but, at the same time, I had huge faith in our players. Over the years, their response to the big challenge has always been to take it on with courage, genuineness and conviction. A flick here, a touch there, a block somewhere: drive on and see what happens. And, when the opportunity presents itself, make it count.

Ours came in the form of a penalty awarded for a foul on Richie Power. I don't care whether it was inside or outside the square – the referee awarded it, and his is the only opinion that counts. Had it been at the other end we would have had to accept it, too. Such are the tiny margins in such a tight contest.

Once again, Henry was thrust centre stage. There isn't a guy on earth you'd want more than Henry Shefflin in that situation. The pressure on him was absolutely enormous, but you could tell from his demeanour before he took the penalty that he had everything sorted out neatly in his head. He was cool and concentrated, making sure that he did everything right to give himself the best possible chance of scoring a goal.

The strike was good, the goal was scored and, suddenly, we were in the lead. A minute later and we were four points clear when Martin Comerford finished a move with a trademark goal. It reminded me of the crucial goal he scored against Cork in the 2003 All-Ireland final – he'd started that final, unlike yesterday when he came on as a sub around the three-quarter mark.

We also sent on TJ Reid and Michael Fennelly, and the response from all three was brilliant. They switched straight on to the pace and tempo of a high-intensity game and, for good measure, they all scored. Martin has been scoring that type of goal for years but, few can have been more crucial that this one as it gave us an advantage we weren't going to surrender over the closing minutes.

Martin would have been disappointed not to be on the starting team but, when his chance came, he took it – brilliantly. Despite not starting, he will always look back on this game with the special sense of achievement that scoring a goal in an All-Ireland final engenders. Martin and Noel Hickey spoke in the dressing room before the game, which is another example of the quality of leaders we have on our panel.

Neither Martin nor Noel would be starting but, in a squad sense, that didn't matter. They – and the other subs – were just as important as the lads who started. Everybody appreciates that. You couldn't buy that sort of spirit and unity and, as manager, I feel privileged to be part of it. It has made Kilkenny what we have been over the last decade.

It's a fabulous feeling to have won yesterday, not just because it completes the four-in-a-row but, also, because it shows exactly what this group of Kilkenny hurlers are all about, both as individuals and as a group. They scored 2-3 in the last seven or eight minutes yesterday, which answered a lot of questions about their ability to keep on striving for more success.

Everybody knows that the day will come when Kilkenny will be beaten, but we're trying to postpone it for as long as we possibly can. We're not using any magic formula, but simply continuing to work off a basic honesty that remains the glue in the entire project. We haven't been beaten in the Championship since the 2005 All-Ireland semi-final, when we lost to Galway and, when I look back on what happened immediately after that amazing game, it makes me laugh. We were reliably informed by a whole range of 'experts' that we were heading into a transition phase from which we would take quite a long time to emerge.

Some transition! Eighteen straight Championship wins, four All-Ireland, four Leinster and two National League titles in four seasons. Thank God, we didn't listen to the prophets of doom. We were told, quite regularly, too, that we had a handy run towards All-Ireland finals on the basis that Leinster wasn't competitive. I have never bought into that – and certainly not this year once Galway arrived from across the Shannon.

How many counties would fancy drawing Galway in the first round of the Championship? I've made the point repeatedly that, if we hadn't been ready for every game, we would have been beaten, and that certainly applied on that June evening in Tullamore against Galway. The idea that we could stroll through Leinster and peak for August and September is totally off the mark, but it's still being sold by some people. Will they ever learn?

We beat Galway, Dublin and Waterford to reach yesterday's final, and if we hadn't got ourselves right for each game we would have been caught. Given Tipperary's rate of progress over the last two seasons, there was every chance we would be meeting them in an All-Ireland final, and an even greater likelihood that it would be a massive battle.

The National League final in May proved just how competitive they were, and it was the same yesterday. We weathered a lot of storms in the first half to secure a two point lead at half-time: I was happy enough with that. Tipperary put it up to us in exactly the way we thought they would, but we still led at half-time. We had also created two goal chances which didn't yield anything, but at least it showed that we were capable of making things happen around the Tipperary goal.

Tipperary came into that game with a great reputation as goal scorers, having put a total of fourteen past Cork, Clare, Waterford and Limerick, so it was always likely they would create a few chances against us – which they did in the second half. Cometh the hour, cometh the man! PJ Ryan's saves were quite spectacular but, to be honest, that's what we would expect of him.

He is an outstanding goalkeeper, just as James McGarry was before him. Everybody saw PJ in his true light yesterday, and he is now a shoo-in for an All Star award. At least, I presume he is, but you never know. McGarry went through his career without getting an All Star, so consistent excellence and a serious knowledge and understanding of the goalkeeping craft guarantee you nothing when it comes to the All Stars.

Hell, no Kilkenny goalkeeper has won an All Star since Michael Walsh in 1993. How mad is that? That particular run is surely about to end.

PJ really enjoyed himself yesterday. Goalkeepers love making saves like those, even if they like to give out to their backs for putting them in that position in the first place. Shot-stopping is a major part of the goalkeeping craft and, while I would have been much happier if PJ hadn't had to touch the ball all day, I'd no doubt he would be ready if, and when, the tests came. And boy, did they come, but we managed to hold out which was crucial in determining the second-half pattern.

The end result was that we didn't concede any goals: ironically, that's something we didn't manage against Limerick or Waterford in the last two All-Ireland finals, which we won much more easily.

The amount of success we have enjoyed throughout this decade is outrageous. We know that, but we never take it for granted, nor have we ever, once, shown a lack of respect to any opposition. It's not how we do things, so it's disappointing that there seems to be an agenda out there among some people to do us down.

All we're striving towards is to be the best we can be, for as long as we can. When we lose, we don't complain and, when we win, we don't gloat. Still, we've been the target for some pretty snide comments, ranging from claims that we haven't been refereed "by the book" (whatever that means) since the 2007 National League final, to references that we engage in "pulling and dragging".

I have to say, I find that sort of stuff disgusting. Referees are only human and, if they keep hearing and reading about how our game is "on the edge", it's not easy for them to ignore. Look back on the free count in our games, and I think you'll find we don't tend to pick them up very easily.

It was 19-8 for Tipperary yesterday and, while I'm not complaining because I leave referees to get on with their job, it's an interesting statistic. For all that, it was Tipperary who had a man sent off. These things happen, but cast your mind back to the immediate aftermath when Tommy Walsh went down.

He had taken a heavy wallop but he was back up on his feet in seconds. There were no theatrics and there was no attempt to put pressure on the referee to send off Benny Dunne. It was up to Diarmuid Kirwan to make his decision based on what he had seen, and Tommy wanted no part in it. It was real manly stuff, yet here is a guy who has been vilified all year. As I've written throughout this book, this has really annoyed me and brings no credit to those who are trying to depict Tommy as something he's not. There's nothing wrong with hurling as played by Tommy Walsh. In fact, he epitomises the very best of what it's about so, instead of experimenting with new rules which detract from the game, we should be holding Tommy up as a role model for how the game should be played.

I know that I'm looking back on yesterday's final with rose-tinted glasses but, if it's an indication of where the standard of hurling stands at present, then it's in a pretty good place. That was a smashing contest in so many ways and, of course, it had a special resonance for Kilkenny people beacuse beating Tipperary in an All-Ireland final is new territory for this team.

It means that we have beaten all five Munster powers – Cork, Tipperary, Limerick, Clare and Waterford – in All-Ireland finals, since 2000. Finishing the decade with a win over Tipperary was the perfect scenario for a squad that simply won't take "no" for an answer.

They're caught up in something that nobody could have envisaged happening a few years ago. Winning one All-Ireland takes a huge effort, but to retain it not once, not twice, but three times, is almost beyond belief.

It's difficult to take it all in today. There's a sense of joy and relief among all Kilkenny people as this team has now achieved something none of their predecessors ever did. That such an incredible peak was reached by beating Tipperary, in a high-quality final, adds to the intense satisfaction.

Let's just enjoy it. The past brought us to where we are, the future is out there, but doesn't have to be addressed just yet. Kilkenny hurling is in previously unexplored territory, so let's get used to our new surroundings. Right now, the view from the peak is absolutely spectacular.

STATISTICS
THE CODY YEARS

EARLY DAYS, HEAVY LIFTING

At the end of it all, I was left facing the unquestionable truth – that I had failed my first All-Ireland test as a manager. Already, the pressure was increasing. Fail in 2000, and my days as Kilkenny manager would probably be over.

Kilkenny 6-21 Laois 1-14, Croke Park (Leinster semi-final)

Kilkenny: James McGarry; Tom Hickey, Canice Brennan, Willie O'Connor; Michael Kavanagh (0-1), Eamonn Kennedy, Peter Barry; Denis Byrne, Andy Comerford (1-0); DJ Carey (2-3), John Power (1-1), Brian McEvoy (0-2); Ken O'Shea (2-1), Henry Shefflin (0-10), Charlie Carter (0-3).
Subs: John Costello for Kennedy, PJ Delaney for McEvoy, Niall Moloney for Carey.

Laois: Ricky Cashin; PJ Peacock, Bill Maher, Seamus Dooley; Darren Rooney, Paul Cuddy, Andy Bergin; Declan Conroy (0-1), Cyril Cuddy; Eamonn Fennelly (0-1), Niall Rigney (1-8), David Cuddy (0-1); Donal Russell, John Shortall (0-1), Fionan O'Sullivan (0-2).
Sub: Nicholas Lacey for Fennelly.

Kilkenny 5-14 Offaly 1-16, Croke Park (Leinster final)

Kilkenny: James McGarry; Tom Hickey, Canice Brennan, Willie O'Connor; Michael Kavanagh, Eamonn Kennedy, Paddy Mullally; Andy Comerford (0-1), Denis Byrne; DJ Carey (2-3), John Power, Brian McEvoy (1-1); Ken O'Shea, Henry Shefflin (1-6), Charlie Carter (1-3).
Sub: Niall Moloney for Power.

Offaly: Stephen Byrne; Simon Whelahan, Kevin Kinahan, Martin Hanamy; Brian Whelahan (0-3), Hubert Rigney, Kevin Martin; Johnny Pilkington (1-3), Paudie Mulhare (0-2); Johnny Dooley (0-5), John Ryan, Joe Dooley; Billy Dooley, John Troy (0-2), Michael Duignan (0-1).
Subs: Joe Errity for Billy Dooley, Daithi Regan for Joe Dooley, Ger Oakley for Errity.

Kilkenny 2-14 Clare 1-13, Croke Park (All-Ireland semi-final)

Kilkenny: James McGarry; Philip Larkin, Canice Brennan, Willie O'Connor; Michael Kavanagh, Pat O'Neill (0-1), Peter Barry; Andy Comerford (0-1), Denis Byrne; DJ Carey (1-3), John Power (0-2), Brian McEvoy (0-4); Ken O'Shea (1-0), Henry Shefflin (0-3), Charlie Carter.
Subs: Niall Moloney for O'Shea, PJ Delaney for Carter.

Clare: Davy Fitzgerald; Brian Quinn, Brian Lohan, Frank Lohan; Liam Doyle, Sean McMahon, Anthony Daly (0-1); Ollie Baker, Colin Lynch; Jamesie O'Connor (0-5), Conor Clancy, PJ O'Connell (0-1); David Forde (0-1), Niall Gilligan (0-3), Alan Markham (0-1).
Subs: Stephen McNamara (1-0) for Forde, Barry Murphy for Clancy, Enda Flannery (0-1) for O'Connell.

Cork 0-13 Kilkenny 0-12, Croke Park (All-Ireland final)

Cork: Donal Og Cusack; Fergal Ryan, Diarmuid O'Sullivan, John Browne; Wayne Sherlock, Brian Corcoran, Sean Og O hAilpin; Mark Landers (capt) (0-1), Mickey O'Connell; Timmy McCarthy (0-3), Fergal McCormack, Neil Ronan; Seanie McGrath (0-3), Joe Deane (0-3), Ben O'Connor (0-1).
Subs: Alan Browne (0-1) for Ronan, Kevin Murray (0-1) for Landers.

Kilkenny: James McGarry; Philip Larkin, Canice Brennan, Willie O'Connor; Michael Kavanagh, Pat O'Neill, Peter Barry; Andy Comerford (0-2), Denis Byrne (0-1) (captain); DJ Carey, John Power (0-1), Brian McEvoy (0-1); Ken O'Shea, Henry Shefflin (0-5), Charlie Carter (0-2).
Subs: Niall Moloney for O'Shea; PJ Delaney for Carter.

National Hurling League
Cork 0-14 Kilkenny 1-9, Kilkenny 2-15 Laois 0-16, Kilkenny 1-16 Waterford 1-12, Kilkenny 3-14 Tipperary 1-13, Kilkenny 2-20 Down 0-14, Kilkenny 3-12 Wexford 3-8, Galway 2-15 Kilkenny 1-15 (semi-final).

League and Championship
Played 11: Won 8, Lost 3.

Titles: Leinster.

MILLENNIUM MAGIC

There were whispers about how we had won the All-Ireland without beating any Munster opposition, but that wasn't our fault. Would Cork or Tipperary have done better against us than Galway or Offaly? I don't know, and I don't care. Results don't lie. I said it a year earlier when Cork beat us in the final and the same applied in 2000 when we won.

Kilkenny 3-16 Dublin 0-10, Croke Park (Leinster semi-final)

Kilkenny: James McGarry; Philly Larkin, Sean Meally, Noel Hickey; Michael Kavanagh, Eamonn Kennedy (0-2), Peter Barry; Paddy Mullally (0-1), Denis Byrne; Henry Shefflin (0-6), Stephen Grehan (0-2), Brian McEvoy (0-1); Charlie Carter (2-3), DJ Carey (0-1), Eddie Brennan (1-0).
Subs: John Power for Byrne, Jimmy Coogan for Brennan, John Paul Corcoran for Carter, Aidan Cummins for Barry.

Dublin: Brendan McLoughlin; John Finnegan, Sean Power, Conor McCann; Dave Sweeney, Stephen Perkins, Liam Walsh; Mick Fitzsimons (0-1), Shane Martin (0-1); Gordon Glynn, Diarmuid McInerney, Damien Russell (0-2); Tomas McGrane (0-4), Sean Duignan (0-2), David Henry.
Subs: Ger Ennis for Fitzsimons, Darragh Spain for Perkins, Derek McMullan for Glynn, Liam O'Donoghue for McInerney.

Kilkenny 2-21 Offaly 1-13, Croke Park (Leinster final)

Kilkenny: James McGarry; Michael Kavanagh, Noel Hickey, Willie O'Connor; Philip Larkin, Eamonn Kennedy, Peter Barry; Andy Comerford (0-1), Brian McEvoy (0-1); Stephen Grehan (0-3), John Power (0-1), Denis Byrne (0-2); Charlie Carter (1-4), DJ Carey (1-3), Henry Shefflin (0-6).
Subs: Aidan Cummins for Comerford, John Hoyne for Power, Eddie Brennan for Shefflin.

Offaly: Stephen Byrne; Simon Whelahan, Kevin Kinahan, Niall Claffey; Barry Whelahan, Brian Whelahan, Kevin Martin; Johnny Dooley (0-5), Johnny Pilkington; Paudie Mulhare, Gary Hanniffy (0-3), Brendan Murphy (0-4); Michael Duignan (0-1), Joe Errity, Joe Dooley (1-0).
Subs: Aidan Hanrahan for Duignan, John Troy for Errity, David Franks for Mulhare, John Ryan for Pilkington.

Kilkenny 2-19 Galway 0-17, Croke Park (All-Ireland semi-final)

Kilkenny: James McGarry; Michael Kavanagh, Noel Hickey, Willie O'Connor; Philip Larkin, Eamonn Kennedy, Peter Barry; Andy Comerford (1-0), Brian McEvoy; Denis Byrne (0-8), John Power (0-1), Stephen Grehan; Charlie Carter (0-1), DJ Carey (1-2), Henry Shefflin (0-7).
Sub: John Paul Corcoran for Grehan.

Galway: Michael Crimmins; Liam Hodgins, Brian Feeney, Ollie Canning; Finbar Gantley, Cathal Moore; Paul Hardiman; David Tierney (0-1), Rory Gantley (0-4); Joe Rabbitte, Mark Kerins, Alan Kerins (0-5); Fergal Healy (0-1), Ollie Fahy (0-1), Eugene Cloonan (0-5).
Subs: Kevin Broderick for Kerins, Brian Higgins for Hardiman, Vinnie Maher for Hodgins, Joe Cooney for Healy.

Kilkenny 5-15 Offaly 1-14, Croke Park (All-Ireland final)

Kilkenny: James McGarry; Michael Kavanagh, Noel Hickey, Willie O'Connor (captain); Philip Larkin, Eamonn Kennedy, Peter Barry; Andy Comerford (0-1), Brian McEvoy; Denis Byrne (0-4), John Power, John Hoyne; Charlie Carter (1-3), DJ Carey (2-4), Henry Shefflin (1-3).
Subs: Canice Brennan (1-0) for McEvoy, Eddie Brennan for Canice Brennan.

Offaly: Stephen Byrne; Simon Whelahan, Kevin Kinahan, Niall Claffey; Brian Whelahan (0-1), Joe Errity, Kevin Martin; Johnny Dooley (0-8), Ger Oakley; Johnny Pilkington (1-1), Gary Hanniffy (0-1), Brendan Murphy (0-1); Michael Duignan, John Ryan, Joe Dooley (0-1).
Subs: David Franks for Claffey; John Troy for Ryan; Paudie Mulhare (0-1) for Murphy.

National Hurling League
Kilkenny 1-13 Cork 0-12, Kilkenny 3-20 Laois 0-9, Waterford 1-15 Kilkenny 1-13, Kilkenny 2-14 Tipperary 2-9, Kilkenny 3-12 Derry 1-9, Wexford 3-14 Kilkenny 2-11.

League and Championship
Played 10: Won 8, Lost 2. **Titles: All-Ireland and Leinster.**

CRASH LANDING

Somewhere along the line, the standards that we had carefully set together had dropped. Without realising it, we had gone a little soft. We were one grand, happy bunch who had won the All-Ireland a year earlier and, as we discovered in the most painful manner imaginable, the day you get cosy is the day you hit the wall.

Kilkenny 3-21 Offaly 0-18, Croke Park (Leinster semi-final)

Kilkenny: James McGarry; Michael Kavanagh, Noel Hickey, JJ Delaney; Philip Larkin (0-1), Eamonn Kennedy (0-2), Peter Barry; Andy Comerford (0-1), Canice Brennan; Denis Byrne, John Power (0-2), John Hoyne (1-0); Charlie Carter (0-6), DJ Carey (0-1), Henry Shefflin (1-6).
Subs: Eddie Brennan (1-2) for Power, Brian McEvoy for Canice Brennan, Stephen Grehan for Byrne, Derek Lyng for Barry, Jimmy Coogan for Carter.

Offaly: Stephen Byrne; Simon Whelahan, Kevin Kinahan, Hubert Rigney; Brian Whelahan, Joe Errity (0-1), Kevin Martin; Barry Whelahan, Johnny Pilkington; Johnny Dooley (0-9), Gary Hanniffy (0-1), Ger Oakley; Rory Hanniffy (0-2), John Troy (0-2), Brendan Murphy (0-2).
Subs: Joe Brady for Oakley; Colm Cassidy (0-1) for Troy.

Kilkenny 2-19 Wexford 0-12, Croke Park (Leinster final)

Kilkenny: James McGarry; Michael Kavanagh, Noel Hickey, JJ Delaney; Philip Larkin, Eamonn Kennedy, Sean Dowling; Andy Comerford, Canice Brennan (0-2); Denis Byrne, John Hoyne (0-1), Brian McEvoy (0-4); Charlie Carter (0-7), DJ Carey (1-0), Henry Shefflin (0-4).
Subs: Eddie Brennan (1-0) for Byrne, Stephen Grehan (0-1) for Carter.

Wexford: Damien Fitzhenry; Colm Kehoe, Darragh Ryan, Sean Flood; Declan Ruth, Liam Dunne, Larry O'Gorman; Adrian Fenlon, 'Mitch' Jordan (0-1); Darren Stamp (0-2), Larry Murphy (0-1), Ryan Quigley (0-1); Rory McCarthy, Paul Codd (0-5), Barry Goff (0-1).
Subs: Martin Byrne for Murphy, Rory Mallon for Kehoe, Murphy for Quigley, Garry Laffan for Goff, Trevor Kelly (0-1) for Fenlon.

Galway 2-15 Kilkenny 1-13, Croke Park (All-Ireland semi-final)

Galway: Michael Crimmins; Gregory Kennedy, Michael Healy, Ollie Canning; Derek Hardiman, Liam Hodgins, Cathal Moore; David Tierney, Richie Murray (0-1); Alan Kerins, Mark Kerins (0-1), Kevin Broderick (0-2); Joe Rabbitte (0-1), Eugene Cloonan (2-9), Fergal Healy.
Sub: Brian Higgins (0-1) for Fergal Healy.

Kilkenny: James McGarry; Michael Kavanagh, Noel Hickey, JJ Delaney; Philip Larkin, Eamonn Kennedy, Peter Barry; Andy Comerford, Brian McEvoy; John Hoyne, John Power (0-2), Stephen Grehan; Charlie Carter (0-1), DJ Carey (1-1), Henry Shefflin (0-9).
Subs: Eddie Brennan for McEvoy, Denis Byrne for Comerford.

National Hurling League
Kilkenny 3-16 Laois 0-11, Kilkenny 2-14 Waterford 0-8, Cork 1-10 Kilkenny 0-12, Kilkenny 1-12 Tipperary 0-15, Kilkenny 2-20 Derry 1-7, Kilkenny 0-19 Wexford 0-16, Clare 2-21 Kilkenny 3-8 (semi-final).

League and Championship
Played 10: Won 6, Drew 1, Lost 3. **Titles: Leinster.**

TITLE TREATS

We started with a clean slate after 2001 and built a team from the bottom up, not from the top down. If we weren't good enough in 2001 we wouldn't be good enough in 2002, unless we made some adjustments.

Kilkenny 2-20 Offaly 1-14, Thurles (Leinster semi-final)

Kilkenny: James McGarry; Michael Kavanagh, Noel Hickey, Philip Larkin; Richie Mullally, Peter Barry, JJ Delaney; Derek Lyng (0-1), Pat Tennyson (0-1); John Hoyne (1-0), Henry Shefflin (0-11), Andy Comerford; Eddie Brennan (1-1), Martin Comerford, Stephen Grehan.
Subs: Brian McEvoy (0-2) for Tennyson, Charlie Carter (0-4) for Grehan, Brian Dowling for Brennan.

Offaly: Stephen Byrne; Mick O'Hara, Joe Errity, JP O'Meara; Joe Brady, Brian Whelahan, Niall Claffey; Barry Whelahan, Hubert Rigney; Gary Hanniffy, Kevin Martin, Brendan Murphy (1-2); Rory Hanniffy (0-1), Stephen Brown (0-2), Simon Whelahan (0-7).
Subs: Brian Carroll (0-2) for Martin, Damien Murray for Brown, John Ryan for Murray.

Kilkenny 0-19 Wexford 0-17, Croke Park (Leinster final)

Kilkenny: James McGarry; Michael Kavanagh, Noel Hickey, Philip Larkin; Richie Mullally (0-2), Peter Barry, JJ Delaney; Derek Lyng (0-2), Andy Comerford; John Hoyne, Henry Shefflin (0-8), Brian McEvoy (0-4); Eddie Brennan (0-2), Martin Comerford, Charlie Carter.
Subs: Stephen Grehan for Carter, Alan Geoghegan for Andy Comerford, Sean Dowling for Larkin, Brian Dowling (0-1) for Brennan..

Wexford: Damien Fitzhenry; Colm Kehoe, Darragh Ryan, 'Doc' O'Connor; Darren Stamp, Declan Ruth, Liam Dunne; Rory Mallon, MJ Furlong (0-1); Rory McCarthy, Larry Murphy (0-1), Paul Codd (0-13); Barry Lambert (0-1), Larry O'Gorman, 'Mitch' Jordan (0-1).
Subs: Nicky Lambert for Murphy, Rory Jacob for O'Gorman.

Kilkenny 1-20 Tipperary 1-16, Croke Park (All-Ireland semi-final)

Kilkenny: James McGarry; Michael Kavanagh, Noel Hickey, Philip Larkin; Richie Mullally, Peter Barry, JJ Delaney; Andy Comerford (0-2), Derek Lyng (0-2); John Hoyne (0-1), Henry Shefflin (0-7), Brian McEvoy; Eddie Brennan (0-1), Martin Comerford (0-1), DJ Carey (0-4).
Subs: Charlie Carter (0-1) for Brennan, Jimmy Coogan (1-1) for McEvoy.

Tipperary: Brendan Cummins; Thomas Costello, Philip Maher, Paul Ormond; Noel Morris, Eamonn Corcoran (0-1), Paul Kelly (0-3); Tommy Dunne (0-1), Eddie Enright; Mark O'Leary (0-3), John Carroll (1-0), Brian O'Meara (0-1); Eoin Kelly (0-4), Eugene O'Neill (0-2), Benny Dunne.
Subs: Conor Gleeson for Enright, Lar Corbett for Benny Dunne, John O'Brien (0-1) for O'Neill.

Kilkenny 2-20 Clare 0-19, Croke Park (All-Ireland final)

Kilkenny: James McGarry; Michael Kavanagh, Noel Hickey, Philip Larkin; Richie Mullally, Peter Barry, JJ Delaney; Andy Comerford (captain) (0-1), Derek Lyng (0-1); John Hoyne, Henry Shefflin (1-7), Jimmy Coogan (0-1); Eddie Brennan (0-1), Martin Comerford (0-1), DJ Carey (1-6).
Subs: Charlie Carter (0-1) for Coogan, Brian McEvoy (0-1) for Hoyne, John Power for Brennan.

Clare: Davy Fitzgerald; Brian Quinn, Brian Lohan, Frank Lohan; David Hoey, Sean McMahon (0-6), Gerry Quinn; John Reddan, Colin Lynch (0-2); Jamesie O'Connor (0-4), Tony Griffin (0-1), Alan Markham; Tony Carmody, Niall Gilligan (0-2), David Forde.
Subs: Ollie Baker (0-1) for Reddan, Gearoid Considine (0-2) for Forde, Andrew Quinn (0-1) for Markham, Conor Plunkett for Baker.

National Hurling League
Kilkenny 1-12 Waterford 0-12, Galway 0-15 Kilkenny 0-9, Kilkenny 2-22 Meath 0-9, Kilkenny 3-14 Clare 2-12, Kilkenny 3-18 Dublin 0-8, Kilkenny 2-14 Limerick 0-15, Kilkenny 2-15 Cork 2-14 (final).

League and Championship
Played 11: Won 10, Lost 1.

Titles: All-Ireland, Leinster and National League.

ANOTHER CLEAN SWEEP

DJ Carey was captain, which was entirely appropriate given how much he had contributed to Kilkenny for so long. I'll make no apologies for saying that I was delighted DJ got a chance to captain the team to an All-Ireland win, because he deserved it.

Kilkenny 3-16 Dublin 0-10, Nowlan Park (Leinster semi-final)

Kilkenny: PJ Ryan; Michael Kavanagh, Noel Hickey, JJ Delaney; Richie Mullally (0-2), Peter Barry, Aidan Cummins; Derek Lyng, Pat Tennyson; Conor Phelan (1-0), Henry Shefflin (1-4), Tommy Walsh (0-5); DJ Carey (0-2), Martin Comerford (0-3), Eddie Brennan (1-0).
Subs: John Hoyne for Lyng, Walter Burke for Cummins.

Dublin: Brendan McLoughlin; Philip Brennan, Stephen Perkins, Darragh Spain; Stephen Hiney (0-1), Kevin Ryan, Derek O'Reilly; David Sweeney, Carl Meehan; Conal Keaney (0-2), Shane Martin (0-1), Kevin Flynn (0-2); Tomas McGrane (0-4), Keith Horgan, Ger Ennis.
Subs: Tommy Moore for O'Reilly, Damien Russell for Horgan, Michael Carton for Ennis, Ronan Fallon for Meehan, John McGuirk for McGrane.

Kilkenny 2-23 Wexford 2-12, Croke Park (Leinster final)

Kilkenny: James McGarry; Michael Kavanagh, Noel Hickey, James Ryall; Sean Dowling (0-2), Peter Barry, JJ Delaney; Derek Lyng (0-3), Conor Phelan (0-1); John Hoyne, Henry Shefflin (1-8), Tommy Walsh (0-3); DJ Carey (0-3), Martin Comerford (0-2), Eddie Brennan (1-1).
Subs: None.

Wexford: Damien Fitzhenry; Colm Kehoe, Darragh Ryan, 'Doc' O'Connor; Keith Rossiter, Declan Ruth, Liam Dunne; Adrian Fenlon (0-1), Darren Stamp (0-1); Rory McCarthy, Donal Berry, 'Mitch' Jordan (0-1); Barry Lambert (1-1), Paul Codd (0-4), Rory Jacob (0-1).
Subs: Barry Goff (0-1) for McCarthy, Michael Jacob (0-2) for Berry, Chris McGrath (1-0) for Jordan, Tomas Mahon for Rossiter.

Kilkenny 3-18 Tipperary 0-15, Croke Park (All-Ireland semi-final)

Kilkenny: James McGarry; Michael Kavanagh, Noel Hickey, James Ryall; Sean Dowling, Peter Barry, JJ Delaney; Derek Lyng (0-2), Paddy Mullally; John Hoyne (0-1), Henry Shefflin (1-7), Tommy Walsh (1-0); DJ Carey (0-3), Martin Comerford, Eddie Brennan (1-4).
Sub: Jimmy Coogan (0-1) for Walsh..

Tipperary: Brendan Cummins; Thomas Costello, Paul Curran, Martin Maher; Eamonn Corcoran, Tommy Dunne, Paul Kelly (0-1); Benny Dunne, Eddie Enright (0-1); Mark O'Leary, Conor Gleeson (0-2), John Carroll (0-1); Eoin Kelly (0-8), Lar Corbett, Brian O'Meara (0-1).
Subs: Noel Morris for Corbett, Paddy O'Brien (0-1) for O'Leary, Brian Horgan for Enright, David Kennedy for Costello, Eoin Brislane for Tommy Dunne..

Kilkenny 1-14 Cork 1-11, Croke Park (All-Ireland final)

Kilkenny: James McGarry; Michael Kavanagh, Noel Hickey, James Ryall; Sean Dowling, Peter Barry, JJ Delaney; Derek Lyng (0-1), Paddy Mullally; Henry Shefflin (0-6), John Hoyne, Tommy Walsh (0-3); DJ Carey (captain), Martin Comerford (1-4), Eddie Brennan.
Subs: Conor Phelan for Walsh, Andy Comerford for Ryall, Richie Mullally for Paddy Mullally, Jimmy Coogan for Brennan.

Cork: Donal Og Cusack; Wayne Sherlock, Diarmuid O'Sullivan, Pat Mulcahy; Tom Kenny, Ronan Curran, Sean Og O'hAilpin; John Gardiner, Mickey O'Connell; Ben O'Connor (0-1), Niall McCarthy (0-2), Timmy McCarthy (0-1); Setanta O'hAilpin (1-0), Joe Deane (0-5), Alan Browne.
Subs: Jerry O'Connor (0-1) for O'Connell; Seanie McGrath (0-1) for O'Connor.

National Hurling League
Kilkenny 4-11 Waterford 0-12, Kilkenny 0-20 Galway 1-12, Kilkenny 1-17 Laois 1-8, Kilkenny 2-22 Clare 1-13, Kilkenny 2-22 Dublin 2-8, Tipperary 2-19 Kilkenny 2-16, Kilkenny 4-17 Cork 3-12, Kilkenny 0-23 Wexford 2-17, Kilkenny 5-14 Tipperary 5-13 (final)

League and Championship
Played 13: Won 11, Drew 1, Lost 1. **Titles: All-Ireland, Leinster and National League.**

BLANKS ALL ROUND

We lost by eight points which, apparently, was the biggest defeat suffered by Kilkenny in an All-Ireland final since 1964. That's hurling for you. You go into Croke Park chasing an All-Ireland treble and leave with the biggest trimming for forty years. Crazy game, this.

Wexford 2-15 Kilkenny 1-16, Croke Park (Leinster semi-final)

Kilkenny: James McGarry; Michael Kavanagh, Noel Hickey, JJ Delaney; Sean Dowling (0-2), Peter Barry, Brian Hogan; Derek Lyng, Pat Tennyson (0-1); John Hoyne (0-1), Henry Shefflin (0-5), Tommy Walsh (0-2); Eddie Brennan (1-1), Martin Comerford (0-2), Jimmy Coogan (0-1).
Subs: DJ Carey (0-1) for Coogan, Aidan Fogarty for Hoyne.

Wexford: Damien Fitzhenry; 'Doc' O'Connor, Darragh Ryan, Malachy Travers; John O'Connor, Declan Ruth, Rory McCarthy; Adrian Fenlon (0-1), Tomas Mahon; Barry Lambert (0-4), Eoin Quigley (0-1), Paul Carley (0-3); 'Mitch' Jordan (0-3), Michael Jacob (1-2), Rory Jacob (1-1).
Subs: Larry Murphy for Lambert, Paul Codd for Mahon, Colm Kehoe for Ryan.

Kilkenny 4-22 Dublin 0-8, Dr Cullen Park (All-Ireland Qualifier)

Kilkenny: James McGarry; Mark Phelan, Noel Hickey, Tommy Walsh; Richie Mullally, Peter Barry, JJ Delaney; Derek Lyng (0-1), Ken Coogan; Martin Comerford (0-2), Jimmy Coogan (1-2), Eddie Brennan (1-3); Aidan Fogarty, DJ Carey (0-4), Henry Shefflin (2-8).
Subs: 'Cha' Fitzpatrick (0-1) for Fogarty, John Maher (0-1) for Carey, James Ryall for Barry, Sean Dowling for Lyng, Conor Phelan for Brennan.

Dublin: Gary Maguire; Philip Brennan, Stephen Perkins, Simon Daly; Stephen Hiney, Ronan Fallon (0-1), Kevin Ryan; Aodhan de Paor (0-3), Carl Meehan; Sean O'Shea (0-1), Gearoid Keogh, Sean McCann; David O'Callaghan (0-2), Michael Carton, Padraig Fleury.
Subs: David Kirwan for McCann, Cormac O'Brien for Philip Brennan, Risteard Brennan for Meehan, Ger O'Meara (0-1) for Ryan, Maghnus Breathnach for Keogh.

Kilkenny 4-20 Galway 1-10, Thurles (All-Ireland Qualifier)

Kilkenny: James McGarry; James Ryall, Noel Hickey, Tommy Walsh; Richie Mullally (0-1), Peter Barry, JJ Delaney; Derek Lyng (0-1), Ken Coogan; Martin Comerford (0-2), Henry Shefflin (2-11), Conor Phelan (0-1); Eddie Brennan (1-3), DJ Carey (0-1), Jimmy Coogan.
Sub: John Hoyne (1-0) for Comerford.

Galway: Liam Donoghue; Damien Joyce, Diarmuid Cloonan, Ollie Canning; Derek Hardiman, David Hayes, Fergal Moore; Fergal Healy, Tony Og Regan; Alan Kerins, David Forde, David Tierney; Damien Hayes (1-2), Eugene Cloonan (0-7), Kevin Broderick (0-1).
Subs: Adrian Cullinane for Healy, David Collins for Alan Kerins, Mark Kerins for Tierney.

Kilkenny 1-13 Clare 1-13, Croke Park (All-Ireland quarter-final)

Kilkenny: James McGarry; James Ryall, Noel Hickey, Tommy Walsh; Richie Mullally, Peter Barry, JJ Delaney; Derek Lyng, Ken Coogan; Martin Comerford, Henry Shefflin (0-9), Pat Tennyson (0-1); Eddie Brennan, DJ Carey (0-1), Jimmy Coogan (0-1).
Subs: John Hoyne (1-0) for Brennan, Sean Dowling (0-1) for Tennyson, Paddy Mullally for Richie Mullally.

Clare: Davy Fitzgerald; Brian Quinn, Frank Lohan, Gerry O'Grady; David Hoey, Sean McMahon (0-3), Alan Markham; Colin Lynch, Diarmuid McMahon (0-1); Andrew Quinn (0-1), Gerry Quinn, David Forde; Niall Gilligan (1-7), Tony Griffin, Tony Carmody.
Subs: Jamesie O'Connor (0-1) for Forde; Ollie Baker for Andrew Quinn; Daithi O'Connell for Diarmuid McMahon.

Cont'd overleaf.

Kilkenny 1-11 Clare 0-9, Thurles (All-Ireland quarter-final replay)

Kilkenny: James McGarry; Michael Kavanagh, Noel Hickey, James Ryall; Tommy Walsh, Peter Barry, JJ Delaney; Derek Lyng, Ken Coogan; Eddie Brennan (1-2), John Hoyne (0-1), DJ Carey (0-3); Martin Comerford (0-2), Henry Shefflin (0-3), 'Cha' Fitzpatrick.
Subs: John Maher for Shefflin; Sean Dowling for Coogan.

Clare: Davy Fitzgerald; Brian Quinn, Brian Lohan, Gerry O'Grady; David Hoey, Sean McMahon (0-2), Frank Lohan; Diarmuid McMahon, Colin Lynch; John Reddan, Gerry Quinn, Andrew Quinn; Niall Gilligan (0-3), Tony Griffin (0-1), Alan Markham.
Subs: Conor Plunkett for Brian Lohan, Jamesie O'Connor (0-2) for Andrew Quinn, David Forde (0-1) for Hoey, Barry Murphy for Reddan, Ollie Baker for Markham.

Kilkenny 3-12 Waterford 0-18, Croke Park (All-Ireland semi-final)

Kilkenny: James McGarry; Michael Kavanagh, Noel Hickey, James Ryall; Tommy Walsh, Peter Barry, JJ Delaney; Derek Lyng, Ken Coogan (0-1); Eddie Brennan (1-1), John Hoyne, DJ Carey (0-2); 'Cha' Fitzpatrick (0-1), Martin Comerford (0-3), Henry Shefflin (2-4).
Subs: None.

Waterford: Ian O'Regan; Eoin Murphy, Declan Prendergast, James Murray; Tony Browne, Ken McGrath, Brian Phelan; Dave Bennett, Eoin Kelly (0-1); Dan Shanahan, Michael Walsh (0-1), Paul Flynn (0-13); Shane O'Sullivan, Seamus Prendergast, Eoin McGrath.
Subs: Jack Kennedy (0-3) for O'Sullivan, Paul O'Brien for Eoin McGrath.

Cork 0-17 Kilkenny 0-9, Croke Park (All-Ireland final)

Cork: Donal Og Cusack; Wayne Sherlock, Diarmuid O'Sullivan, Brian Murphy; John Gardiner, Ronan Curran, Sean Og O'hAilpin; Tom Kenny (0-1), Jerry O'Connor (0-1); Ben O'Connor (0-3), Niall McCarthy (0-3), Timmy McCarthy; Kieran Murphy (0-2), Brian Corcoran (0-2), Joe Deane (0-5).
Sub: John Browne for Brian Murphy.

Kilkenny: James McGarry; Michael Kavanagh, Noel Hickey, James Ryall; Tommy Walsh, Peter Barry, JJ Delaney; Derek Lyng (0-1), Ken Coogan; Henry Shefflin (0-5), John Hoyne, DJ Carey; 'Cha' Fitzpatrick (0-1), Martin Comerford (captain) (0-2), Eddie Brennan.
Subs: Conor Phelan for Fitzpatrick, Sean Dowling for Coogan..

National Hurling League
Waterford 0-15 Kilkenny 1-10, Galway 0-18 Kilkenny 1-12, Kilkenny 2-14 Laois 2-10, Kilkenny 2-10 Clare 1-12, Kilkenny 1-15 Dublin 0-9, Kilkenny 2-13 Offaly 0-11, Kilkenny 3-31 Antrim 3-7, Kilkenny 3-22 Wexford 1-17.

League and Championship
Played 15: Won 10, Drew 1, Lost 4.

Titles: None.

Our preparations were supposed to be out-dated, lacking in method and finesse. By comparison with Cork and their sophisticated ways we were pre-historic. Yet, a year later, we were All-Ireland, Leinster, National League and Walsh Cup champions and had remained unbeaten in all competitions throughout the year. Not bad for a squad in transition.

Kilkenny 6-28 Offaly 0-15, Croke Park (Leinster semi-final)

Kilkenny: James McGarry; James Ryall, Noel Hickey, Jackie Tyrrell; Richie Mullally (0-1), Peter Barry, JJ Delaney; Bryan Barry (0-1), Derek Lyng (0-2); Martin Comerford (1-3), Eoin Larkin, Tommy Walsh (0-5); Richie Power (1-1), DJ Carey (1-2), Henry Shefflin (2-11).
Subs: Conor Phelan (0-1) for Lyng, John Hoyne for Carey, Michael Kavanagh for Mullally, Eoin McCormack (1-1) for Power, John Tennyson for Hickey.

Offaly: Brian Mullins; Barry Teehan, Ger Oakley, David Franks; Daniel Hoctor, Kevin Brady, Colm Cassidy; Michael Cordial, Brendan Murphy; Gary Hanniffy (0-2), Rory Hanniffy (0-1), Dylan Hayden (0-1); Brian Carroll (0-3), Joe Brady, Damien Murray (0-7).
Subs: Paul Cleary for Teehan, Stephen Brown for Franks, Aidan Hanrahan for Murray, Paul Molloy for Cordial, Cathal Parlon (0-1) for Hayden.

Kilkenny 0-22 Wexford 1-16, Croke Park (Leinster final)

Kilkenny: James McGarry; Jackie Tyrrell, Noel Hickey, James Ryall; Richie Mullally (0-1), Peter Barry, JJ Delaney; Bryan Barry, Derek Lyng; Martin Comerford, Eoin Larkin (0-3), Tommy Walsh (0-4); Richie Power (0-3), Conor Phelan (0-1) Henry Shefflin (0-8).
Subs: Eoin McCormack (0-1) for Phelan, Eddie Brennan (0-1) for Bryan Barry, Michael Kavanagh for Ryall, John Hoyne for Larkin.

Wexford: Damien Fitzhenry; 'Doc' O'Connor, Darragh Ryan, Keith Rossiter; Malachy Travers, Declan Ruth (0-1), Diarmuid Lyng; Adrian Fenlon, Rory McCarthy (0-2); Paul Carley (0-1), Eoin Quigley (0-2), Des Mythen (1-1); Michael Jacob (0-1), 'Mitch' Jordan (0-2), Rory Jacob (0-5).
Subs: Redmond Barry (0-1) for Fenlon, Tomas Mahon for Carley, Barry Lambert Michael Jacob.

Kilkenny 0-18 Limerick 0-13, Croke Park (All-Ireland quarter-final)

Kilkenny: James McGarry; Michael Kavanagh, John Tennyson, James Ryall; Richie Mullally, Peter Barry, JJ Delaney; Bryan Barry (0-1), Derek Lyng (0-1); Martin Comerford (0-2), Eoin Larkin, Tommy Walsh (0-2); Richie Power, DJ Carey (0-3), Henry Shefflin (0-9).
Subs: Eddie Brennan for Power, Eoin McCormack for Bryan Barry, John Hoyne for Larkin.

Limerick: Timmy Houlihan; Damien Reale, Stephen Lucey, Mark Foley; Ollie Moran, Brian Geary, Peter Lawlor (0-3); Paul O'Grady (0-1), Niall Moran (0-1); Donie Ryan, James O'Brien (0-1), Michael Cahill; Patrick Kirby, TJ Ryan (0-6), Andrew O'Shaughnessy (0-1).
Subs: Alan O'Connor for Cahill, Pat Tobin for Kirby.

Galway 5-18 Kilkenny 4-18, Croke Park (All-Ireland semi-final)

Galway: Liam O'Donoghue; Shane Kavanagh, Ollie Canning, Damien Joyce; Derek Hardiman, Tony Og Regan, David Collins; Fergal Healy (0-1), David Tierney (0-2); Richie Murray (0-2), David Forde (0-2), Alan Kerins; Ger Farragher (2-9), Niall Healy (3-0), Damien Hayes (0-1).
Sub: Kevin Broderick (0-1) for Niall Healy.

Kilkenny: James McGarry; Michael Kavanagh, John Tennyson, James Ryall; Richie Mullally, Peter Barry (captain), JJ Delaney; Derek Lyng, Tommy Walsh (0-1); Martin Comerford (0-1), Henry Shefflin (1-9), John Hoyne (1-0); Eddie Brennan (2-4), DJ Carey, Eoin Larkin (0-1).
Subs: Richie Power (0-2) for Hoyne, Brian Hogan for Barry, Eoin McCormack for Lyng, Jackie Tyrrell for Larkin.

National Hurling League
Kilkenny 2-16 Waterford 0-17, Kilkenny 4-16 Galway 1-21, Kilkenny 0-19 Laois 1-9, Clare 2-13 Kilkenny 1-8, Kilkenny 2-27 Dublin 0-11, Kilkenny 1-14 Cork 1-11, Kilkenny 3-26 Wexford 0-5, Kilkenny 3-18 Tipperary 2-16; Kilkenny 3-20 Clare 0-15 (final).

League and Championship
Played 13: Won 11, Lost 2.

Titles: Leinster and National League.

We had to be in their faces, behind their backs and coming in from the side, too. I wanted the black-and-amber to be a blur in front of their eyes all the time. I wanted it to look big, powerful and utterly confident. Wherever Cork players turned, they were to see a Kilkenny man approaching. And, if they turned the other way, another Kilkenny man was to be steaming in. There would be no let-up, no hesitation, no compromise.

Kilkenny 1-23 Westmeath 1-9, Mullingar (Leinster semi-final)

Kilkenny: James McGarry; Michael Kavanagh, JJ Delaney, Donncha Cody; Jackie Tyrrell, John Tennyson, Tommy Walsh; Derek Lyng (0-1), Richie Mullally (0-2); Willie O'Dwyer (0-1), Martin Comerford (0-3), Eoin Larkin; Eoin McCormack (1-3), Henry Shefflin (0-8), 'Cha' Fitzpatrick (0-2).
Subs: Michael Rice (0-3) for Comerford, PJ Delaney for Tennyson, Peter Cleere for Larkin, John Dalton for Walsh.

Westmeath: Mark Briody; Conor Jordan, Christy Murtagh, Paul Greville; John Shaw, Darren McCormack (0-1), Noel Gavin; Brian Connaughton (0-1), Enda Loughlin (0-1); Greg Gavin, Brendan Murtagh, Andrew Mitchell (0-5); Barry Kennedy (1-0), Derek McNicholas, Joe Clarke (0-1).
Subs: Daniel Carty for McNicholas, Donal Devine for Gavin, Martin Williams for Jordan, Philip Gilsenan for Connaughton, Dermot Faulkner for Clarke.

Kilkenny 1-23 Wexford 2-12, Croke Park (Leinster final)

Kilkenny: James McGarry; Donncha Cody, JJ Delaney, Noel Hickey; Jackie Tyrrell (0-1), John Tennyson, Tommy Walsh; Derek Lyng (0-1), Richie Mullally (0-1); Eddie Brennan (0-2), 'Cha' Fitzpatrick (0-2), Michael Rice (0-1); Martin Comerford (0-4), Eoin Larkin, Henry Shefflin (1-7).
Subs: Michael Fennelly (0-1) for Mullally, Richie Power (0-3) for Larkin, Willie O'Dwyer for Fitzpatrick.

Wexford: Damien Fitzhenry (0-1); Malachy Travers, Keith Rossiter, 'Doc' O'Connor; Richie Kehoe, Declan Ruth (0-1), Diarmuid Lyng; Darren Stamp, Ciaran Kenny; Rory McCarthy, Eoin Quigley (0-1), PJ Nolan; Stephen Doyle (0-3), Rory Jacob (1-2), 'Mitch' Jordan (1-4).
Subs: MJ Furlong for Jordan, Michael Jacob for Kenny, Tomas Mahon for Stamp, Michael Doyle for Nolan.

Kilkenny 2-22 Galway 3-14, Thurles (All-Ireland quarter-final)

Kilkenny: James McGarry; Michael Kavanagh, JJ Delaney, Noel Hickey; James Ryall, John Tennyson, Tommy Walsh; Derek Lyng (0-1); 'Cha' Fitzpatrick (1-2); Eddie Brennan (0-1), Martin Comerford (0-3), Eoin Larkin (0-4); Eoin McCormack, Henry Shefflin (0-11), Aidan Fogarty (1-0).
Subs: Michael Fennelly for McCormack, Michael Rice for Fogarty.

Galway: Liam Donoghue; Damien Joyce, Tony Og Regan, Ollie Canning; Derek Hardiman, Shane Kavanagh, Ger Mahon; Fergal Healy, Conor Dervan (0-1); Cathal Connolly, David Forde, Alan Kerins (0-2); Damien Hayes (0-2), Ger Farragher (0-5), Niall Healy (1-1).
Subs: Richie Murray (0-1) for Connolly, Eugene Cloonan (1-0) for Mahon, David Tierney (1-2) for Fergal Healy, Eoin Lynch for Forde, Kerril Wade for Farragher.

Kilkenny 2-21 Clare 1-16, Croke Park (All-Ireland semi-final)

Kilkenny: James McGarry; Jackie Tyrrell, Noel Hickey, JJ Delaney; James Ryall, John Tennyson, Tommy Walsh; 'Cha' Fitzpatrick (0-1), Derek Lyng (0-1); Eddie Brennan (0-1), Martin Comerford (0-2), Eoin Larkin (0-2); Michael Rice, Henry Shefflin (1-13), Aidan Fogarty.
Subs: Brian Hogan for Tennyson, Eoin McCormack (1-0) for Rice, Willie O'Dwyer for Fogarty, Richie Power (0-1) for McCormack.

Clare: Davy Fitzgerald; Gerry O'Grady, Brian Lohan, Frank Lohan; Brian O'Connell, Sean McMahon (0-5), Gerry Quinn; Jonathon Clancy, Colin Lynch; Niall Gilligan (1-3), Tony Carmody (0-2), Diarmuid McMahon (0-1); Derek Quinn (0-1), Alan Markham, Tony Griffin (0-4).
Subs: David Hoey for Gerry Quinn, James McInerney for Derek Quinn, Pat Vaughan for Clancy, Declan O'Rourke for Diarmuid McMahon, Daithi O'Connell for Markham.

Cont'd overleaf.

Kilkenny 1-16 Cork 1-13, Croke Park (All-Ireland final)

Kilkenny: James McGarry; Michael Kavanagh, Noel Hickey, Jackie Tyrrell (captain); Tommy Walsh, John Tennyson, James Ryall; Derek Lyng (0-1), 'Cha' Fitzpatrick (0-1); Eddie Brennan (0-1), Martin Comerford (0-1), Eoin Larkin; Richie Power (0-1), Henry Shefflin (0-8), Aidan Fogarty (1-3).
Subs: Willie O'Dwyer for Larkin, Richie Mullally for Lyng.

Cork: Donal Og Cusack; Pat Mulcahy, Diarmuid O'Sullivan, Brian Murphy; John Gardiner (0-1), Ronan Curran, Sean Og O'hAilpin; Tom Kenny, Jerry O'Connor (0-1); Timmy McCarthy, Niall McCarthy (0-1), Neil Ronan; Ben O'Connor (1-4), Brian Corcoran, Joe Deane (0-6).
Subs: Kieran Murphy for Ronan, Wayne Sherlock for Mulcahy, Cathal Naughton for Timmy McCarthy, Cian O'Connor for Kieran Murphy, Conor Cusack for Kenny.

National Hurling League
Kilkenny 1-26 Laois 1-13, Kilkenny 0-19 Tipperary 0-10, Kilkenny 0-14 Limerick 1-11, Kilkenny 0-12 Antrim 1-7, Kilkenny 1-16 Galway 0-10, Kilkenny 3-20 Tipperary 2-11, Kilkenny 3-11 Limerick 0-14 (final).

League and Championship
Played 12: Won 11, Drew 1.

Titles: All-Ireland, Leinster and National League.

A manager has to trust his players to work their way through whatever problems they encounter in a game. They won't always be able to do that because they're up against a better team, but the one thing you can't do is fill their heads with complicated theories. Hurling is a simple game and should be treated as such.

Kilkenny 1-27 Offaly 1-13, Portlaoise (Leinster semi-final)

Kilkenny: PJ Ryan; Michael Kavanagh, Noel Hickey, Jackie Tyrrell; Tommy Walsh (0-1), Brian Hogan, JJ Delaney (0-1); Derek Lyng (0-1), 'Cha' Fitzpatrick (0-3); Willie O'Dwyer, Henry Shefflin (0-12), Eoin Larkin (1-0); Eddie Brennan (0-2), Martin Comerford (0-3), Aidan Fogarty (0-2).
Subs: Conor Phelan (0-1) for Lyng, John Hoyne for Carey, Michael Kavanagh for Mullally, Eoin Subs: Michael Fennelly (0-1) for Lyng, Eoin Reid (0-1) for Fogarty, James Ryall for Delaney, John Tennyson for Hickey, Michael Rice for Larkin.

Offaly: Brian Mullins; Conor Hernon, Paul Cleary, David Franks; Kevin Brady, David Kenny, Ger Oakley; Barry Teehan, Brendan Murphy (0-2); Gary Hanniffy (0-1), Rory Hanniffy, Derek Molloy; Brian Carroll (0-1), Joe Bergin, Damien Murray(1-8).
Subs: Michael Cordial (0-1) for Teehan, Shane Dooley for Bergin, Cathal Parlon for Rory Hanniffy, Eddie Bevans for Carroll.

Kilkenny 2-24 Wexford 1-12, Croke Park (Leinster final)

Kilkenny: PJ Ryan; Michael Kavanagh, Noel Hickey, Jackie Tyrrell; Tommy Walsh, Brian Hogan (0-1), JJ Delaney; 'Cha' Fitzpatrick (0-2), Michael Fennelly; Martin Comerford (0-5), Eddie Brennan (0-1), Eoin Larkin (0-2); Eoin Reid, Henry Shefflin (0-9), Willie O'Dwyer (2-3).
Subs: James Ryall for Walsh, John Dalton for Delaney, John Tennyson for Hogan, Michael Rice (0-1) for Reid, Donncha Cody for Hickey.

Wexford: Damien Fitzhenry; Paul Roche, Declan Ruth, Malachy Travers; Richie Kehoe (0-2), Keith Rossiter, Ciaran Kenny; Diarmuid Lyng, Eoin Quigley (0-1); Michael Jacob, 'Doc' O'Connor, Stephen Nolan (1-5); Nigel Higgins, Darren Stamp (0-1), Rory Jacob (0-3).
Subs: Willie Doran for Ruth, Rory McCarthy for Michael Jacob, Barry Lambert for Higgins, Pierce White for Kenny, 'Mitch' Jordan for O'Connor.

Kilkenny 3-22 Galway 1-18, Croke Park (All-Ireland quarter-final)

Kilkenny: PJ Ryan; Michael Kavanagh, Noel Hickey, Jackie Tyrrell; Tommy Walsh, Brian Hogan, JJ Delaney; Derek Lyng (0-2); 'Cha' Fitzpatrick (0-3); Martin Comerford (0-2), Eddie Brennan (2-2), Eoin Larkin (0-2); Willie O'Dwyer (0-1), Henry Shefflin (0-8), Aidan Fogarty (0-1).
Subs: Richie Power (1-1) for Fogarty, James Ryall for Delaney, John Tennyson for Hogan, Michael Fennelly for O'Dwyer.

Galway: Colm Callanan (0-1); Gregory Kennedy, Ger Mahon, Fergal Moore; Derek Hardiman, John Lee, Shane Kavanagh; Damien Hayes, David Collins; Alan Kerins (0-4), Fergal Healy (0-2), Richie Murray (1-0); Kerril Wade (0-7), Iarla Tannian (0-1), Niall Healy (0-3).
Subs: Damien Joyce for Moore, David Forde for Hardiman, Eugene Cloonan for Murray, Kevin Broderick for Tannian.

Kilkenny 0-23 Wexford 1-10, Croke Park (All-Ireland semi-final)

Kilkenny: PJ Ryan; Michael Kavanagh, Noel Hickey, Jackie Tyrrell; Tommy Walsh, Brian Hogan, JJ Delaney; Derek Lyng, 'Cha' Fitzpatrick (0-2); Eddie Brennan, Henry Shefflin (0-14), Eoin Larkin (0-2); Willie O'Dwyer (0-1), Martin Comerford (0-2), Richie Power (0-1).
Subs: John Tennyson for Hickey, Richie Mullally for Lyng, Aidan Fogarty (0-1) for Brennan, John Dalton for Kavanagh, Eoin Reid for Comerford.

Wexford: Damien Fitzhenry; Malachy Travers, Keith Rossiter, Paul Roche; Richie Kehoe, Declan Ruth, Diarmuid Lyng; Rory McCarthy (0-1), Darren Stamp (0-1); Eoin Quigley, 'Mitch' Jordan, 'Doc' O'Connor (0-1); Barry Lambert (0-5), Michael Jacob (1-1), Rory Jacob.
Subs: Paul Carley for Jordan, Ciaran Kenny for Rossiter, Stephen Nolan for O'Connor, Pierce White for Rory Jacob, PJ Nolan (0-1) for Carley.

Cont'd overleaf.

Kilkenny 2-19 Limerick 1-15, Croke Park (All-Ireland final)

Kilkenny: PJ Ryan; Michael Kavanagh, Noel Hickey, Jackie Tyrrell; Tommy Walsh (0-2), Brian Hogan, JJ Delaney; Derek Lyng, 'Cha' Fitzpatrick (0-1); Willie O'Dwyer, Martin Comerford, Eoin Larkin (0-4); Eddie Brennan (1-5), Henry Shefflin (1-2) (captain), Aidan Fogarty (0-1).
Subs: John Tennyson for Hickey, Richie Power (0-4) for O'Dwyer, Michael Fennelly for Shefflin.

Limerick: Brian Murray; Damien Reale, Stephen Lucey, Seamus Hickey; Peter Lawlor, Brian Geary, Mark Foley; Donal O'Grady (0-2), Mike O'Brien; Michael Fitzgerald (0-1), Ollie Moran (1-3), Sean O'Connor (0-1); Andrew O'Shaughnessy (0-7), Brian Begley, Donie Ryan.
Subs: Niall Moran (0-1) for Mike O'Brien, James O'Brien for O'Connor, Pat Tobin for Fitzgerald, Kevin Tobin for Ryan, Mark O'Riordan for Lawlor.

National Hurling League
Kilkenny 0-19 Dublin 2-13, Tipperary 3-13 Kilkenny 2-13, Kilkenny 2-17 Limerick 0-12, Kilkenny 2-21 Antrim 0-11, Kilkenny 1-19 Galway 0-18, Kilkenny 2-22 Wexford 2-7, Waterford 0-20 Kilkenny 0-18 (final).

League and Championship
Played 12: Won 9, Drew 1, Lost 2. **Titles: All-Ireland and Leinster.**